FORTY-EIGHT MINUTES

Bob Ryan and Terry Pluto

FORTY-EIGHT MINUTES

A Night in the Life of the NBA

Macmillan Publishing Company
New York
Collier Macmillan Publishers
London

Macmillan Publishing Company
866 Third Avenue, New York, N.Y. 10022
Collier Macmillan Canada, Inc.

Library of Congress Cataloging-in-Publication Data
Ryan, Bob.
Forty-eight minutes.
Includes index.
1. National Basketball Association. I. Pluto,
Terry, 1955–   . II. Title. III. Title: 48 minutes.
GV885.515.N37R9   1988   796.32'364'0973   87-21966

ISBN 0-02-597770-9

Macmillan books are available at special discounts for bulk purchases for sales promotions, premiums, fund-raising, or educational use. For details, contact:

Special Sales Director
Macmillan Publishing Company
866 Third Avenue
New York, N.Y. 10022

10 9 8 7 6 5 4 3 2 1

Designed by Jack Meserole

Printed in the United States of America

To Jeff Neuman:
The only editor who
could have imagined
a book like this.
—TERRY PLUTO

To Elaine Ryan:
In the next life, maybe
you'll get a nine-to-five man
who makes seven figures.
—BOB RYAN

Contents

Acknowledgments

Cleveland Cavaliers coach Lenny Wilkens took a deep, personal interest in this book. He gave about a dozen hours of interviews on all facets of game preparation and strategy, and spent close to eight hours going over the videotape of the game. Furthermore, Wilkens permitted his huddles during the game to be taped.

Cavs assistant coach Dick Helm opened up his scouting report on the Celtics and supplied some play diagrams.

Cavs general manager Wayne Embry supplied a list of all the players he considered signing when Mark Price got hurt. Embry also discussed in depth what it took to get Craig Ehlo signed to a ten-day contract.

Agent Ron Grinker was a big help in giving a great deal of useful background information about how players are signed to ten-day contracts.

Others who deserve a special thanks are Cavs trainer Gary Briggs, broadcaster Joe Tait, Phil Hubbard, John Williams, Ben Poquette, Brad Daugherty, Ron Harper, Craig Ehlo, John Bagley, and Mark West. Roberta Pluto and Pat McCubbin contributed greatly in terms of transcribing tapes and helping to prepare the manuscript.

—TERRY PLUTO

To Terry Pluto, for involving me in what has turned out to be an extremely rewarding project. To Jimmy Rodgers, who provided much-needed insight into a complex game, and who cheerfully gave me his valuable time. To Jeff Neuman, who quarterbacked this book from day one. To Ernie Roberts, Fran Rosa, the late Jerry Nason, Dave Smith, and Vince Doria, the *Boston Globe* editors who have put up with my eccentricities over the many years I've covered the Celtics. To the members of the Cleveland Cavaliers and Boston Celtics, who provided us with such a rich writing vehicle. As always, to Elaine Ryan, for her unwavering support during a seemingly endless basketball season. Thank you, all.

—BOB RYAN

FORTY-EIGHT
MINUTES

Prologue

It was Sunday night, January 11, five days before the Cavaliers were to play the Boston Celtics in Boston, and Cleveland coach Lenny Wilkens and his wife Marilyn were in the kitchen of their Brecksville, Ohio, apartment. Marilyn had her hands in the sink, Lenny had his on a towel.

The phone at the Wilkenses' apartment had been ringing for much of Sunday evening. Cavalier trainer Gary Briggs was calling; so was Cavalier public relations director Bob Price. But Wilkens and his wife had gone out and missed the calls. When they returned home, the dishes were waiting and so was the telephone. This time it was a sportswriter, a beat man who covers the Cavaliers.

"What do you think about Mark Price?" asked the writer.

"What about Price?" asked Wilkens.

There was a long silence, and the writer finally said, "So you don't know about Price."

"What happened?" asked Wilkens.

"He had an appendicitis attack," said the writer. "About now, he should be on the operating table at Cleveland Clinic."

Wilkens was silent.

"They say he'll be out at least a month, maybe six weeks," said the writer.

"After surgery, that sounds about right," said Wilkens. "Is he doing okay?"

"I suppose so. At least I didn't hear about any complications."

"That's good."

1

This time it was the writer's turn to pause. Finally, he broke the silence by asking, "What are you guys going to do?" "We have four games this week," said Wilkens. "With Price out, we have only one point guard [John Bagley]. We have to make a move for someone."

That pretty much was the end of the conversation, although the writer could almost hear Wilkens mulling the options, running the names of available point guards through his head.

For the Cavaliers, losing Price was not quite on par with the Los Angeles Lakers' having to go without Magic Johnson for a month. But it was a significant problem, for Price was more than just another six-foot white guard. He was a player Wilkens had come to respect and rely on. Yes, Bagley was the starter and played about thirty minutes a night, but Price was often on the floor in the fourth quarter, running the team in close games. That says a lot about a rookie point guard, especially when the rookie's coach was a great point guard, a player whose main attribute was his intelligence and maturity. In other words, though Price would not be Rookie of the Year, though he wouldn't even start for the Cavaliers, he was no ordinary rookie.

"We aren't a very good outside shooting team in the first place," said Wilkens. "But Price has the best range of anybody on the team."

What Wilkens left unsaid was the fact that other teams had been playing sagging defenses (read: tight zones) on the Cavs. Sure, there is no such thing as a zone defense in the NBA. No one ever hedges on his tax returns, either. At the time of his operation, Price was eighth in the NBA in three-point shooting, hitting 40 percent. Ironically, he was shooting only 39 percent overall, meaning his most accurate shot was from at least twenty-two feet. Also, while the Cavs were the worst foul shooters in the NBA—69 percent—Price was hitting 81 percent from the line.

Dish towel in hand, Wilkens started thinking about bodies.

"We don't have enough guards," he said. "John Bagley is my only point guard. My other guards are Ron Harper and Johnny Newman. A year ago, they were both playing small forward in college."

A game against the world champions was looming at the end of what now looked like a very long week. Wilkens would have loved to have the luxury of thinking about the Celtic game. Imagine being a football coach, Wilkens said. Imagine having a whole week to prepare for one game. Imagine what that would be like. It was as if Wilkens were imagining heaven. Instead, he had the Detroit Pistons on his mind, as he thought about not one but two games with the Pistons—Tuesday night in Cleveland and Wednesday night at the Silverdome in Pontiac.

"After we're done with those two games, I'll start to pay attention to the Celtics," said Wilkens. "Hey, we're not good enough to look by anyone, and I mean anyone."

On this Sunday in January, the Cavaliers had a 14–20 record and had lost five of their last six games. They were coming off a 129–104 pounding in Atlanta the night before, a twenty-five-point game that wasn't even that close. It was over in the second period.

"I know Atlanta is a good team, but we just were awful," said Wilkens. "I didn't like anything about the game."

•

Cavaliers general manager Wayne Embry arrived at his Moreland Hills, Ohio, home about 11:30 Sunday night. Embry's wife, Teri, was waiting for him. Earlier in the evening, she had received a call from Bob Price, who delivered the news about Mark Price.

"Bad news, Wayne," she said. "Mark Price had an appendicitis attack."

Embry rubbed his head, trying to clear away the jetlag and make sure that his wife had indeed said something about Price and an appendix. Slowly, Embry learned the details. Price was in Cleveland Clinic. He would be out for at least a month.

Sighing, Embry picked up the phone and dialed Lenny Wilkens's number.

"Well, coach, what are we going to do?" said Embry.

"We've got to get another guard," said Wilkens.

Embry sighed again. He had just gotten off a plane from Seattle, where he had been scouting a college game between Washington and Arizona.

"Coach, I went across the country to see Christian Welp and all I saw was some seven-foot, 250-pound guy shoot eighteen-foot jumpers," said Embry, with the tone of a man expected to see Hulk Hogan and instead ended up at the ballet.

"It's been that kind of day," said Wilkens.

The two men hung up, saying they would talk again Monday morning.

•

In Cincinnati, it was midnight when the phone rang at the home of Ron Grinker, a veteran NBA agent. All Grinker will say was that a "friend" was calling.

"I've been in the business twenty-three years and you develop contacts, almost a network all over the league," said Grinker. "There are guys who keep me posted on anything that happens."

When Grinker picked up the telephone, the friend said, "Did you hear about Mark Price?"

"What happened?" asked Grinker.

"An appendicitis attack."

"How long?"

"At least a month."

"Cleveland could use Jerry Eaves," said Grinker. "Or maybe Sedric Toney. They need a guard."

The friend agreed.

"I'll call Wayne Embry first thing in the morning," said Grinker, hanging up.

•

Embry arrived at his office at the Coliseum about 9 a.m. Monday. He sat down at his desk and began to look at his telephone messages and mail. Embry is a massive man—6-foot-8 and much closer to three hundred pounds than he would like. He shuffled through his messages with his huge hands, the hands that were considered the largest in the NBA when he played in the 1960s.

This went on for five minutes, when the phone rang. Embry's secretary said Ron Grinker was on the line. Embry wasn't surprised.

"Grinks, how you doing?" asked Embry.

"Just fine," said Grinker. "I was wondering how were things with you."

"Not good," said Embry. "But I expect you already know."

"I heard about Price."

"Then you know."

"Sedric Toney and Jerry Eaves are both playing very well in the CBA."

"Ron, I just don't know what we're going to do."

"But you have to make a move."

"That's right."

"Toney and Eaves both belong in the league," said Grinker. "They're both good kids, and they'd really help you."

"Oh, Grinks, I just don't know."

"You know who could be a real asset? Lancaster Gordon."

"I just don't think . . ."

"Wayne, the kid just needs to get away from the Clippers. He'll be a good player, but never in Los Angeles. He's buried on the bench. He just needs a change of scene. You wouldn't have to give up much to get him."

"I'll be frank with you," said Embry. "I don't think these guys are what we're looking for."

"You may think I'm crazy," said Grinker. "But the kid who might be able to help you at the point is already on your roster."

"And who's that?" asked Embry, knowing the answer.

"Scooter McCray," said Grinker.

"I knew you were going to say that," said Embry. "Look Ron, I know Scooter is one of your boys and he's a good kid, but . . ."

"Until he hurt his knee at Louisville, he handled the ball as well as his brother [Houston's Rodney McCray]," said Grinker.

"I don't think Scooter is the answer," said Embry.

The conversation went on for a few more minutes before breaking off.

•

While Embry and Grinker were talking, Wilkens was starting practice without Mark Price.

John Bagley was the point guard, and he was guarded by Scooter McCray, a 6-9 small forward who was trying to show Wilkens that he could play point guard. McCray was the Cavs' twelfth player, a good guy, a practice player.

"Practice player" is a nice name for "a body," the common term used for the players on the end of the bench. A pro basketball team has a twelve-man roster, and only ten men can practice at a time, so that means two are left sitting on the side watching the action. But in the real world of the NBA in January, seldom are all twelve players ready to practice. Some guys have to sit out because of injuries, and others because their knees and/or legs can barely take the pounding of eighty-two regular season games, much less two-hour practices in between.

That's where the practice players, or the bodies, come in. They are usually the eleventh and twelfth players, and their job is to keep the regulars sharp. Their games are the practices as they permit the injured to heal, the old to rest, and the rest of the team to have ten players to scrimmage and prepare for the next opponent.

Attitude more than ability is the crucial element for the practice player. He must be willing to work his hardest in the mornings and afternoons, while knowing that he won't play at night unless the game is totally out of hand and the fans are heading for the parking lot.

Wilkens watched McCray at the point. He shook his head. Wayne Embry was right—as far as backup point guards went, Scooter McCray was not the answer.

•

As practice was taking place, Embry remained in his office and was joined by Gary Fitzsimmons, the Cavaliers' director of player personnel and chief scout. They were talking about Lester Connor, a 6-6 guard who had been with Golden State for four years. He was now a free agent and had not signed with anyone.

"If we sign Lester, we'll have to deal with George," said Embry.

"George" was George Karl, the Golden State coach. From June 1984 to March 1986, Karl coached the Cavaliers. When he was fired, Karl was bitter, vowing, "One day, I'll come back to this building [the Richfield Coliseum] and beat the Cavaliers, and I'll be very happy about it."

The Cavs liked Connor for his size and defensive skills. But to sign him, they would have to give Connor an offer sheet. Under the NBA's collective-bargaining agreement, players are free agents at the end of their contracts, but their old teams retain a right of first refusal. An interested team must sign the player to an "offer sheet" detailing the terms of a proposed contract. His old team has fifteen days to decide whether to match the offer or let him go. Often, the team would match the offer and then immediately deal the player to the interested club, at least getting some compensation for him.

In the case of Connor, Karl's presence as coach was a complicating factor. Golden State would surely ask for compensation for Connor, or at least make the Cavs wait fifteen days before freeing him to join Cleveland. The consensus was that Karl would not make it easy for the Cavs to get Connor.

"There is one other thing to think about," said Embry. "What's Lester been doing for the last couple months? He's not in the CBA, he's not playing in Europe. Is he in shape? Who knows?"

Embry had a yellow legal pad in his lap. Fitzsimmons was paging through the latest statistics from the Continental Basketball Association. The CBA is basketball's version of the minor leagues. But instead of one NBA team having a corresponding farm club, any NBA team can sign any CBA player at any time. The NBA helps subsidize the CBA.

The phone rang again, and again it was Grinker.

"You're not going to tell me about Jerry Eaves and Sedric Toney again," said Embry.

"What about Craig Ehlo?" said Grinker.

"Go on," said Embry, remembering Ehlo as a 6-6 blond guard who spent the last three years on the Houston bench.

"You have to understand that I don't represent Ehlo, I'm just doing this as a favor for Tom Nissalke," said Grinker. "Tom is coaching Ehlo in Jacksonville [of the CBA] and he's really high on him. Tom said Ehlo is a tough kid, he can shoot the ball, and I think he'd be a natural for you."

"I kind of like Ehlo," said Embry. "I'll talk to Lenny [Wilkens] and get back to you."

Embry wrote down the number and hung up. Then he and Fitzsimmons began making a list.

Alone on the right side of the yellow legal pad was Connor's name. At the left were these names, all CBA guards—Jerry Eaves and Sedric Toney (Grinker's guys), Craig Ehlo, Bryan Warrick, Rick Wilson, Kevin Henderson, Bill Martin, and Bruce Douglas.

By that time, "the word was out on Price," said Embry. "It seemed like a hundred agents were calling. I didn't talk to most of them."

When practice ended, Wilkens and his assistants—Dick Helm and Brian Winters—joined Embry and Fitzsimmons. They eliminated Connor because of problems that might arise if they had to deal with Golden State. Wilkens also wondered about Connor's condition, since he wasn't playing.

The coaching staff glanced at the other names, and they all liked Ehlo. Or, more accurately, Ehlo finished first and the rest were either tied for second or last.

•

"About an hour after our last conversation, I got a call back from Wayne," said Grinker. "He wanted to sign Ehlo to a ten-day contract. Ehlo was playing in Biloxi, Mississippi, and I gave Wayne the number at his hotel."

"It was funny," Ehlo recalled, "because early that Monday morning I had talked to Grinker, and he told me to get my bags packed and be ready, something might break. A little while later, Wayne Embry called and said that I was his choice and that they needed someone quick and someone who was ready to play. I told Wayne that I was really ready."

After hanging up with Embry, Ehlo called Grinker. About the same time, NBA Commissioner David Stern announced that Houston guards Mitchell Wiggins and Lewis Lloyd had been banned from pro basketball because of drug use.

"Ron, Cleveland wants to sign me," said Ehlo. "What should I do?"

"You probably should know that Houston needs guards and [Coach] Bill Fitch will probably want you back," said Grinker. "That is something to consider, but I can't make this decision for you."

"Well, I'm taking Cleveland's offer," said Ehlo, who hung up with Grinker and then called Embry. That wasn't the last call Ehlo would make.

"I called my friend David Nortstrom, who is the equipment manager for the Rockets," said Ehlo. "He was in the dressing room in Houston, and I was telling him how Cleveland wanted me and I was all fired up about it. He yelled to the guys in the dressing room that I got a job with Cleveland, and at that moment, Bill Fitch walked by.

"Then Fitch called me and offered me a chance to go back to the Rockets. He was going to try to sign me anyway, because they needed guards. I guess hearing that Cleveland wanted me just speeded up his call. I told Fitch that I had committed to Cleveland, and I was going. I realized that the Cavs were only offering a ten-day contract and Houston would sign me for the rest of the year, but I needed a new team."

.

All of this may sound like a lot of fuss over a marginal player, but it is business as usual in the NBA. When someone is hurt, the search is on to find a body . . . yesterday.

Ehlo (pronounced EE-low) had been the twelfth man on the Rockets for three years. He averaged 2.4 points and never played more than fourteen minutes in any game. He was a nice guy, a good practice player.

"Insurance policy, that's how Bill Fitch looked at me," said Ehlo. "I was happy to be in Houston. In fact, during the summer [of 1986], I saw Fitch and he told me that as long as he was in Houston, I'd be there. So I signed a contract for $125,000."

There was a hitch. It was a make-good deal. In other words, Ehlo had to make the team or he wouldn't be paid.

"Fitch cut me at the end of training camp, one hour before the deadline for the opening-day rosters," said Ehlo. "I couldn't believe it. I didn't see it coming. Fitch talked about the numbers game and contract obligations, the usual garbage. Basically, they kept Connor Henry over me."

The same Connor Henry would later be cut by Houston and picked up by Boston when the Celtics needed a warm body at guard.

"After I got cut, Tom Nissalke called me and asked me to play in the CBA for him in Jacksonville," said Ehlo. "But my old agent [Steve Blick] didn't think I should go to the CBA. For two months, I moped around the house. I still had friends at the Summit, and I'd go down there and shoot around by myself or with a few of the Rockets. I played a lot of ball at the local YMCA. By Christmas, I just couldn't stand it anymore. I was tired of waiting for the NBA to call, because I knew the call was never coming. Then Tom Nissalke called, and I went to play for him. Two weeks later, I got the offer from Cleveland.

"It was Nissalke who put me on to Ron Grinker. Ron always says that if you're a guy like me, a guy who never had anything guaranteed because I was a third-round draft pick, that I should always play somewhere so that people can find me. I need all the exposure I can get. Hey, I was with the Rockets for three years and no one ever saw me play in real game situations. It was always garbage time, so how could I be judged playing those kind of minutes?"

But Wilkens said, "I saw enough of Ehlo in Houston to know that he could help us. Wayne and I also looked at him as more than a body who'd be there for ten days. We were thinking that if he looked good, we'd sign him for the rest of the season."

The Cavs did just that, on day nine of Ehlo's ten-day contract. By then, Ehlo had officially named Grinker as his agent, and Grinker convinced the Cavs to pay Ehlo $50,000 for the remaining forty-six games on the schedule.

•

Ehlo signed with the Cavaliers Tuesday. A few hours later, the telephone again rang at Wayne Embry's office. It was about three hours before the Cavaliers were to play the Detroit Pistons.

"There was a guy on the line named Steve Blick," said Embry. "He said he was Ehlo's agent and he wanted to know if I had an interest in him."

According to Embry, the conversation went like this:

"I'm not just interested in Ehlo, but I already signed him," said Embry.

"But I'm his agent," said Blick.

"I don't care who you are, I'm signing Ehlo, not you."

"I'd think that the least you could have done would be to call the Players' Association and find out who represents Ehlo."

"Look, whatever is between you and Ehlo is between you guys. I signed the kid and he will be in uniform tonight."

Thinking about that conversation a few weeks later, Embry found himself laughing.

"The thing about signing one of Grinks's guys is that you usually end up in some sort of adventure," said Embry. "I mean, Grinks says he isn't representing Ehlo, he's just doing a favor for Nissalke. And Ehlo says that Grinks is his agent, and Grinks tells me that he isn't taking a commission for the kid."

Embry shook his head.

"It's none of my business," said Embry. "I don't know anything about Blick, but I do know that Ehlo is Grinks's kind of player."

In NBA circles, Grinker is legendary. Not for his fat contracts or his ability to get players commercial endorsements, but for his sheer persistence. He is the Broadway Danny Rose of basketball.

"First of all, I've never heard of any agent in any sport who handles more marginally talented players," said Embry. "If someone gets hurt, you can bet that Grinks will be calling you, trying to get one of his guys a ten-day contract. He has a bunch of guys whose chances are, at best, remote of playing in the league. And he sticks by the same guys, year after year. He does a lot of things from the goodness of his heart. I suppose there might be some ulterior motives involved, but offhand I can't see what they are."

Grinker does represent a few stars, or at least players with glittering contracts—Cedric Maxwell, Derek Smith, and Louis Orr. But most of his players are the likes of Hank McDowell, Bill Martin, Scooter McCray, Dirk Minniefield, Kevin McKenna, Richard Anderson, and Granville Waiters. In January 1987, he had ten players in the CBA and fourteen more in Europe.

"The funny thing is that you look up in the middle of February and Grinker has a lot of his guys in the league," said Embry. "A lot of those guys don't belong in the league, but he has found a place for them."

Ehlo also noticed this.

"I got to be pretty good friends with Hank McDowell," said Ehlo. "We used to work out together. There is no way Hank should have played in the NBA, but he kept getting ten-day contracts."

Indirectly, McDowell played a role in Ehlo's switching agents.

"Grinker got McDowell a contract to play in Italy," said Ehlo. "But when Hank got over there, he was injured, couldn't play, and got cut. When Hank got back to the States, Grinker gave Hank back his agent's commission: $10,000. Grinker didn't have to do it, but he knew Hank needed help."

Embry said, "Every summer, Grinks has his camp. I mean, his camp is famous among us GMs. Grinks will have the usual guys down there—McDowell, Jerry Eaves, Richard Anderson, and the rest—and he'll have a couple third- or fourth-round draft choices and a few new guys.

"Then Grinks will call all of us [general managers] up and ask us to come look at his players. He'll say that [Celtics assistant coach and Grinker's good friend] Ed Badger is running it, so I guess that is supposed to make it official. All I know is that he's got a bunch of players who don't have a snowball's chance in hell of lasting in the league, but he works like crazy for them. Ron is a genuinely nice guy, who is, for the most part, honest. Most agents dump a kid the minute it seems the kid won't make a lot of money. For them being an agent is a commercial endeavor and they're always trying to maximize their earnings. But Grinks is just the opposite. He is interested in the underdog, and that makes him more human. Besides, he's a character and fun to talk with on the phone."

Ehlo said, "My first game with the Cavs was in Detroit. About one in the morning, my phone rings and it's Grinker. He wanted to know how I played, was I doing all right. I mean, Ron didn't even get a commission from me signing with Cleveland. It made me feel good to know he was thinking about me."

Grinker said, "What do I care about getting 4 percent of

Ehlo's $4,800 for ten days? I wanted to find a place for Ehlo where he could get established, last the season, and build a career. That's why I advised him to go to Cleveland."

A forty-seven-year-old attorney, Grinker has an office in Cincinnati. His specialty is divorce, personal injury, and labor issues.

"My main income comes from my law practice," said Grinker. "I've been in basketball for twenty-three years, but I never started charging anything until seven or eight years ago. I never asked a player to sign an agreement with me until the league passed a rule a few years ago saying that agents had to have a contract with their clients."

Chicago Bulls assistant Gene Littles said, "On and off, Ron has represented me for twenty years. He never took a cent from me. That's true of a lot of guys I know. At least, now he takes the standard 4 percent of a guy's contract. But I had been telling him to charge for years before he finally started doing it."

Grinker said, "I suppose I really don't do business like most agents. Like with Ehlo. I'm not even sure I'm involved with him now. As I keep saying, he was a favor for two people—Wayne Embry and Tom Nissalke. In fact, Craig asked me to represent him and I told him not yet. I said he really didn't know me. That we had to sit down and talk first. He was really surprised when I said there was no fee involved in his deal with Cleveland."

Why take time with Ehlo, Granville Waiters, and the others?

"Anyone can represent Ralph Sampson or Michael Jordan," said Grinker. "That's not to say I wouldn't like to do it. I'd love it. But the highest draft picks I ever had were Jim Ard [no. 6] and Lancaster Gordon [no. 8]. Representing a guy that high in the draft is a no-brainer, anyone can do it. When I talked to Rodney McCray as he was coming out of Louisville, I told him that he really didn't need an agent, being the third player in the draft. I said, 'Rodney, I can teach you enough to do your own contract and get a good deal in an hour.' I like the challenge of finding other guys jobs, of getting them in the right place."

Grinker loves to tell success stories.

"Take Derek Smith. I had NBA people telling me his natural position was power forward, but he wasn't big enough to play there. His college coach, Denny Crum, said Derek couldn't play in the NBA and he set up Derek with a $14,000 job playing in France. But one summer, I brought Derek to my home in Cincinnati. I got him to lose thirty pounds and he worked day and night with Ed Badger. Ed Badger made a player, a big guard, out of Derek Smith. Now the guy no one wanted is making almost $1 million a year with Sacramento."

Then there's Denver Broncos kicker Rich Karlis, the only football player represented by Grinker.

"Karlis was a walk-on at the University of Cincinnati. One day, I get a call from a friend I had at the university, and he said that Rich was looking for an agent. I went down to see the kid and we went out to the field. I was wearing a three-piece suit, holding the ball and he was kicking it out of my hand. Moments like that, working with a kid like Karlis, that's what makes this great."

But great is not the word Grinker uses for other agents. "I think the majority are whores and prostitutes. All they care about is the bottom line and what's in it for them. I mean, why do they keep signing kids to contracts that aren't guaranteed? They tell you that Joe Blow got $200,000 a year, and you wonder why any team would pay that much. Then you find out that not a nickel is guaranteed, so they can cut Joe Blow without it costing them anything.

"This can be a dirty business. When the tenth player in the draft gets $500,000 a year for four years, you're talking about an agent's cut of 4 percent of $2 million. And that doesn't include all the cuts some agents take for handling a guy's money and making investments. If I were a businessman instead of a lawyer, would there be anything wrong with giving a blue-chip college player a brand new Mercedes so he would sign with you? Where's the risk? It's a good investment. But I look at it like this—either you do it right or you join the rest and buy your kids.

"Maybe I don't represent the best players, but I represent the best people. I've never had a kid busted on drugs or get in real trouble. I have one player who I thought might have been shaky, and in the contract I signed with him is a clause that I can demand that he take a drug test at any time, and I have the right to inform every NBA team of the result of the test, all of it written so that it is free from lawsuits and liability. The kid doesn't know if I'll ever use the clause or not, and that's how it's supposed to be. Right now, he's playing well, making a lot of money, and he's with a team and in a city where I think he'll stay out of trouble.

"I've never signed for any loans for my kids. Nor will I even accept a collect call from them. I've bought them meals, and that's it. The only time I've ever given money was $404 to John Schweitz, who was staying with me in Cincinnati and he needed to go home to California to see his girlfriend. It was an emergency situation."

Grinker's favorite expression is that he doesn't treat Sedric Toney any different from Cedric Maxwell.

"Basketball people say I fall in love with my clients, and I suppose I still do," said Grinker. "But now, I can tell a kid to give up the game. Before, I used to think that everyone could play somewhere. My goal isn't to get every one of my kids into the NBA. It is to give them the chance to make it, to let them find out for themselves if they can play. Sure, I've lost clients or had them stolen from me over the years. I started out representing Pat Cummings and Johnny Davis, but they switched agents.

"All I know is that this is a great job. I get up in the morning and I'm excited. Where can I find a team for Jerry Eaves, can I get Dirk Minniefield traded from Cleveland to Houston or Cedric Maxwell from the Clippers to Houston?

Doing it my way means there's always a crisis for some player, but I like that. I like being the guy who can help.

"I'm always on the phone. Bill Fitch and I like to call each other at 2:30 in the morning. The phone will ring in the middle of the night, I'll bitch and complain and then I'll answer it and talk for ninety minutes. My phone bill is $2,000 a month—easy. I'll make five hundred calls a year in which I'll try to find a job for a Jerry Eaves or a Sedric Toney."

This is the story that reveals the most about Grinker: "I went to California for a wedding and stayed at a Marriott, where they keep a computer log of incoming and outgoing calls, including the ones that came in while I was on the line with someone else. It was during the Derek Smith negotiations with Sacramento. I was on the phone from 7 a.m. to 2 a.m. After two days, I checked out, and I asked for the log of my calls. The total was 419 calls. I still have a copy of that log in my office."

•

Ehlo was in uniform on Tuesday night, as the Cavaliers played Detroit at the Richfield Coliseum. And Grinker had another idea for Wayne Embry.

"Did you ever think about trading Ben Poquette?" asked Grinker.

"Why is that?" asked Embry.

"I was thinking," said Grinker.

There was a long pause.

"Okay, Ron, let's hear it," said Embry.

"I would think that some teams would want Poquette. He's 6-9, he's been in the league ten years," said Grinker.

"He'd be a great player for the Celtic bench," said Embry.

"So I asked myself this question," said Grinker. "What's the difference between Ben Poquette and Hank McDowell?"

"You're not going to say what I think you're going to say," said Embry.

"Wayne, you're building for the future," said Grinker.

"Ben Poquette makes \$284,000. You can trade him for a draft pick and . . ."

"Sign your boy Hank for the minimum," said Embry.

"Exactly," said Grinker.

"Ron, I'm disappointed," said Embry.

"Why's that?" asked Grinker.

"I would have thought you could have done better than this thing with McDowell," said Embry. "Ben Poquette and Hank McDowell are not in the same class."

"It's something to consider," said Grinker.

"Not this time, Ron," said Embry, and that pretty much ended the conversation.

•

While Embry fielded Grinker's latest brain storm, Wilkens was in the Cavs' dressing room knowing that he would face the Pistons with only three guards—John Bagley, Ron Harper, and Johnny Newman. Yes, Ehlo was in uniform, but he hadn't practiced and he didn't know the plays.

"It would take some unusual circumstances [read: blowout] for me to use Ehlo," said Wilkens before that Tuesday game with Detroit.

Wilkens did try to look at the bright side: "The fact that we've been home Sunday and Monday nights, at least we got to sleep in our own beds. Being at home just makes you a little looser, a little more comfortable. The crowd will be with us, the guys won't be quite as afraid to try something. If you make a bad play on the road, you sometimes think the whole game can blow up in your face. You do it at home, you figure it's just one play. It is easier to keep the momentum on your side at home."

So the Cavs went out and played the Pistons at home and lost, 103–101. Bagley played 45 minutes of point guard and was 3 for 12 from the field. Harper had a tremendous game with 37 points on 15 for 24.

But it was an agonizing game for Wilkens. With four

seconds left and Detroit ahead, 103–101, the Cavs had the ball out at midcourt. Wilkens drew up a play whereby Harper got the ball isolated on the far wing. On his playboard, it looked great. On the floor, it looked even better than great. Harper was freed by a double pick on the baseline; Phil Hubbard hit the rookie with a long, perfect pass. Harper took two dribbles and was floating to the basket. About five feet away, he flipped up a bank shot.

"Ninety-nine out of a hundred times, I make that shot," said Harper.

Well, this was the hundredth time; the ball banged against the board and off the front of the rim as the buzzer sounded.

"It was a great play," said Harper. "I got the ball where I wanted it. I just didn't make the shot."

And in that sentence lies the truth that all coaches have such trouble accepting—they can do a lot for their teams, but they can't put the ball in the basket. That job belongs to the players.

•

Wilkens was talking over that game with his assistant Dick Helm Wednesday morning at 8 a.m. as the Cavs assembled at Cleveland Hopkins Airport to catch a flight to Detroit, where the two teams would do it again.

"I don't like to dwell on injuries," said Wilkens. "But if we had Mark Price, we would have won that game. You know that Price would have been worth more than two points for us."

Then there was the subject of foul shooting.

"Okay, we don't have Price, but we still were 23 for 36 at the line," said Wilkens. "It's tough to win when you shoot 64 percent at the foul line. We make our foul shots, it doesn't matter that Price is hurt or what happened to Harper on that last play."

The Cavs arrived at the Detroit Airport at 10 a.m. They were at the Northfield Hilton an hour later. Most of the players sort of staggered off to their rooms, talking about naps.

Cavs trainer Gary Briggs said that back-to-back games are especially difficult for a young team. "Our rookies seem to have trouble adjusting to these situations. Even some of the guys who've been in the league a couple of years have problems. They're all right the first night, but the second night they play like they're in a funk. I think it's because they haven't figured out how to deal with getting themselves mentally and physically ready for the second time in twenty-four hours.

"People say a lot about jetlag and switching time zones. But I think it's more mental than physical. I don't care what anyone says, traveling is tedious. You get up in a hotel and wait for a bus. After you get off the bus, you wait at the airport for your flight. And these days, you just know your flight is going to be at least forty-five minutes late. Then you finally get on the plane, and you find out you can't land when you're supposed to because they're having air traffic control problems at the airport so you start circling and circling. Finally, you land and it's another twenty-thirty minutes waiting to get the luggage and then there's a forty-five-minute ride from the airport to your hotel. It's all little things, and none of it is hard. But it all adds up to a pain in the ass. If you want to find reasons to be tired, a lot of these things can be used as excuses. But the good players have their heads in the game. Phil Hubbard knows exactly who he will be guarding and what that man does. In this case, it's Adrian Dantley. He knows that Dantley is right-handed, that he likes to use head and pump fakes to draw fouls. In Hubbard's head, he can see Dantley's moves before he actually makes them on the court. But there are some guys on this team that if you walked right up to them and asked who they had to guard, they couldn't tell you, and we just played the same team the night before."

•

In Wednesday's game, most of the Cavs seemed to remember the Pistons, and the Pistons remembered the Cavs, but

what both teams seemed to remember most was that they had
played the night before and they were tired.

Cleveland scored nineteen points in the first quarter and
fourteen in the fourth period, but the issue still wasn't decided
until the Pistons broke it open with four minutes left. Dantley
and Cleveland's Mark West went for a loose ball; West hit the
floor and got to it first, then Dantley gave West a Puma to the
side of the head. West and Dantley and Bill Laimbeer and
several other players ended up in something that resembled a
Big-Time Wrestling cage match as guys made a lot of grunting
sounds while having each other arm-in-arm in something that
was more of a dance than a fight.

The final was Detroit 104, Cleveland 87. The Cavs made
26 turnovers, shot 52 percent from the foul line and 38 percent
from the field. Harper went from a career-high 37 points
Tuesday night to a career-low 10 points. Yes, this was the
same Ron Harper and it was the same Detroit Pistons, but if
you compared films of the games, you'd never believe it.

"That's how it is with rookies," said Wilkens. "Up and
down. But you know what? I firmly believe that we'll play a
very close game in Boston."

And why is that?

"I can feel it coming," said Wilkens. "These kids don't
give up and they respond to challenges like their first game in
Boston. They won't embarrass themselves."

•

Thursday morning at 7:15, the Cavaliers met in the lobby
of the Northfield Hilton and boarded a bus that took them to
the Detroit Airport where they caught a 9 a.m. flight to Boston.
Cleveland had lost three in a row and seven of its last eight
games.

"Don't you think I know that?" asked Wilkens when the
losing streak was mentioned.

Wilkens continued to fret about the foul shooting. "It has
been killing us," he said. "When we go to the line, I've been

getting indigestion. We move the ball well, make four, five passes. Then we get the ball to somebody open, somebody who has a lane to the basket. He makes a good drive, gets fouled, and then goes to the line. Then we miss both shots and it feels like we got nothing out of the play. The problem isn't bad execution, it's bad foul shooting."

But was this the best time to play Boston?

"It all depends on your attitude," said Wilkens. "If you don't think you can win the Garden, there's never a good time to play there."

There were plenty of statistics to back Wilkens's statement that maybe never is the best time when it came to the Celtics. They had won fifty-three of their last fifty-four home games. The Cavs hadn't won in Boston since 1978 and had lost twenty-one in a row at the Garden. Since Bird joined the Celtics, Cleveland had never beaten them more than once in a season, and the Cavs' 88–86 victory on December 6, 1986, seemed to have filled the quota for this season.

The scheduling computer hadn't exactly done the Cavaliers a large favor by placing them in Boston at this time, either. The Celtics had won 9 of 10 games in a roll that would stretch to 21 of 24 and 26 of 31, and they had the extra incentive of wishing to pay back the Cavaliers for that defeat. Included in those nine Boston victories were four straight on the West Coast immediately after Christmas; a game in New Jersey in which all five starters had over twenty points (something that happens in the NBA approximately once or twice a year); a victory at home over Sacramento in which Robert Parish racked up twenty-eight points and twenty-five rebounds; and, finally, a relatively easy 117–108 decision over Dallas two nights earlier.

"Look, I'm telling you that it will be a close, well-played game," said Wilkens. "That's all I have to say about it now."

•

As the Cavaliers sat in the Detroit Metro Airport, Cavs trainer Gary Briggs started to talk about the upcoming trip to Boston.

"Pain in the ass," said Briggs. "Every trainer in the league will tell you the same thing."

In five years with the Cavaliers, Briggs had lived through five coaches and three general managers. He attended Troy State in Alabama and the University of Florida, and he speaks with a distinct deep Southern (the players call it red-neck) accent. During the games, Briggs sits at the far end of the bench nearest the scorer's table. His job is to keep track of the personal fouls on both team's players and the timeouts for both teams. He also puts himself in charge of yelling "Three seconds" at the officials, "Just to make them pay attention."

Briggs relishes being a character. He is conscientious, hardworking, and dedicated. He knows when to shoot off his mouth and get a laugh, and he knows when to keep quiet. Most of all, he knows how to keep his players healthy and his coach happy. A wide variety of coaches from Bill Musselman to George Karl to Wilkens have great respect for Briggs.

"Okay, you might think I've got an attitude problem about the Celtics because I've been in this league for five years," said Briggs. "But if you're a trainer in the league for five minutes, you'll end up bitching about Boston."

So what's the problem?

"About everything," said Briggs.

Such as?

"Well, they always give you the runaround," he said. "At most places, you usually get to practice in the arena. In Boston, you never do, not even for the shootaround on the morning of game day. They end up sending you out to some crummy little college [Hellenic College] in Brookline. And when you complain to them about not getting into the Garden, the Celtics say, 'Hey, it's not our fault. The hockey team did it. The hockey team controls the building.' I think that if they ever drop an atom bomb on Boston, the Celtics will blame it on the hockey team."

What else?

"Generally, they jack you around," said Briggs.

Examples, please.

"Take today," said Briggs. "I try to set up my practice sessions in advance so I don't have to mess with them at the last minute. About three weeks ago, the Celtics said we could practice from 2 to 4 p.m., which would leave us time to go lift weights at a health club. A week ago, they changed it to noon to 1 p.m. at Boston Garden. Then yesterday [Wednesday], they tell me it is 4 p.m. today at Hellenic College. They have a lady who sets up the practice times, and I think she's 105 years old or something. Anyway, you get the idea—they always change it on you. They tell you that you can get into the Garden, then you never do."

And what about when you finally get into the Garden?

"The first time I went there, I was appalled," said Briggs. "I mean, the whole joint smelled like a big dumpster."

What else?

"The dressing rooms, if you can call them that. You get bounced between these two small rooms, and each one is about eight feet wide. Our seven-foot guys can sit on one bench, spread out their legs, and put them on the bench across the room. And it's always so damn hot in there, I've got to open the windows. Sometimes, the heat is so oppressive it smells like someone threw up in there about a week ago. I know the building is old and maybe they can't control the heat that well, but I bet they could do better than this if they cared just a little bit."

And what else?

"There's the floor," said Briggs. "It's that nice parquet and it looks great on television, but it's the worst in the league. I remember during the playoffs in 1985 when we were playing Boston. The game was on CBS, and right before it started, I walked on the floor and I stepped on something and heard it pop. I heard the same noise coming when some of our players dribbled a ball near that spot during the layups drills. One time, a ball hit the floor and three bolts popped up. It was fifteen minutes before a playoff game was to start and they hadn't even tightened down all the bolts on the floor. They brought a maintenance man out and he went around checking all the bolts, tightening them with a screwdriver."

Briggs says that the Celtics are a favorite topic at the trainers' summer convention.

"The last couple years, the standard opening line to our bitch session begins with [Portland trainer] Ron Culp saying, 'Does anyone have any complaints about anyone besides Boston?' It's become a damn joke, but one of those sick jokes that are painful, too. The two major complaints about Boston is that they jerk you around with practice time and they have the worst ballboys in the league. I call them 'Caspers,' like the ghost. You walk into the dressing room and you might see one. You'll say hello to the kid and then he's gone for the rest of the day. You need a ballboy for errands, but in Boston, you can't find one. Then you look for a kid in the hall, and some usher comes over and stares as if he's saying, 'What the hell are you doing in my hallway?'

"When a team comes to Cleveland, I always make sure there is a ballboy in the visitors' locker room until the coach has his pregame meeting and tells everyone to leave. You may need some extra tape, scissors, or whatever. There is a kid there to get it for you."

Then there is the subject of tickets.

"When you go into the dressing room at most places, they have the complimentary tickets ready for you. All the players have to do is fill out the envelope with the names of who they are leaving the tickets for, and then a ballboy takes the tickets upstairs to the office. But in Boston, they sometimes wait until forty minutes before the game. I can't figure out why they do it, other than to be a pain in the ass. The same guy always brings the tickets into the dressing room and he looks at you like, 'You better know we're doing you this big favor giving you these tickets. We'd really like to sell them, but the league won't let us.' Think about it for a minute. The coach gets four tickets, the assistants, the trainer, and the players get two each. That comes to thirty-four tickets, big deal.

"I know a lot of the guys on the Lakers, and they don't act like this just because they've won a few championships. But in Boston, it's like they think, 'I hate dealing with you. You're lower than something that comes out the rear end of a dog.' That gets real old after a while."

•

The Cavs assembled in the lobby of the Cambridge Hyatt waiting to board the 4 p.m. bus to practice. Briggs was still moaning about the Celtics' canceling Thursday's practice at Boston Garden and telling the Cavs that they were more than welcome to use Hellenic College's gym.

"A barn is more like it," said Briggs. "And I don't care if the Celtics do practice there. If the place is so great, why don't they tell the hockey team to practice there?"

Pro basketball is the only sport where the players dress for practice at the hotel, and they wear their warmups in the lobby. And when there is no practice, players often wander through the hotel wearing at least their team warmup jacket, and often matching sweat pants. Conspicious? You bet. But the players are used to being stared at, anyway. If you're black and 6-foot-10 and staying in places that are havens for upper-middle-class businessmen, you stand out. If you wear your warmup, at least the others in the lobby won't have to ask if you're a basketball player.

"But they'll still ask you how the weather is up there," said 6-foot-9 Ben Poquette.

The Cavs made the half-hour bus ride from the Cambridge Hyatt to Brookline in the middle of the afternoon. It was a cold but sunny day, which was fortunate, since most of the streets around the gym were built more for a burro than a bus.

Wilkens watched the bus driver closely, a young blond guy who seemed pretty new to the job. Why not? A rookie driver for a rookie team.

"I'm getting a strange feeling that our driver can't go to his right," Wilkens whispered to a writer.

"Well, you ought to know," said the writer. "You spent thirteen years in the league and never drove to your right."

"That's just a myth," said Wilkens. "I'm telling you, this driver only makes left turns."

Wilkens wasn't upset, just intrigued. And indeed it seemed that the driver went out of his way to make left turns as the bus seemingly went in circles before finally arriving at the gym.

"I'm telling you, he didn't make one right turn," said Wilkens as he got off the bus.

•

As Wilkens walked into the gym, he said this would be a light practice.

"It's been a brutal week," said Wilkens. "First, we got beaten up pretty badly in Atlanta on Saturday night. Then we lost Mark Price on Sunday. Tuesday and Wednesday, it was back-to-back with Detroit. We're just tired. I've had some coaches who couldn't see it. They always thought that you had to apply the heavy hand after you lose a few games, run the guys up and down the court until they about drop. But that just makes it worse. You can't tell me that practicing your team until they fall over is teaching, it's just punishment. Maybe it makes the coach feel better, but it just makes the players worse. We need to lighten the tone, work on a couple of specific areas, and rebuild our confidence."

Wilkens also said the travel schedule was a factor.

"We had a 6:30 a.m. wake-up call in Detroit, and by the time we got to Boston and settled in our rooms, it was 12:30," said Wilkens. "Now, it's 4 p.m. and we're practicing.

On a day when you travel, it's just plain stupid to have a very physical practice, and I don't care how many games you've lost or who you're playing the next night."

•

A single banner hung in the gym, and it had nothing to do with the Celtics. In fact, it was more like a road marker, letting you know where you were: "Hellenic College, a Holy Cross School of Theology."

The only pro aspect of the gym was the floor, which was about NBA size and had an NBA three-point line. There were only eight rows of wooden bleachers on one side of the floor and an elevated stage at the other side. The stage looked like a nice place for Hellenic's next production of *The Music Man*. There were no seats under the basket, just cement block walls. The main baskets had glass backboards, but the four side baskets all had wooden backboards. Two of the rims dipped to the left as if they had endured too many dunks from Robert Parish.

"When you think about it, it really is strange that a good team like Boston would practice in this place," said Phil Hubbard. "It's just so small."

And so hot. Inside, the temperature must have been eighty degrees. Gary Briggs was mumbling as he went around opening windows.

And so dark. It appeared that all the lights weren't turned on, but maybe it was too dark to tell. It was gray, much like the final moments before an afternoon thunderstorm.

Wilkens told the players to take it easy and shoot around.

"But guys, work on the shots you take in a game," said Wilkens. "Forget the hooks from half-court, okay?"

Wilkens joined the players and shot at a side basket.

"Hey, who said I never went right?" said Wilkens to a couple of writers. The coach then took three dribbles and made a right-handed layup. Yes, he went to his right, but it didn't look right for Lenny Wilkens.

"Hey, Coach, let's see the J," said Ron Harper.

Wilkens took an eighteen-footer.

"I didn't see it," said Harper.

"You didn't look close enough," said Wilkens, taking another shot.

Technically, it was a jump shot. He did leave his feet, and you probably could have slid a penny between his shoes and the floor at the height of his jump.

"You just be nailed to the ground," said Harper, after seeing Wilkens's second jumper.

•

After ten minutes of relaxed shooting, Wilkens, his assistant coaches, and all the players lay down on the floor and started a series of stretching exercises. Wilkens always stretches with his players.

"It's good for you," said Wilkens.

Good for you and a good example for the players was more like it. Wilkens was well aware that most players don't like to stretch, and when they are forced to do it, some try to cut corners. But with the coach on the floor, turning his forty-eight-year-old body into a pretzel, they were almost embarrassed into stretching. It was sort of like a general eating in the same mess hall with the enlisted men.

When the fifteen-minute stretching was finished, Wilkens had the players run three-on-two fast-break drills. That's three men on offense—a player in the middle with the ball and two players filling the wings—going against two defenders. The idea is to get the players loose and playing basketball at the same time.

Next, Wilkens had the team work on its transition offense. There were five players on the floor, set up in a half-court defense. Assistant coach Dick Helm shot the ball, making sure to miss. One of the Cavs rebounded and passed out to a guard, who set up the fast break. The idea was to get the ball up the court and start the offense as quickly as possible.

"We need to get our big men involved, get them running," said Wilkens. "Our big men can beat McHale and Parish down the floor."

You could see the Cavs were still cold. The drill was five on zero, and they were only making half of their shots.

After fifteen minutes of transition, Wilkens broke the team up, with the five starters—John Bagley, Ron Harper, Brad Daugherty, John Williams, and Phil Hubbard—at one end of the court and reserves Johnny Newman, Keith Lee, Craig Ehlo, Ben Poquette, and Scooter McCray at the other. Wilkens had them run through the plays.

"I want us to remember that we have options off every play," said Wilkens. "If we make a pass or two and there's no good shot, make a couple more passes. Ball movement. That's the key. When we move the ball, we get more open shots and we hit 'em."

Reviewing the plays was especially important to Ehlo, who was having his first practice since signing a ten-day contract before the first game with Detroit on Tuesday.

"Craig's a smart kid," said Wilkens. "I sat next to him on the plane and went over our offense. He caught on well. Some guys just have a feel for the game and he's one."

Finally, Wilkens had the players break down into groups of two and practice foul shots. While losing seven of their last eight games, the Cavs shot a rip-roaring 63 percent at the line. The average NBA team hits 75 percent, the Celtics were at 85, and the Cavs were the worst in the NBA at 68 percent with the figure seemingly dropping by the day.

Ron Harper stood at the foul line pantomiming his shot.

"I don't know, sometimes the ball goes out of my hand sideways," said Harper. "Sort of like a football."

Harper was hitting 65 percent, which would be fine if he were a quarterback throwing spirals but was embarrassing for an NBA guard.

"Think about your wrist," Wilkens told Harper, "Don't twist your wrist when you shoot."

Wilkens also worked with Mark West, who was even more of a challenge than Harper. The 6-10 West was a career 49-percent foul shooter, and he was at 38 percent in his last eight games. West also had a problem with his wrist. At the foul line, his right arm and wrist stayed stiff as he shot, almost as if he were throwing a fastball. So Wilkens had one guy shooting foul shots like a football and another guy getting the ball up to the rim at ninety miles per hour.

"You can't make a terrible foul shooter into a great one," said Wilkens. "But we can do a lot better than this. Lately, some of the problems we've had are due to nothing but a lack of concentration. These kids get to the line and they're thinking that they're tired, or that they missed their last shot or they're trying to remember what they're supposed to do on defense. That's why the Celtics are so good at the line. They stand there with the ball and all they see is the rim. That comes with experience. Most players become much better foul shooters after they've been in the league a few years."

Former NBA forward turned WTBS broadcaster Rick Barry watched the Cavs uncork brick after brick from the foul line in Detroit, inspiring him to say, "I don't see why these kids don't understand that foul shooting is where you can be the most selfish, greedy guy in the world and still help your team. If Harper could get up to 80 percent, he could add three to five points to his scoring average."

Harper said, "I know I'm not shooting them real good right now, but I'm doing better than I did in college."

Such was the case, as Harper was a 64-percent shooter at Miami of Ohio. In fact, eight of the Cavs' twelve players were shooting better at the line than they did the year before.

"I suppose you could say that's scary," said Wilkens. "But I look at it from the perspective that at least these guys are showing they can improve."

As the team boarded the bus to go back to the hotel,

Wilkens talked about a fine and reward system he had instituted for the team.

"It began with the two games with Detroit," said Wilkens. "We've already got $100 in the kitty after two games."

Every missed foul shot costs the player $3, but any player who can make it through the game without missing makes $5.

"I don't believe in fines and I don't use them," said Wilkens. "I prefer to handle each discipline problem man-to-man, on an individual basis. But maybe I can at least make the guys see each foul shot as possibly costing them three bucks. Hopefully, they'll think about it before they shoot."

1

Game Day

Friday, 8:30 a.m.

Cavaliers coach Lenny Wilkens was having breakfast in the coffee shop of the Cambridge Hyatt. He talked about a lot of things, starting with Boston coach K. C. Jones.

"We're not extremely close friends," said Wilkens. "But I think we have a lot of respect for each other, going back to when we played. When you were guarded by K.C., it was like a war. I tease him about it, saying I still have the bruises on my arms from his defense. He doesn't like to hear you say that he fouled you, but that was K.C. He guarded you so close, it was like wearing a sports coat during the game. You just couldn't shake him off you. He never said a word, but you knew that K.C. couldn't be intimidated. He was tough and smart, a guy who knew where the ball should go and who should get it. And his hands, K.C.'s hands were so strong and quick."

This was one of Wilkens's favorite moments. He likes sitting in a coffee shop, talking with friends, whether the subject is K. C. Jones, the stock market, or strategy for that night's game. Some coaches are bar coaches; others are coffee-shop coaches. Wilkens falls into the second category. He can be found in the coffee shop for an early breakfast, for a late lunch (about 2 or 3 p.m.), and after the game for a snack and perhaps a beer.

"I guess it comes down to the fact that I just don't like bars," said Wilkens. "I don't mind having a drink, but you

33

won't find me closing down some joint. There are some guys in this league, a certain element of coaches, who usually can be found in the bars. I'm not saying they're right or wrong, I'm just saying it's not right for me. I just don't like to sit around and have eight beers while shooting the breeze."

Wilkens said he had a lot in common with the man who would be coaching the Celtics that night.

"I don't think K. C. Jones and I fall into any of the coaching cliques. Neither one of us believes in self-promotion, and both of us never forget that it's the players who win games for you. Some guys say that, but then they tell you how smart they are and about all the great moves they made. Well, there are times in games when K.C. and I will do something pretty good, a move that helped win a game, but we're not about to stand up and tell the world about it."

There are certain coaching cliques in the NBA. Milwaukee's Don Nelson was the driving force behind Portland's hiring Mike Schuler and Golden State's hiring George Karl, both Nelson disciples. Then there is the Hubie Brown school, which spawned Mike Fratello in Atlanta and Bob Hill with the New York Knicks.

"I feel I'm on good terms with all the coaches," said Wilkens. "But I've never thought I had to please any one of them so they'd say something nice about me. Maybe that has hurt me at times, because there is a network of coaches who help find each other jobs. That has been the case since the league began. Only the names have changed."

Wilkens and Jones are black, and in January of 1987, there were only two other black head coaches—Bernie Bickerstaff in Seattle and Don Chaney with the Los Angeles Clippers. Interestingly, when Wilkens was pushed into the front office as general manager of the Sonics in 1985, his first job was to find a man to replace himself as coach. That man turned out to be Bickerstaff. Jones and Chaney also have something in common—they both were defense-oriented guards for the Boston Celtics.

So being black coaches automatically put Wilkens and Jones in the minority. Being former players also did.

"It's not as bad as it was about ten years ago, but there still is a feeling by some people that guys who played in the league can't be good coaches," said Wilkens. "For example, I think Jack Ramsay has done a great job where he has been, but in one of his books he writes that he doesn't think ex-players should become pro coaches. There were a group of guys who came out of the college ranks—Bill Fitch, Jack Ramsay, and others—who became known as great teachers and geniuses. Some of these people are very bright and can teach, but it's not because they came out of college. But what really upsets me is that some coaches try to put down the ex-players. They say all Doug Moe and Gene Shue ever did was roll out the ball and get out of the way. Well, those guys won a lot of games. They must know something.

"So much of it is image. Some guys make a point of letting everyone know that basketball is all they think about. They act like they watch films twenty hours a day. I'm not going to pass judgment on them. I watch video, but I don't do it all day long. I'll watch a game a couple of times and I'll analyze it, and once I understand what happened, I'm done. No matter if you watch the game once, twice, or ten times, it doesn't change. Either you see what you need to see or you don't. I was the same way in college. I took good notes in class. When I went back to the dorm, I rewrote them and looked them over. By midnight, I was in bed. Other guys would stay up all night studying, but I still got A's and B's so what's the big difference? Let me put it to you like this—I love basketball but most of my friends have nothing to do with the game. I like to read novels, I go to the theater and to concerts. When the season's over, I concentrate on spending time with my family. They're the most important thing to me. As I said before, I have spent a long time in this game and I love basketball, but it's only a part of my life, not all of it by a long shot. I know what I've done in basketball. I feel as though I've made an impact in the game and anyone who takes the time to look at the record can see it."

The forty-eight-year-old Wilkens had been in the NBA since 1960, when he came out of Providence College armed with an economics degree and already having the reputation as a shrewd point guard. But Wilkens never received the recognition he deserved, either as a player or a coach. That's because his career has been spent in the NBA backwater towns of St. Louis, Portland, Seattle, and Cleveland.

"I'm from Brooklyn and I went to Providence, so if I had played or coached the Celtics or the Knicks, I would have been closer to the media centers and I suppose. . . . look, I really don't spend much time thinking about 'what if?' It may sound corny, but I refuse to worry about things that are out of my control."

The record shows that at the start of the 1986–1987 season, only nine coaches in the history of the NBA had won more games than Wilkens. His .530 winning percentage was fifth best among active coaches. He took Seattle to the championship finals in 1977–78, and then he won the NBA title with the Sonics in 1978–79.

The NBA title is something else Jones and Wilkens share.

"When I took over the Sonics [for Bob Hopkins on November 30, 1977], we were 5–17 and the starting lineup was Fred Brown, Slick Watts, Paul Silas, Marvin Webster, and Bruce Seals. On the bench were Dennis Johnson, Gus Williams, and John Johnson. Right off, I knew there had to be some changes made."

To the bench went Brown, Watts, and Seals. Into the lineup came Dennis Johnson, John Johnson, and Williams. The Sonics finished that season 42–18 under Wilkens and lost to Washington in the last minute of the seventh game of the NBA finals. The next year, the Sonics won it all, defeating Washington for the championship.

"It was like a love-in," said Wilkens. "There were 25,000

people at the airport to meet us after the finals and the next day, there was a parade with 300,000 people in the streets. After a while, the championship team takes on legend status. It's something people in that city never forget."

While Wilkens won a world title in Seattle and Jones won two with the Celtics, neither has ever been voted Coach of the Year.

"As I said before, I think part of that has to do with politics," said Wilkens. "K.C. and I believe your record should speak for itself, but I guess that isn't the case. That first year with the Sonics, some people said they didn't vote for me because the balloting was before the playoffs and they had no idea we'd play that well in the playoffs. But wasn't that team 5–17 when I took over and weren't we playing some of the best basketball in the league by the end of the season? And the next year, we win the whole thing and everyone says, 'Well, Lenny should. He had the talent.' But two years before, when the team was 5–17, writers were whining about the Sonics having no talent. When I first got the job, there was a story in the Denver paper quoting several coaches and general managers saying they felt sorry for me because I had so little to work with. Then we start to win, and all of sudden everyone said the Sonics were loaded with players."

Wilkens said race also may be a factor.

"I know it's hard to believe, but there still could be some prejudice toward blacks in coaching. I hate to say it, but there still are some people in the game who think blacks can't coach, or they think blacks aren't as honest or as intelligent as the whites who coach. I've been astonished by some of the remarks I've overheard that have been made by NBA people. K. C. Jones has won championships and he never was Coach of the Year. Al Attles won a championship with Golden State and he didn't get the award. Neither did I. It does make you wonder.

"What I really admire about K.C. is that he knows how to

use his players. Okay, you have Larry Bird. Everyone says he's the coach on the floor, the guy who runs the team. Maybe, but someone was smart enough to set up an offense where the ball ends up in Bird's hands. Some coaches couldn't do that. They couldn't let Bird play such a dominant role, because it would take the spotlight away from them. They want to put too much of themselves in the game. Well, it's the talent that wins, not the coach's name. The Celtics reflect K.C.'s personality. They are mean, tough, and smart, a smooth-running machine. People can say all they want, but who is making the substitutions? Who is calling the timeouts? Who is in charge of the practices? Somebody on that Boston bench is obviously doing something right."

Wilkens has been a coach in thirteen of the last seventeen years, starting in 1969 when he was a player-coach in Seattle at the age of thirty-one. He was the Sonics' coach–point guard for three seasons until he was replaced as coach by Tom Nissalke at the end of the 1971–72 season. Wilkens had a home in Seattle and his last team was 47–35, the best record in Sonics history to that point. Wilkens and Nissalke had a meeting in which Wilkens thought they agreed that Wilkens would stay with the Sonics as a point guard and leave the coaching to Nissalke. Two weeks later, Wilkens was traded to Cleveland, a recent expansion team, a last-place team with the worst attendance playing in the worst arena in the league.

"Len had to feel betrayed by what the Sonics did to him," said Cavs broadcaster Joe Tait. "But he never said anything to embarrass Seattle. And when he was with the Cavs, Len knew a lot more about basketball than Bill Fitch. If he wanted to, he could have caused a mutiny, taken the team right away from Fitch. But Len kept his mouth shut and worked hard. He was the first legitimate star this franchise ever had. He was the first guy who came in here with that quiet determination and fire to win."

After two years with the Cavs, he moved to Portland as a

player-coach in 1974. After two years with Portland, he did a stint with CBS as a broadcaster and then returned to Seattle, first as player personnel director, then as coach.

By some who know him, Wilkens has been dubbed "The Good Soldier" or "The Organization Man." He never complained when he was traded to Cleveland, and he never complained when he was relieved as coach of the Sonics in 1985. He was "promoted" to general manager, but anyone familiar with the situation knew that Wilkens still wanted to coach and that the front-office position was an easy way of moving him off the bench.

In 1984–85, his last season as coach of the Sonics, they were 31–51, but he had winning records in six of his previous seven seasons. In Seattle, they were upset that only six of Wilkens's last eight teams made the playoffs. But in Cleveland, only one of the last eight teams made the playoffs, which made Wilkens's record look very attractive.

After Wayne Embry was named the Cavs' general manager in June 1986, Wilkens spoke to him and mentioned that he wanted to return to coaching. It wasn't long before he had the job.

"Cleveland has been great for me, exactly what I needed," said Wilkens. "Sometimes, you can stay somewhere too long. I think that is the essence of whatever problems I had in Seattle. We had a great team, but it got old. We were picking low in the draft, and some of our picks and trades didn't work out for the best. They spent a lot of time in the newspapers writing about who drafted who and who wanted to trade what player and why. For me, it wasn't a good situation. But in Cleveland with these kids, it really is what coaching is all about. I love teaching and I love how these kids so want to learn. I mean, during a timeout, all their eyes are on the board and the play being drawn up, not on the scoreboard or some chick in the stands. It's a good feeling, because all the players and coaches know we're in this together."

10:30 a.m.

Larry Bird is flipping through the morning paper. "Look at this," he says. "Michael Jordan was 17 for 43 last night. Time for me to have a forty-shot game."

Teammate Dennis Johnson hears him. "I'm the man you have to talk to," Johnson points out.

The Celtics are preparing for the morning day-of-game shootaround at Hellenic College, their normal practice site. Despite Gary Briggs's paranoia, it is true that the only time the world champion Boston Celtics get to use Boston Garden for a shootaround is during the playoffs, and then only if the Boston Bruins have already been eliminated from the Stanley Cup playoffs. The Celtics are tenants—beggars, actually—when it comes to their relationship with the owners of the Boston Garden.

The Celtics are in a jovial mood as they prepare for that night's game with the Cleveland Cavaliers. They have won ten of their last eleven games and are in first place in the Atlantic Division by five full games over Philadelphia. Moreover, they are looking forward to the game with Cleveland, since the Cavaliers defeated them in the season's only meeting five weeks earlier.

"Our team," says assistant coach Jimmy Rodgers, "has a tremendous collective memory. Any time we lose to someone, no matter who, it seems to have a positive effect on us."

10:45 a.m.

Bird emerges from a side room inside the gymnasium brandishing an orange Cavaliers jersey, number 35. That number belongs to Phil Hubbard, the Cavalier he will be matched up with in the game. Apparantly Gary Briggs has been doing some laundry at Hellenic.

11:00 a.m.

The Cavaliers gathered in the lobby of the Cambridge Hyatt as they prepared to board a bus that would take them to Hellenic College for the shootaround.

"I thought we might get to use the Garden," said Lenny Wilkens.

"Same old crap about the hockey team," said Briggs.

Wilkens just nodded. He had heard this explanation before—about a million times, to be exact.

•

On the bus, Briggs started telling more Celtic stories.

"They made us practice at Hellenic College when we made the playoffs in 1985. No one knew how to get there and the driver was the worst. We kept going in circles and finally got there real late, leaving only twenty-five minutes on the time they set aside for us to practice.

"So when we finally get there, the door is locked, just like you'd figure. We spent another five minutes looking for a janitor to unlock the place. We were supposed to practice from 10 to 11 a.m. When we finally got on the floor, there was only twenty minutes left to practice. The guys loosened up and then [former Cavs coach] George Karl had the team stand under the basket for a little meeting. Exactly at eleven, Bird and Ainge came storming onto the court and just started shooting at the basket where George and the team were standing.

"So George said, 'Hey, you guys mind? We're trying to have a meeting.'

"And Bird said, 'It's eleven o'clock and you're on my court.'

"Then Bird took another shot at the basket. McHale showed up and he had his usual arrogant 'I'm better than you slimeballs' attitude. Finally we just broke off practice and gave them the floor. I just hate those guys for that kind of crap."

11:15 a.m.

The Celtics have gone through their stretching exercises and a few warm-up drills. Now they are listening as Rodgers goes over some things they can expect from the Cavaliers.

"They like to push the ball down quickly," Rodgers says.

"You've got to find your man. Get back and match up. They like calling a set play off the secondary break. It's by position number. If they call a '2,' look for the 2 guard, [Ron] Harper. We can change up on defense, 'fist' or 'open hand.' If 'fist,' I want some fronts. We should body check. We should scramble."

Rodgers does most of the talking. K. C. Jones is the head coach, but he is by nature a taciturn man. His coaching expertise lies more in his overview of the game and his one-on-one communication skills. Something about him is immediately endearing to jocks, who sense that K.C. would never lie to them or betray them in any way. Those players old enough to remember are aware that he was a tenacious defender and clever playmaker who was good enough to warrant having his number 25 retired and hoisted to the Boston Garden rafters, right next to the Russells, Cousys, and Havliceks. The younger players perceive K.C. as a players' coach, a man who asks little of them as humans and expects a lot of them as players.

Rodgers, meanwhile, is the acknowledged X-and-O man,

the technical expert. He came to the NBA in 1970 as the assistant to Bill Fitch when Fitch became the Cavaliers' first coach. The two had forged a relationship at the University of North Dakota and were viewed as the NBA's resident Lone Ranger and Tonto for twelve years, nine in Cleveland and three in Boston, until Fitch left following the 1982–83 season to take over the Houston Rockets. The only year they had not been together was 1979–80, Fitch's first in Boston, when Rodgers, by then the Cavaliers' player personnel director, was contractually bound to Cleveland. But he hustled over to Boston for the '80–81 season and has been here ever since.

At forty-three, Rodgers probably knows as much about the inner workings of the NBA as anyone in the league. Respected as a premier advance scout, Rodgers is cheerful and polite. For many years he was viewed as Fitch's "Bobo," or yes-man. When Fitch left, he naturally asked Rodgers to follow. Rodgers surprised just about everyone by staying in Boston, in part because he liked the organization, in part because he didn't want to yank his family out of a very pleasant living situation, in part because his younger son, Matt, had great promise as a football player and was fortunate enough to be playing for a great high school coach, and in part because he sensed it was time to cut the cord with Bill Fitch.

K. C. Jones has the final say, of course, but many of his decisions are heavily influenced by the advice of both Rodgers and the other assistant, Chris Ford, a ten-year NBA guard who has been identified as a future coach since the onset of puberty. Much of the Celtics' pregame preparation is handled by Rodgers.

11:25 a.m.

The Cavs arrived at Hellenic College five minutes before the scheduled start of their practice. Most of the Celtics remained on the floor, and Red Auerbach was standing under the basket. Most of the Cavs remained in the hallway, peeking inside at the Celtics.

"Hey, you guys don't have to genuflect before walking in here," Briggs said to a couple of rookies.

By 11:30 Bird was the only Celtic still on the floor. No one made a move to throw him off. Five minutes later, Bird finally left.

•

As the Cavs took the floor to loosen up, Wilkens was interviewed by a few Boston writers.

"I really think it's going to be a good game," he said.

The writers nodded condescendingly.

Then Wilkens said, "We're starting to come around. I think Ehlo gives us real stability and experience in the backcourt."

Think about that for a moment. Ehlo had been with the Cavs for four days. In three years with Houston, he never played more than fourteen minutes in a game or scored more than fourteen points.

"When I got into the game, you knew it was garbage time," said Ehlo. "In Houston, we'd get a big lead and the fans would start chanting my name. I was like Auerbach's victory cigar. Finally, when we were far enough ahead, [Houston coach Bill] Fitch would call my name and throw the white child to the fans."

•

Ron Harper was at the foul line, practicing his foul shots. Bang, bang, bang.

"Hey, Ron, cut the sides off those bricks," yelled Briggs.

Harper laughed and clanked another shot against the rim.

•

John Bagley was walking across the court and stopped, grabbing his knee. He stood there, holding his knee. Briggs ran out to him.

"What's wrong?" asked the trainer.

"I don't know," said Bagley. "I was just standing there and it started to hurt. I didn't do anything."

Briggs helped Bagley limp off the court. He had Bagley sit down and ice his knee.

"All we need, a mysterious knee injury," said Briggs. "We don't get injuries, we get mysteries. The thing is, I know Bags has to be hurting. He's a tough little guy and he doesn't complain unless something is really wrong. But I ask you, whatever happened to the regular old sprained ankle?"

Briggs shook his head, trying to figure out how the Celtics could be blamed for this latest debacle.

•

The idea of the shootaround is to get the players thinking about the team they play that night. It also prevents them from sitting around the hotel all day, eating and watching soap operas.

"That's the easiest way to end up with legs that feel like lead," said Wilkens. "If you rest too much during the day, you feel tired when you walk onto the court."

•

Wilkens called the players to half-court and told them about the Celtics for the first time since the two teams last met.

Here were his main points:

"1. We have to take away the long pass. Boston loves to throw the baseball pass to start a fast break, even after a made basket. When they get a rebound, jump them with your arms up so they have to stop and look before getting the ball upcourt.

"2. As soon as the Celtics get a rebound, match up with someone as they run downcourt. Guard them as if you were a defensive back and they were wide receivers.

"3. Remember, take away that first outlet pass. Make them dribble the ball up the court.

"4. Always see the ball. If your man doesn't have the ball, make sure you know where he is and you know who has the ball and where. The Celtics wait for you to turn your back on the ball. Then your man breaks for the basket and they hit the guy with a pass and he ends up with the lay-up. See the ball. Always.

"5. This point applies to both Ainge and Dennis Johnson. If they want to set up and take a shot, that's all right. That doesn't mean you completely ignore them, but if they feel like taking twenty-footers, we can live with that. Both Ainge and D.J. are more effective when they drive and either take a lay-up or pass off to one of the big guys. The big thing with these guys is when you're playing off them and they catch a pass, don't go running at them because they will drive right by you.

"6. When Parish catches the ball, try to force him to turn to his left and take a jumper. Whatever you do, don't go running out at him. He'll give you a little fake, you'll run by, and he'll end up with a lay-up. Stay up and on him, keep your arms up. Brad [Daugherty], you can beat him down the court. Think about running him.

"7. The big thing is to try to deny Bird the ball. If he gets it, try to play him as tough as you can. Phil [Hubbard], you've played him before, so . . .

"8. We've got to take the ball at them. We want to run the ball whenever we can. Make them stop us. Keep thinking, push the ball, push the ball, take it to the basket on them.

"9. Pay attention to when their second team comes in. Guys like Greg Kite and Fred Roberts, they don't get the calls that the first team does. We can take it to the basket on those guys, force them to foul us. Remember that Roberts is a garbage player, he likes to get the stuff off the boards so block him out. Also, Roberts is pretty much a right-handed player, He seldom goes to his left."

•

His talk finished, Wilkens had the team run some lay-up drills to let them loosen up their legs. Wilkens stood on the sidelines watching his players. He was wearing a white sports shirt and bright red sweatpants and drinking coffee from a styrofoam cup.

Briggs approached Wilkens.

"Well?" asked Wilkens.

"Bags said the knee hurts," said Briggs. "As far as tonight goes, it's iffy right now. I can't tell what's wrong with it other than it's sore, maybe some inflamation."

Wilkens nodded. Suddenly, he was going to get to find out just how much stability and leadership Craig Ehlo had.

Wilkens broke the team down into two units again. The starters—Daugherty, Hubbard, Harper, and Hot Rod Williams—stayed at one basket with Wilkens. The rest of the players went to the far basket to work out with assistant Dick Helm.

"I want us to go through the plays," said Wilkens. "I don't mean walk, I mean move, like you would in the game."

Realizing that Bagley was out for the rest of the practice, Wilkens put down his coffee cup and walked on to the court. He held up his hand, Harper threw him the ball, and Wilkens took over for Bagley at point guard.

After five minutes, Harper said, "Look, guys, the coach knows the plays."

"Too bad he couldn't start tonight," said Cavs broadcaster Jack Corrigan as he watched Wilkens.

•

The last twenty minutes were spent on foul shooting. Thursday, Harper and his football spirals were Wilkens's project. On this Friday morning, it was Brad Daugherty, who was shooting only 53 percent from the line in his last nine games.

"I don't know what happened to me," said Daugherty. "I wasn't anything like this in college."

Daugherty was a 70-percent foul shooter in his four years at North Carolina.

"I think the problem is my hands," said Daugherty. "They're getting bigger."

How's that?

"I think they've been growing," said Daugherty.

So?

"The ball has been sticking to them, staying in my hand too long," said Daugherty. "It messes up my release."

Wilkens took the ball from Daugherty and held the ball out in front of him. He broke down the foul shot into the grip, the wrist action, and the release. It was almost like saying, "Here's the ball, there's the rim, and here's how we put it in."

Wilkens said, "It's his release. Brad is shooting the ball too much out of his palm, and not getting the ball up on his fingers."

Could it be that his hands had grown too much?

"That's what he said?" asked Wilkens, shaking his head.

Daugherty took about two hundred foul shots as Wilkens watched, and he was making about 70 percent when practice ended.

•

With an ice pack wrapped around his knee, Bagley limped on to the bus.

"I still don't know what happened," he said. "All I know is that my knee hurts. I don't know if it was because I played all those minutes against Detroit [forty-five and thirty-seven] or what. Right now, I don't think I can play."

That prospect seemed to pain Bagley as much as his knee did. Bagley is from Bridgeport, Connecticut, and he played for Boston College.

"The last thing I want to do is miss a game in the Garden," he said.

3:00 p.m.

The only person traveling with the Cavaliers who saw their last victory in Boston Garden was radio broadcaster Joe Tait. The score of that Cavs win was 115–101 on October 13, 1978.

"You know what?" asked Tait. "I've been racking my brain trying to remember that game, but I can't. All I can remember about coming to the Garden with the Cavs is taking beating after beating after beating."

Tait was in his room at the Cambridge Hyatt, preparing his scorebook. He used a pen with four different colors, and he drew lines on a regular-lined sheet of notebook paper. He wrote in each player's name, height, weight, years in the league, and college.

"Eighty-two times a year I write in the same thing for the Cavaliers, and I've been doing it pretty much the same way since I started doing the Cavs in 1970," said Tait. "Obviously, I can do this blindfolded, but I have the feeling that the one night I don't do this kind of review of the players in the game is the one night I'll end up with some kind of mental block and I'll blank out on the air."

In Cleveland, Tait has become a legend. He represents everything right about professional basketball in that city, because he was there when the franchise began in 1970, and he has done the Cavs ever since with the exception of a two-year hiatus during the ownership of Ted Stepien in 1981 and 1982. After a game, Tait will sign more autographs than most of the players. Radio talk show host Larry King has called Tait "the best basketball play-by-play man in the business."

Tait's opinions on the Cavs carry a great deal of weight in Cleveland, and Tait is not a house man. He was highly critical of Bill Musselman, and that former Cavs coach once challenged Tait to a fight in the middle of a coffee shop at the

Dallas Hyatt. Tait also came down hard on George Karl, when Karl said he still wanted to coach the Cavaliers and yet was interviewing at the University of Pittsburgh for a college coaching job. Also, one of the Cavs' owners, Gordon Gund, is blind; Tait is Gund's eyes during the game. Gund lives in Princeton, New Jersey, and he has Tait's broadcasts wired into most of the rooms of his home.

After finishing his scorebook, Tait leaned back in his chair and lit up a cigar.

"I hope this game doesn't end up how I think it might," he said. "But as a broadcaster, you have to go into the night understanding you could be dealing with a twenty- to twenty-five-point beating, because I've sat through so many of them here. But you can't become overwhelmed by that. For example, what if the Cavs play well? It's not all that likely, but they are a young team, Lenny is a very good coach, and they're liable to rise up and give Boston a game. So if that happens, you can't end up on your own personal downer because the team is playing better than you thought they would. You can't be caught by surprise by any kind of game—a close one or a blowout."

In most arenas, Tait broadcasts the games from the floor. In Boston Garden, he is at the top level, near the roof.

"I have no idea how high they have me up there, but planes landing at Logan airport have been known to fly between me and floor," said Tait. "Let's put it this way— being that high is a good place to get a nose bleed and you can tell which players use Selsun Blue. You're so high, you spend the whole game leaning forward over the table in front of you, trying to figure out what those little specks on the floor are doing down there."

Tait said that Boston sells as many seats as possible on the floor, which is why the broadcasters have ended up much closer to the roof than to Larry Bird.

"It's pure economics, and more and more teams are going to do it," said Tait. "I don't say I agree, but they figure the press doesn't pay for those courtside seats, and they can sell them for a ton of money to corporations."

Tait said that he liked games with the Celtics, but not at the Garden.

"I prefer it when they come to Cleveland. First, it usually is a sellout, and second, we at least have a chance to beat them. In Boston, we've lost twenty in a row and after a while, it borders on tradition. Therefore, it's difficult not to think, 'Here we go again,' especially when you're dealing with a club that, even though it's getting long in the tooth, still has some of the best talent in the league.

"When I was a kid, I always wanted to go to the Garden for a game. In the infancy of the NBA on television, you saw three teams—the Lakers, the St. Louis Hawks, and the Celtics. For a while, I thought the NBA was a three-team league and they played only on Sundays, because that seemed to be the rotation. I'd watch those games from the Garden with the parquet floor, and I'll tell you, I thought it was something. But when I walked into the Garden for the first time in 1970, I was flabbergasted. I couldn't believe how bad it was. I mean, the rats were the size of cats, and the cats had to travel in packs for protection from the rats. They still have cats or rats running around. I know I've seen something furry scurrying about.

"Then there is the floor itself, great to look at and awful to play on. I've even been out there and shot a few baskets, and I can tell you that the floor ought to be used for kindling wood at the earliest possible moment. Everything they say about the floor being full of gaps and dead spots is so true. Thinking about the building and the effect the Celtics have on teams here, I don't know what kind of game it will be."

What if someone put a gun to your head and made you guess?

"I'd say the Celtics would win by fourteen points," said Tait. "The reason I picked fourteen points was because the Celtics often get up twenty-some points and K. C. Jones decides to let his bench play a lot longer than he usually does.

Let's face it, Boston has won nine of ten, we've lost seven of eight. At practice, John Bagley came up with some kind of knee injury. Mark Price had an appendicitis attack. Lately, we just can't make a foul shot. It could be a fourteen-point game that would seem like a lot more."

The bookies basically agreed with Tait; Boston was a 15-point favorite.

•

The man assigned to scout the Celtics was Cavs assistant Dick Helm. Helm saw Boston play three times during the first three months of the season, the latest being on January 9, 1987, when Boston played host to Sacramento.

"That was a week before we were to play the Celtics, so that was current enough," said Helm. "Besides, Boston isn't the kind of team you need to see a lot. They aren't a gimmick club, one of those teams that's always changing offenses and defenses, a team that is always bringing in new players. They have pretty much done the same things since Bird, McHale, and Parish got there. The reason to periodically check up on the Celtics is to see if they've added any new plays or made any subtle changes."

His scouting report ran as follows:

Boston's philosophy

"With some teams, you wouldn't address this point because it changes from year to year and coach to coach," said Helm. "But the Celtics have been playing the same way since Red Auerbach was coach. Now he is team president, and they still do the same things.

"I've heard Auerbach say he drafts players who are intelligent and who are used to winning. You can see those traits on the floor because the team plays conceptually. On offense, they pass the ball so much. Guys just don't take bad shots, and if they do, their butts are on the bench. And if the guy keeps it up, they get rid of him. It's almost a privilege to play for the Celtics. Guys take less money to play there because they know they will win. The attitude always has been, 'If you stick with us, we'll take care of you. If you play really well, we'll hang your jersey from the rafters. This isn't a team, it's a family.' For the most part, the Celtic players accept this and they accept the system. And when you play them in Boston Garden, you walk out of the dressing room and it hits you—it's almost like the Basketball Hall of Fame. There's all those banners and jerseys. You come through this haze and you can almost see all the great seventh playoff games that have been here, you can see Auerbach lighting up that victory cigar. You can just feel something special about the place—the ghosts of all the old games and great players.

"Then you see the current Boston team, and you know they are right out of that mold with Bird and McHale. You know that they won't get rattled. You know that they will come at you hard, that they won't just put it into third gear and coast. In our case, that will be very significant because they will remember that we beat them the last time we played. I can see exactly how it will be in that dressing room before the game, because I saw the Celtics a few years ago in a similar situation. I was with Seattle and we beat them in Boston. Then they came to our place and I happened to be going through their dressing room. They had all of our plays on the blackboard; the guys were intently watching a videotape of our last game. It was quiet, intense. You could feel the electricity, the determination. This was business, these guys were getting ready to go to work. No one said it, but you could feel the message—'These guys beat us last time. It won't happen again.' That's part of the philosophy, the mystique. They don't want anyone to beat them twice in a row. The Celtics don't want any team to think they own Boston. Rather, you see that the Celtics honestly believe they are number one, like they are destined to be on top, and they refuse to let anyone challenge them, especially a team like us with five rookies."

What Cleveland must do: "The only reason I talked about the Celts and the Garden is that it might be a factor when our kids go out there for the first time. But what the coaches will remind the players is that we did beat them in Cleveland. Bird didn't play, but everyone else did. Furthermore, in that one game, we had more poise than Boston because we made fewer mistakes down the stretch. So yes, the Garden can be an intimidating place, especially if you're not ready for it. But on the court, things are pretty much the same as they were in Cleveland. It's their guys against our guys, and I think our players have a lot of the traits Boston looks for—they come from winning programs. They are unselfish and they expect to succeed. I say get out on the floor early, look around, feel the Garden, and get it out of your system. When the game comes, just think and play hard."

The fast break

"Boston will run every chance it can, and the Celtics have their big men moving, knowing that if they run down the court, they'll get the ball. So that is the first thing we must be aware of—their running game. Brad Daugherty has to know that if he starts to loaf, Parish is going to take off down to the other end. I scouted a game early in the season against Washington and Moses Malone had been on the floor too long. Moses started sucking air, and the next thing you know, Bird had hit Parish with three seventy-foot baseball passes. They got six points in about three minutes that way just because Robert beat Moses down the floor.

"I love Boston's fast break. You don't see their guards or Bird dribbling up the floor with their heads down. They are always looking around, seeing if their big men are filling a lane. Suppose you're 6-2 and you're going to the basket; you may score or you may not. It depends on the defense. But if you have seven-foot Robert Parish or 6-11 Kevin McHale filling a lane, and they get the ball so that all they need to do is take one dribble and go up for a slam, who is going to stop them?

"The Celtics are always looking to push the ball because that's what leads to easy points. They hit the boards, they take pride in their defense, and then they get the ball down the floor. In the three Boston games I've scouted, they've gotten 30 percent of their points off fast breaks. By comparison, we've gotten 15 percent. So the fast break is a tremendous weapon for them."

What Cleveland must do: "First, if they don't rebound, they can't fast break. That means we have to fight them for every rebound. When they do get a rebound, we need to get right up on the players, force them to hold the ball for a few seconds, make a guard come back to get the ball. This will prevent the long baseball pass. Also, we can't run around with our heads down on defense. Like Lenny always says, 'See the ball.' That's what we've got to do, know not only where our men are on the floor, but also be aware of who has the ball. We can't go taking a bunch of three-pointers and long jumpers. Those rebounds tend to go long and are easily converted into fast-break points at the other end of the court. You know what? The more I see Boston, the more I realize that we can run on them. That is the advantage of our youth. We need to take advantage of our young legs, let them worry about *our* fast break."

Passing

"I don't think any team dribbles as little as Boston. They understand that it is much easier to move the ball around with a pass than by dribble. They keep swinging the ball from one side of the court to the other, waiting and probing the defense, looking for a breakdown. It starts with Bird. He loves to see the ball go from guy to guy until someone gets an open shot. Whenever I watch Boston, I'm always impressed by how often they pass and how little dribbling goes on."

What Cleveland must do: "First of all, we just can't double-team Bird. Seven out of ten players in the league will shoot the ball from the low post even if they are double-teamed. They figure that at least they will draw a foul. But not Bird. He'll kill you with his passing. There is a tendency with some teams to double-team whenever the ball goes into the post. We can't do that to the Celtics, because of their passing skills. In other words, we have to play very good man-to-man defense."

Posting McHale

"The Celtics' first option is to get the ball in Bird's hands, because he moves it around so well. The second option is to get the ball to McHale down low. Of course, the first part of the offense often leads to the second. McHale has such long arms and so many moves, he is almost unstoppable. I mean, it is just about impossible to totally shut him down, but you can keep him from completely dominating the game."

What Cleveland must do: "John Williams is going to cover McHale, and his offense might be the best defense against McHale. Here is what I mean: Hot Rod is about as tall as McHale and he is a little quicker than Kevin. We'll tell John to attack the basket. Put the ball on the floor and go right at Kevin. Maybe Kevin will pick up a few quick fouls. If nothing else, Hot Rod can make Kevin work on defense, wear him down and that can hurt his offense. When Kevin has the ball, I think we'll try to double-team him at least a few times, see if we can force him to pass."

Outside shooting

"Some coaches say let Ainge and Johnson shoot from the outside. I think that's very simplistic thinking because Ainge and Johnson will hit the fifteen-eighteen-footer if you don't even try to guard them. The idea is to force Boston's guards to shoot the ball from, say, twenty feet, and get a hand in their face. A few years ago, the NCAA did a survey about guys taking open shots from about fifteen feet and shots where the player had a defender's hand in his face. The survey found that there was a 6-percent difference between shooting guarded and unguarded. I'm not talking about trying to block the shot, just annoying the shooter a bit. Sure, we'd rather have Ainge and Johnson shoot from the outside than Bird, and we'd rather let Ainge and Johnson shoot from the outside than let McHale operate under the basket.

What Cleveland must do: "We have to guard Bird everywhere. Under the basket, on the wing, at the top of the key. He is their best outside shooter. As for Ainge and Johnson, we aren't going to play them so tight that they can just drive around us. Both players would rather penetrate than shoot from the outside. But we aren't going to just stand there and watch them take eighteen-footers. Those guys are good enough to beat you if you do that."

Trick plays

"As I said before, Boston is not a gimmick team. On defense, they pretty much play you man-to-man; they do very little trapping or pressing. On offense, they go to their strengths because they don't believe you can stop what they do best. But they like to score on sidelines out-of-bounds plays. It is very simple, but it works for them. Bird takes the ball out on the side. They put McHale all alone under the basket and they put their other three players in a straight line in front of Bird. Bird throws the ball in to McHale, who does one of two things:

"1. He just goes up for his shot, figuring no one can stop him one-on-one.

"2. He passes back to Bird, who just stepped in bounds and is in great position to take a three-pointer.

"I've seen the Celtics get six to eight points a game off these plays.

What Cleveland must do: "First of all, we have to pressure Bird taking the ball out. Make it difficult for him to throw that pass down to McHale. Second, we know where Bird likes to go after he throws the ball in. The man guarding Bird should try to stay all over him, force him to another part of the floor, or at least make sure he is covered. The temptation is to forget about the guy who passes the ball in from out of bounds. If the guy is Bird, you'll get burned."

Matchups

POINT GUARDS   John Bagley versus Danny Ainge

Ainge on offense: "Ainge prefers to drive to the basket, and he is capable of taking the ball all the way or passing off to the big man at the last second. This is crucial to know, because some guys tend to penetrate and pass, and when other guys go to the basket, you can be sure they plan to shoot. But Ainge does both, making him very tough. He has also improved his outside shot. He's not a great outside shooter, but he will hit the wide open fifteen- to eighteen-footer. He is a little impulsive. Once in a while, he gets carried away with his shot and takes it a bit too much. He has a very aggressive personality and sometimes he'll try to take the game into his hands and do too much."

Ainge on defense: "This is where Ainge's aggressive personality works so well for him. He is like a terrier that gets right up into your pants leg. He'll pressure you full court, he'll hound you everywhere, and he's so hard to shake. He's always pushing and grabbing and hanging all over you. He fights you for every inch."

What Bagley must do: "John has to be aware that Ainge will start off the offense by bringing the ball up the floor. He doesn't go inside, and he won't post up Bags. You have to be aware of his outside shot, but the main thing with Ainge is to stop his drive. I think we need to help Bags by setting some picks for him in the backcourt. That way, he can rub off Ainge and get a little breathing room as he brings the ball up the floor. John should be able to hold his own, because he's strong with the ball and I don't think Ainge's physical style of defense will bother him as much as it does some other guards."

SHOOTING GUARDS   Ron Harper versus Dennis Johnson

Johnson on offense: "D.J.'s outside shooting is underrated. By that, I mean two things:

"1. He is great shooting off the fast break. The Celtics will run the ball up the court, get it to D.J., and he'll stop on a dime and bury the fifteen-footer. He takes that shot off the dribble at full speed with great confidence.

"2. He is a great clutch shooter. He may miss his first six outside shots, but in the fourth quarter, those shots are going in.

"D.J. penetrates well to the basket and he likes to post up and take a turnaround jumper. He is just so smart and so good in close games."

Johnson on defense: "I think he's the best defensive guard in basketball. He gets right in a player's face, and he has such quick hands. He can take away the ball without the player even realizing he has lost it. He is so quick, and he has the knack of beating players to the spot where they want to take a shot. It is almost like he has a movie in his head and he can see the play before it happens. That's why he blocks so many shots."

What Harper must do: "Ron's offense will be a key here. Ron loves to get the ball in the open court and run. I've already said that D.J. is a great defensive player, but I don't think anyone can consistently stop Harper one-on-one in an open-court situation. The first time they played in Cleveland, I think D.J. was surprised about how tough Harper is going to the basket. He will be ready for Ron this time, but I still don't know if he can stop him. Ron needs to be very careful when he has the ball, because D.J. can steal it from anyone. Also, D.J. will probably try to post Ron and get him into foul trouble, so Ron has to be sure he doesn't try to reach in or over the back and get cheap fouls. The main thing is that Ron has to get his offense in gear and really make D.J. run and work. It is an interesting matchup—D.J.'s strength is defense, Ron's is offense. D.J. is a veteran, Ron's a rookie. But I think Ron will come through pretty well because he's so talented."

CENTERS   Brad Daugherty versus Robert Parish

Parish on offense: "Robert is so good in post-up situations. He has such long arms and the ability to catch the ball, turn quickly, and shoot it. He is dependable on the boards. What I like about Parish is that he is so team-oriented, but he does have to see the ball every other possession in order to stay in the game. He always keeps the ball high over his head, and he has a quick, one-dribble move to the basket. Keeping the ball over your head means a lot because suddenly the ball is 8 1/2 feet off the ground. A smaller player can't sneak by and steal it because he can't reach it. A bigger player will probably have to reach in and foul to get it. Robert has learned this lesson well. He also runs well on the fast break."

Parish on defense: "He is a fine shot blocker and very good on the defensive boards. He blocks shots sometimes because players forget how tall he is and how long his arms are. He is so stoic out there, you tend to forget he is a very intense player."

What Daugherty must do: "First of all, I know Parish runs the court well, but Daugherty can beat him down the floor for some fast-break layups. Second, he has to remember to block Robert off the boards, or else Robert will slip in and get some offensive rebounds. Robert is very deceiving. When Robert posts up, Brad has to play good position defense with his body. He can't reach in and get silly fouls. I expect them to go to Parish early, and a key to the game will be keeping Brad out of foul trouble."

POWER FORWARDS   John Williams versus Kevin McHale

McHale on offense: "He gets open for a shot better than any big man in the league. He does it before he gets the ball by moving or faking or just running to an open area of the floor. In other words, most of Kevin's work is done before he ever receives the ball, and when he gets it, it is relatively simple to score. Most big guys just stand in the post with their hands up, and they don't get in real position to take a good shot until after they receive a pass. He has nice little jump hooks and a very good short fallaway jumper. This isn't just another guy whose arms are so long. He doesn't take bad shots, and he has so many fakes when he does get the ball. He does so well getting his body between his man and the basket so he is in position to receive the pass. I mean, he is a great scorer. What else can you say?"

McHale on defense: "His long arms make him a good shot blocker. Like Parish, he is deceiving on defense. He is working harder than you think, and if you relax for a moment, he'll block a shot back in your face or take the ball right out of your hands. He is not as much physically strong as smart enough to know when and where to use his strength."

What Williams must do: "First of all, Hot Rod should not get discouraged if McHale gets some quick baskets early in the game. He does that to everyone. Also, Hot Rod likes to leave his feet to go up for the block. You can't do that with McHale, because you'll end up fouling him and he'll make the field goal, too. I don't think it's wise to play behind McHale and just concede the pass. You need to play McHale a little off to the side, your hand in front of him to cut down on the area where he can get a pass. Offensively, Hot Rod is quicker than McHale and he needs to use his quickness to get to the basket."

SMALL FORWARD   Phil Hubbard versus Larry Bird

Bird on offense: "Where do you start? With his passing? With his outside shooting? With his rebounding? He is the classic point forward, the big man who can handle the ball, see the whole court, hit the open man with a pass, or bury the three-point shot. His whole game centers around making his teammates better players. You have to cover him outside because he is so dangerous from three-point range. And you have to watch him going to the basket because he's liable to do anything—pass, shoot, you name it. He probably is the one player who comes to mind when you talk about having skills in every offensive area."

Bird on defense: "He is another guy who has pictures in his head and can see what will happen next. Almost instinctively, he can see every option off of every play. He knows how much time is on the clock, where his man is, where the ball is, and where the ball is likely to go. Most guys have enough problems just keeping track of who they are supposed to be guarding. He plays defense like a free safety. He loves to leave his man, set up a double-team, or step in front of a guy and intercept a pass. Again, that goes back to his ability to see into the future. Bird loves to roam on defense and you have to be aware of that."

What Hubbard must do: "Defensively, he has to be on Bird everywhere. Make him work for every shot, and every pass. Guard him so closely when he doesn't have the ball that Boston will be forced to look in a different direction. The less Bird has the ball, the better for us. Larry will get his points, but Phil will make him earn them. Phil plays Bird about as well as most guys because he's quick, tough, and surprisingly strong. Phil gets a lot of fouls, but the officials have respect for him. For every five he is called for, he gets away with ten or fifteen. On offense, Phil needs to look to score so that Bird will have to watch him and not wander so much."

2
Pregame

The Cavaliers gathered in the lobby of the Cambridge Hyatt for the bus to Boston Garden.

Craig Ehlo was telling a few players, "Did you know that I was the last guy to score a basket in the playoffs last year?"

None of the players seemed especially interested, but Ehlo was not about to be denied.

"It was the sixth game, and we [the Houston Rockets] were getting beaten up pretty bad by the Celts," said Ehlo. "Bill Fitch put me into the game with two minutes left and I scored six points. Anyway, I get the ball at half-court with five seconds left. By now the fans are going crazy because Boston was winning the title. I'm dribbling to the basket and here come the fans. Well, I said, I'm gonna dunk in the championship game. I elbowed a fan around midcourt and pushed away another guy around the foul line. Then I went up, and boom. Guess what?"

The players were mildly interested, but not enough to answer.

"I'm the first guy in basketball history to dunk on a fan," said Ehlo. "And as I was in midair, I'm thinking that it would be great to have a ball from the championship game. So I slammed it through the rim, and then I tried to get it. But the fan I dunked on, he wanted the ball. Then out of nowhere

63

comes Greg Kite, trying to get the ball for the Celtics. He about tackled me and the fan to get the ball."

Ehlo smiled. The players just shook their heads.

"Hey, it's basketball history," said Ehlo.

.

A few moments later, Ron Harper said to no one in particular, "Okay, Boston wears those green and white uniforms."

There was silence.

"I mean, Ohio U. used to wear green and white," said Harper. "When I was at Miami [Ohio], we beat up on them all the time."

More silence. Harper began to realize that this wasn't the Mid-American Conference.

"I wonder if Larry Bird ever heard of Ohio U.," said Harper.

.

The Cavaliers were the only team that stayed at the Hyatt in Cambridge, and that is the farthest any visiting team's hotel is from Boston Garden. And why is that, asked a writer?

"The place is owned by the same family that owns our uniforms," said Gary Briggs. "It's Gordon and George's brother, Graham Gund. Does that explain things?"

5:30 p.m.

As the players filed on the bus, Scooter McCray asked the writers, "Anybody got a *Post?*"

That's not the *Washington Post*, but the *New York Post*.

"All I've got is the *New York Times*," said sportswriter Joe Menzer. "I got a *Boston Globe*, too."

"Nah, I like the *Post*," said McCray. "I like to get the rumors. I want to see who got his name in Peter Vecsey's column."

•

There was a seating ritual on the bus. Briggs always sat in the front seat directly behind the driver. Wilkens sat in the front seat across the aisle. Behind Briggs was assistant coach Dick Helm, and behind Wilkens was assistant Brian Winters. Then came the writers, with the players in the back. Ben Poquette always sat nearest the front, while Keith Lee was at the rear. The rest of the players were in between, but in no special seats.

The bus crept smack into the middle of Boston's Friday-evening rush hour. Soon, Poquette's head was up against the window as he drifted off to sleep.

In the front seat, Wilkens read a story in the *Boston Herald* that quoted Dallas coach Dick Motta as saying, "I've been coming to the Garden since Bill Russell was the center, and I can tell you that this Celtic team—the team they had last year before Walton and Wedman got hurt—is the best team to have played in the league in the last nineteen years. It is better than the late Russell teams, because those teams were getting old. And it is better than the Dave Cowens teams, because it is bigger. We came to Boston with a 25–12 record, yet we were probably fifteen points inferior to them even before the game started. For us to have any kind of a shot at an upset, all components had to have been functioning above average. If we make a mistake or a ref blows a call, the magnitude seems insurmountable. When Kevin McHale started to beef at the ref, three of his teammates walked over and told him to shut up. That's how mature they are. They police themselves. It's a helluva team."

Wilkens had a blank expression as he put the paper down on the seat next to him.

6:00 p.m.

It took the Cavaliers a half hour to make the five-mile trip from the Cambridge Hyatt to Boston Garden. As the team was stuck on Cambridge Street, Joe Tait pointed to one hotel after another saying, "There's the Sonesta, we used to stay there. And there's the Sheraton, we stayed there, too. And there's the Marriott, we stayed there, too. . . ." In his seventeen years on the beat, Tait has stayed in more hotels than most of the Cavs players have appeared in games.

As the bus stopped in front of Boston Garden, Harper got out, looked around and said, "Is this the gym? It looks like a bus station."

Actually, it *is* a train station.

•

Part dump, part shrine, part House of Horrors, part House of Basketball Worship, the Boston Garden is a singular stop on the NBA tour. The only existing NBA venue anywhere near the Garden's age is Chicago Stadium, six years its junior, but the true mystique in Chicago is all wrapped up in the resident hockey team, not the basketball team.

With the sixteen championship banners and the two sheafs of retired numbers hanging down from the rafters, the Garden has an aura no other NBA arena can match. Visitors are not merely playing a basketball game when they come to Boston. They are more like guests who have been invited over for tea. The banners serve as draperies in this spacious living room. The Celtics and their fans act as if it is a *privilege* to play there. The apparent responsibility of the visiting squad is to provide a certain amount of competition, but only enough to allow the Boston players a proper showcase for a display of basketball expertise.

The business of the Boston Garden on nights when the

Celtics play is basketball, and nothing else. There is no rock music blaring from the loudspeakers (given the wretched quality of the sound system, this is even more of a blessing than the most diehard traditionalist might think). There are no cheerleaders. Public address announcer Andrew Jick does not introduce the team as *"Your"* Boston Celtics, the way so many obnoxious PA men are forced to do around the league. There are, thank God, no mascots.

There is only basketball, and it's played on the hallowed parquet floor. It is basketball as it existed ten, twenty, thirty, and forty years ago. The Boston Garden has had new seats and a new scoreboard installed in recent years, but it's still sitting atop a train station, it's still reached by a screeching overhead transit system, and it's still got the same feel it had when the best player on the team was Ed Sadowski or Fat Freddy Scolari. A fan whose last game here was in 1950 wouldn't feel out of place. He'd just have more company.

The Garden isn't the noisiest building. It is neither the biggest nor the smallest NBA arena. It is, however, one of the more intimate ones. Built in 1928 with ice hockey, indoor track, and boxing in mind, it is more a high-rise than a sloping-back arena. It is said to be a scaled-down version of the famed Madison Square Garden that was located on Fiftieth Street and Eighth Avenue in New York, and, in fact, the official name of the eating and drinking establishment housed inside is the "Boston Madison Square Garden Club."

For years the capacity for basketball at the Garden was 13,909. The number passed into the Bostonian vocabulary as a standard of reference. A man would come back from ten-o'clock Mass on Sunday morning and say to his neighbor, "Geez. Thirteen nine-oh-nine at St. Bartholomew's today." A man would come back to his desk after visiting the company cafeteria and say to his fellow worker, "Watch out. It's thirteen nine-oh-nine up there."

The interesting thing about the 13,909 was that very seldom during any regular-season Celtics game from 1946 to

1972 were that many people actually in the building. There is a great deal of talk about how Bob Cousy saved professional basketball in the town, but it's not as if he made basketball a religion in Boston. Attendance improved from an average of 4,252 a game in 1949–50 to 6,184 the following year, Cousy's first. In the next five years prior to the advent of Bill Russell the largest per-game average in Boston was 8,064 in 1955–56.

People from the outside have never understood that basketball was very much a novelty in Boston back in those days. Wintertime in Boston meant one thing: hockey. The Bruins, not the Celtics, were the team with tradition. The city of Boston was so uninterested in basketball that the sport was not included in the school system's roster of sporting activities for two decades, starting in the mid-twenties. The suburbs, yes; the city, no.

Boston's very presence as a charter member of the Basketball Association of American (the forerunner of the NBA) came about simply because Walter Brown thought it might be a good business proposition. Brown ran the Boston Garden, and his objective, shared by the preponderance of BAA owners, was to fill some dates in his arena on nights when there was no hockey, boxing, wrestling, or indoor track. There was no great clamor for a professional basketball team in Boston in 1946.

Brown was not a wealthy man. He was a sportsman, a gentleman, and a man of honor. Though his entire sports background was in hockey, he grew to love his Celtics as if they were his own offspring. He believed in them, for reasons that were not terribly apparent at the box office.

Truly modern professional basketball came to Boston in 1950 when Brown hired a brash Brooklynite named Arnold J. (Red) Auerbach to coach his team. Auerbach had already coached two professional teams. He was the first coach of the Washington Capitols in 1946, and he had been the coach of the Tri-Cities Hawks in 1949–50. Auerbach was opinionated and autocratic. Walter Brown knew next to nothing about basketball, which was fine with Auerbach; Red liked the idea of running the entire basketball operation.

Auerbach quickly discovered that he had come to a basketball wasteland. The local newspapers had only marginal interest in the team and the entire sport of professional basketball. One paper, the *Boston Post,* refused to cover the team at all for the first few years. There was great fervor in Boston concerning college basketball, however, the hook being a classy Holy Cross outfit. The Crusaders had won the NCAA title in 1947, and they were the focal point of many highly successful doubleheaders in the Boston Garden over the next three years. The Boston press had particularly embraced Bob Cousy, the flashy Holy Cross guard. Cousy was practically a local demigod, and it made perfect sense to the Boston press that he be made a Celtic. Auerbach, however, was an orthodox basketball man who thought Cousy's unique playing style, which included behind-the-back passes and all sorts of individual gestures, was horrifying. He would rather have given up smoking cigars than draft Bob Cousy. His disgust reached a peak at a writers' luncheon shortly after Auerbach was signed to coach the team. "Am I supposed to win," he inquired, "or please the local yokels?"

The joke was on Auerbach, though, because when the Chicago team that had originally selected Cousy folded and the players were dispersed, Cousy's name was drawn out of a hat by Brown. That's how the man the world would soon know as "Mr. Basketball" became a Boston Celtic.

The Celtics' following was small but loyal, and quite ethnic. The core of their fandom came from the Jewish community of the Greater Boston area, specifically the residents of Brookline, a wealthy enclave almost entirely surrounded by the city of Boston. Sellouts were very infrequent. As an example of Boston's professional basketball consciousness, Brown felt it necessary to secure a preliminary game featuring two Boston high schools the night of the first NBA All-Star Game in 1951.

Auerbach didn't help the situation. He was a coach and general manager, not an impresario. His idea of promotion was to get the schedule printed. His theory was that you opened the doors, they came, they liked the show, and they'd come back. He wasn't about to beg. If you didn't like the product, there was obviously something wrong with you, not him, and certainly not with professional basketball.

The Celtics would have gone under were it not for the fighting spirit of Walter Brown. This amazing man, whose memory remains so sacred that people like Auerbach can hardly mention his name without getting misty, did absolutely everything he could to keep the Celtics alive. This included taking out a second mortgage on his home to help finance the team and reaching into his own bank account to give his players the playoff shares they had earned following one season. The players had cooperated by taking Walter at his word that there would be some cash forthcoming. Imagine anything like that happening today.

The five thousand or so diehards who came every night in the early fifties grew to appreciate basketball as much as any other group of fans in the league. Some of them, men such as Harold Furash, who had attended the very first Celtics practice in 1946 and who remains a season-ticket holder today, became friendly with the players and management. They were very much a part of the Celtics "family." They could not understand why more people hadn't learned to love professional basketball as they did, but once the game started their only concern was the basketball being played, not the empty seats alongside them.

Walter Brown attempted to solve his attendance problems by playing home games elsewhere. The Celtics played a number of "home" games in nearby Providence. In the 1952–53 season the "Boston" Celtics played twenty-one of their seventy NBA games in Boston. Granted, playing in homes-away-from-home or neutral sites was not an isolated practice in those days, but few teams spent as much time *not* playing in their own home as the Celtics.

The Celtics in those pre-Russell days were perennial

bridesmaids, mostly because they lacked a rebounder to get them the ball. They had a fine finesse center in "Easy" Ed Macauley, a consummate jump shooter in Bill Sharman, and the man who set the standard for all playmakers in Cousy. They could score when they got the ball, but they lacked any sort of inside defensive presence, and they were often beaten badly on the backboards.

The first time Red Auerbach saw Bill Russell perform for the University of San Francisco, he knew that the rangy center was the answer. Russell was a new type of basketball force. The big men who had come before him featured offense. They had hook shots and their prime thrust was scoring. The 6-9 Russell was a substandard (and uninterested) shooter. His skill lay in rebounding and in defense, where he had a novel concept: Someone would throw up a shot, and Russell would block it. This just wasn't done in those days.

But how to get him? The Celtics didn't have a high enough draft pick in 1956. There was no way Russell would last long enough to reach Boston. The only way was to make a trade.

The first pick belonged to the Rochester Royals. Their owner, Lester Harrison, liked Russell, but wasn't sure he wanted to pay him what he'd ask. The bidding competition in that far different sports world was the Harlem Globetrotters; Russell did have financial leverage. Harrison decided he wouldn't take Russell, and, anyway, he was quite pleased to select Duquesne's Sihugo Green, a superb 6-3 athlete.

Next up was St. Louis. They were owned by a fiery fellow named Ben Kerner. He and Auerbach had been owner and coach, once upon a time, back when the franchise was located in the Tri-Cities of Moline and Davenport, Iowa, and Rock Island, Illinois. Kerner had fired Auerbach. Kerner wasn't sure how well a big black man would go over in St. Louis.

Kerner was amenable to a trade. The deal was this: Macauley and the rights to Kentucky All-American Cliff Hagan (then coming out of the service) for the rights to Russell. Auerbach really hated to trade Macauley, whom he loved dearly, but Macauley said it was all right because he had a sick child, and he came from St. Louis, so it would be a good move for him to go back home. If his playing skill weren't enough, his graciousness at a time of Celtics need would have been enough for Auerbach to get Ed's number 22 retired and hoisted to the Garden ceiling.

The Russell era actually began in December 1956, because he was busy helping the United States win the Olympic gold medal in basketball down in Melbourne, Australia. When he joined the Celtics they were already in first place with a 16–8 record, in large measure due to the contributions of another rookie, Tom Heinsohn. Auerbach had acquired the 6-7 forward via a device known as the "territorial draft choice," which gave each NBA team natural rights to players attending schools within a certain geographic radius. Heinsohn had gone to Holy Cross, about forty-five miles west of the Boston Garden as the crow flies.

Russell immediately acclimated himself to the NBA. But by the time he retired thirteen years later, the league had yet to acclimate itself to him. The Celtics won their first championship on April 13, 1957, defeating the St. Louis Hawks by a 125–123 score in double overtime. They did so before a roaring crowd of, yes, 13,909. It was the first of eleven championships in the Russell era.

Curiously, this was one of only two seasons in which they averaged as many as ten thousand people a game in Russell's time. There have been innumerable theories concerning the low regular-season attendance figures over the next dozen years. One of the most prevalent beliefs was that the Celtics were so good, so *overwhelming*, that people were simply bored. Supporters of that theory point to the fact that the only other season in the Russell era in which the Celtics averaged over ten thousand was 1965–66, when the Celtics lost the Eastern Division regular-season title for the first time since 1955–56, finishing second to Philadelphia by one game. See, they said. People want competition.

There was a lot more to the Boston attendance situation than the lack of good pennant races, however. Start with the Boston Bruins. They may have been infrequent challengers for the Stanley Cup (1941 was their last triumph), but they still pulled in big crowds. As the years went on it became fashionable to follow the Celtics during the playoffs, but the night-in, night-out support was disappointingly limited.

Media coverage was inadequate. None of the Boston papers covered the team on the road until the playoffs. The papers would cover the road games by listening to the radio broadcasts and writing stories based on the colorful and, shall we say, somewhat slanted descriptions of renowned Celtics announcer Johnny Most. It can be argued that skimpy coverage led to uninformed and, ultimately, uninterested fans.

The Celtics gradually became more and more beloved as time went on. People traveling outside Boston learned that the rest of the nation thought the Celtics were something special. People in Ames, Iowa, or Tucumcari, New Mexico, who occasionally got to see the Celtics on television assumed that the Celtics were a hot item locally. In truth they were honored with lip service but basically ignored until special moments, much like another underappreciated Boston treasure, the *Christian Science Monitor*.

Very little of this academic appreciation of the Celtics as a civic bellwether was reflected in the box office. The true believers kept coming, however, and their ranks grew slightly during the Russell years. The pinnacle for these loyal fans came in 1969, when an aging band of Celtics, who had finished a distant fourth during the regular season in the Eastern Division, won successive series over Philadelphia, New York, and Los Angeles to win the eleventh title in thirteen years.

Russell retired that summer, ending one of the great careers in American athletic history. He had played thirteen years and had won eleven championships. He was the only constant on those eleven champions, save Auerbach, of course. Russell had even coached the last two title squads following Auerbach's 1966 retirement from the bench to the front office. With typical Auerbach logic, he had deduced that Russell wouldn't play for anyone else but Russell, so he made him coach. That Russell happened to be the first black coach in one of the four major sports leagues made Auerbach's decision a sociology story as well.

Life without Bill (and without the brilliant Sam Jones) was rocky. The 1969–70 Celtics were impotent in the middle, finishing sixth in a seven-team division. Attendance dropped over 1,400 people a game, to 7,504. There were no sellouts, and the largest crowd of the season came on opening night. The diehards came to cheer for old favorites John Havlicek and Don Nelson, while wondering if they'd ever again enjoy basketball as much without Bill Russell out there blocking shots and igniting fast breaks.

The wait was brief, because in the 1970 draft Auerbach, picking fourth, chose a 6-foot-9 redheaded backboard eater named Dave Cowens. Red wasn't sure exactly what Cowens was (some teams thought he was a forward, others a center); he just knew that Cowens was fast, strong, smart, and as competitive as anyone he had ever encountered and that he could go get the basketball. Sound familiar?

With Cowens in the middle, a thirty-year-old Havlicek playing the king on the Celtics' chessboard, Nelson popping in his soft jumpers, and a young tandem of Jo Jo White and Don Chaney providing the team with some much-needed athleticism in the backcourt, the Celtics brought life back to the Garden. Attendance rose slightly in 1970–71, a little more the next season, and then spilled over the magic ten thousand mark in the '72–73 season, when the Celtics won sixty-eight games and missed winning a championship, they believed, only because Havlicek suffered a shoulder separation during the Eastern Conference finals against New York.

Most Celticologists of the times believed that ten thousand was an optimum figure. Concurrent with the rise of the Celtics was the ascension of the Boston Bruins to an all-time peak of popularity. These were the big, bad bruins of Phil Esposito, Ken Hodge, Johnny (Pie) McKenzie, Ken Hodge, Derek (Turk) Sanderson, Gerry Cheevers, and especially Bobby Orr, the wonderchild defenseman. They owned the town as no athletic team had since the Red Sox of the teens. The Celtics were doing all right, but compared to the Bruins they were a Double A franchise. In the spring of 1973, it was impossible to imagine the Bruins would ever be anything but number one in the winter and the Celtics would ever be anything but number two.

But what did account for the Celtics' appeal? Why were the basketball fans more willing to come see this team than the hallowed Russell teams? No one knew for sure, but there was no shortage of theories:

1. Russell was personally unapproachable, whereas Cowens was an accessible superstar, a real workingman's hero.
2. The Celtics were now attracting second-generation fans for the first time. The children of the original fans now had their own money to spend. They were attracted to the Celtics as kids and now they were consumers. Plus, Dad and Uncle Sid were still around, so everyone went together.
3. Media coverage was more extensive. The Boston papers had expanded their coverage. The Celtics had good local television coverage. Johnny Most was now a certified local legend, and it was chic to listen to his hysterical accounts of the games.
4. The Celtics featured white stars. This last subject is endlessly debated in Boston, a city where race is a very volatile topic. Auerbach was a pioneer in sports, drafting and signing the first black in the NBA (Chuck Cooper, 1950), becoming one of the first two coaches to start five black players (both the '65–66 Celtics and 76ers did so), and hiring the first black coach (Russell) in the NBA. In

addition, he insisted on black-white roommate pairs whenever possible. In terms of his personal record, the Celtics
stood above reproach when it came to fostering the rise of
black players in the NBA.

But while the NBA was getting blacker and blacker, the
Celtics were able to hold on to some superior white players.
Cowens, with his flaming red hair, was a vivid contrast to
Russell. Could the Celtics help it if a particular fan felt more
empathy toward Cowens than Russell? Havlicek was white.
Nelson was white. Paul Westphal, another exciting white
player, joined the team in 1972. The Celtics clearly maintained their appeal in the seventies for the biased consumer.
Only a fool would fail to understand that. The question was
whether or not the Celtics have ever pandered to the bigots
who happened to be basketball fans. The Celtics maintained
then, and maintain now, that they don't.

Rival general managers and owners envied the Celtics for
their good fortune, as they defined it. Blacks were taking over
the game on the court, and the Celtics appeared to be the only
team capable of winning a high percentage of games while
still employing a large number of white players. The professionals found it difficult to criticize the Celtics when they
would gladly have traded half their team to get their hands on
a Dave Cowens or a John Havlicek, players who might have
induced the same white fans who were staying home in their
own cities to come out to the games.

The NBA existed in a frighteningly racist society, and few
doubted that one reason why the NBA had not attained the
stature it deserved was that large segments of white America
didn't want to patronize a sport featuring so many blacks. The
flip side of this was that the blacks who would ostensibly love
to come watch their own heroes simply could not afford
tickets.

The Celtics won championships with Cowens at center
and Havlicek playing a major role in both 1974 and 1976.

These championships meant a great deal to Auerbach, who wanted to show the world that the Celtics could accomplish great things even without Russell. The Celtics had clearly broadened their fan base by now, and they silently cheered when the Bruins and Bobby Orr (by then the owner of two battered knees) had an acrimonious parting in 1976. The Bruins have never recovered from his departure.

But very little went right for the Celtics in the next few years, on and off the court. Cowens took a "leave of absence" after the eighth game of the 1977 season. He returned two months later, and the Celtics were able to extend the Philadelphia 76ers to a seventh game the following spring, but the fabric of the team had been irrevocably damaged. The team won thirty games in '77–78, and the highlight of the season came on the final day of an otherwise dreary year, when a capacity crowd came to bid a teary farewell to thirty-seven-year-old John Havlicek.

Public faith in the Celtics had eroded, although the actual attendance figures could have been worse. From a high of 13,446 in the '75–76 season, the Celtics' average slipped to 10,193 in '78–79, when the only sellout of the season came on opening night. The Cavaliers handled them by fourteen points, and a lot of people said good-bye to the Celtics for the season.

By this time the team was in the hands of John Y. Brown (no relation to Walter), a mercurial Kentucky blowhard who had so alienated Auerbach that the cigar smoker had seriously considered accepting an offer to take over operation of the Knicks, of all people. The Celtics had gone through seven ownership regimes following the sudden death of Walter Brown in the fall of 1964, but all interested parties consider the meddlesome Brown to have been the worst of the lot.

His most egregious act came on February 14, 1979, when, without Auerbach's knowledge or approval, he took three precious number-one draft picks Auerbach had been hoarding and shipped them to New York for the skittish Bob McAdoo, a three-time NBA scoring champion whose style and personality had no chance to fitting in with the Celtics, even a Celtics team as unrecognizeable as that one.

Auerbach has never forgotten or forgiven. Years later, he told an interviewer with regard to John Y. Brown: ". . . and he'd make deals. Well, he made one great big deal that could have destroyed the team, without even consulting me. . . . He did ruin it. We just happened to put it back together again, luckily. One wrong guy can ruin it so fast your head will swim."

Auerbach's outlook brightened considerably when Brown's partner bought him out following the 1978–79 season. Harry Mangurian, in contrast to his bombastic business partner, was from the "speak softly and carry a big stick" school. He was a tough man on the inside, but he kept a very low public profile. And he wasn't foolish enough to make deals without consulting Red Auerbach.

At the conclusion of the 1979–80 season, the Celtics needed to do two things. They needed a coach, and they needed to restore public confidence. Auerbach found his coach in Bill Fitch, who had just resigned after nine successful years in Cleveland. And there was a way to restore public confidence. All the Celtics had to do was sign Larry Bird to a contract.

Auerbach had drafted Bird the previous spring. The Celtics had two high draft choices, number six and number eight. He took Bird, who had a year of eligibility remaining at Indiana State, at number six. He took Freeman Williams, a scoring machine from Portland State, at number eight. Williams would never play a game for the Celtics before being included in a controversial John Y. Brown–inspired trade with the San Diego Clippers, née the Buffalo Braves.

The Celtics had one calendar year to sign Bird, or else he would be thrown back into the 1979 draft pool. In the interim, Bird led Indiana State to a 33–1 record and a berth in the national championship game. When Auerbach drafted him, many knowledgeable experts were saying the 6-9 forward from French Lick, Indiana, could become an All-Pro. By the time the Celtics started negotiating with Bob Woolf, Bird's agent, the opinions had been revised upward. The only question appeared to be whether Bird would become the greatest forward of all time, or the greatest player of any description.

Harry Mangurian was not afraid to spend the money. He signed Bird for the highest salary ever paid a rookie in any major professional sport, a sum in excess of $600,000 a year. Since Boston was something of a backwater outpost when it came to college basketball in those days, not everyone knew what to expect. However, the average fan was pleased to know that there was something resembling a savior out there and that the Celtics had not been timid about obtaining him for their very own.

It took Bird something like two months to become the most popular basketball player Boston had ever seen. Bigger individually than Cousy, bigger than Russell, bigger than Havlicek, bigger than Cowens, bigger than anybody. He combined the best skills of each previous Boston basketball superstar, and he possessed a work ethic unsurpassed in the history of the sport. He demonstrated the ability to shoot, pass, rebound, defend, and make clutch plays. He wasn't afraid to take a charge or dive on the floor for a loose ball, things many gifted players in the league believe are actions best left to the low-price overachievers. Boston's basketball fans, weaned on the best basketball teams that had ever been assembled, recognized that their entire experience had been educating them to appreciate this one man, a player so versatile and compelling that he represented a microcosm of everything good the sport has to offer. Of all the gym joints, in all the towns in the world, he had come to theirs. Watching Larry Bird play became a privilege. Dazed basketball aficionados wandered around asking themselves, "What wonderful thing did I ever do to deserve *this?*"

It didn't hurt, of course, that Bird was white.

Would the Celtics' fans have embraced Larry Bird as they

did if he were black? If, for example, he were Magic Johnson? Probably not. Would they be so in love with Kevin McHale and his wondrous rejections if he were black? Probably not. Would comparable players with darker skin have created such a passion in this racially fractured city? Probably not. Does this change their basketball accomplishments? *Absolutely not.*

Meanwhile, attendance soared. Forgotten were the days when a good season-ticket total was eight hundred. On December 19, 1980, the Celtics defeated the Houston Rockets by a 133–119 score before 14,570, which was 750 below the then capacity figure of 15,320. Those were the last official empty seats for any Celtics game, regular-season, playoff, or exhibition. The Celtics sell over 12,500 season tickets annually in a building that now seats 14,890 (a renovation that added thirty-two luxury boxes reduced the capacity). The waiting list for season tickets is years long. Following the 1985–86 season the Celtics raised their ticket prices substantially. There were eight season-ticket cancellations.

There were championships in 1981, 1984, and 1986, and a loss in the 1985 championship finals. With each passing year the crowd feels more and more a part of a continuum. There are now third-generation followers, fans to whom Nate Archibald, and not Bob Cousy, represents the Good Old Days. This is the Boston Garden, where the Cavaliers will be battling against decades of excellence tonight.

•

The Celtics have been arriving at their place of business for the past fifteen minutes or so. All except one. Larry Bird habitually presents himself anywhere from a half hour to an hour and a half before everyone else, because he likes to go out and shoot hundreds of jumpers on the Garden floor in preparation for the game, usually with assistant equipment manager Joe Qatato retrieving the basketball.

On this particular day, Bird has napped for two hours

("Woke up about 3:30 and lay there until 4") and driven to the Boston Garden, arriving around 5:15. Unlike some of his teammates, Bird has no prescribed eating habits on the day of the game.

Bird's obsession with pregame shooting is one of the great conversational topics in the league whenever coaches gather. "It's tough enough coming in here, anyway," says Knicks coach Bob Hill. "Then you find out *he's* already been out there two and a half hours before the game practicing his jump shot."

K. C. Jones has spent part of the afternoon watching the tape of the first Cleveland game. Bird was unable to play due to a strained right achilles tendon, but that was no excuse for the Celtics' languid effort. "It showed we weren't into it," he said. "Slow motion. We really didn't want to be there. Our second game in two nights. No intensity; that's what I saw."

Rodgers also scoured the tape and has now firmed up his opinion of the Cavaliers, a team he finds fascinating in the extreme, given its extreme youth.

"They've got a good half-court game, surprisingly good," he said. "Good execution, but their first objective still is to push the ball down quickly, especially Harper and Bagley. Harper is ahead of the pack most of the time. Bagley pushes it with Daugherty and Williams trailing.

"I've seen Cleveland five or six times now. What interests me is that they looked very well organized early on. One exhibition game against Detroit was interesting, however. It showed their youth. They had Detroit beaten, but they didn't know how to win the game. I mean, they were really in control and didn't know it. There's some pretty good talent on the Cleveland team, but they don't always know how to use it. In this particular game they had the momentum going, and any kind of positive approach and they would have won the game."

It's a widely held NBA belief that the average rookie has a career crisis somewhere around the thirtieth game of the season. He has played the equivalent of a college season, and he isn't even forty percent through his schedule. This revelation frightens and depresses some players. The Cavaliers, with three rookie starters, are ripe for this effect. Tonight's game is their thirty-seventh.

"Now they face the thirty-game syndrome," Rodgers said. "It's easy to hit that college wall. A team like that will ride some highs and lows. If it's getting some rewards in terms of wins and losses, it can be extremely dangerous."

K.C. has seen enough of the young Cleveland talent to be highly impressed. Number one, there is Ron Harper, the young cheetah masquerading as an NBA guard. He had twenty-six in the earlier game, and no Boston defender appeared physically capable of stopping him. "He's quick *and* fast," said K.C. "Explosive. Innate passing ability. Once he gains some knowledge of the NBA he will be very difficult to deal with. He has a confidence bordering on arrogance, and that's what you need to be great."

Rodgers is equally intrigued with Brad Daugherty, the Cleveland rookie center. "He has a handle of being 'soft,' but I don't think he is. I'm not even sure what that's supposed to mean. He's aggressive, and he seems to play with confidence. I think he's a very good player, and if they wind up getting another center, he could become a nice two-position man." Indeed, Marty Blake, the NBA's director of scouting, had rated Daugherty as both the number-one senior center and the number-one senior power forward prior to the 1986 draft.

This is the first visit to the Boston Garden for Harper, Daugherty, Williams, and substitute guard Johnny Newman, and the ancient second-story barn can be an intimidating place. This particular Celtics team has only lost one game in the building since December 6, 1985, and no previous group, whether led by Bill Russell, Dave Cowens, or anybody else, has ever established such hegemony. Rodgers wondered to what extent, if any, the young Cavaliers will be affected.

"I don't know," Rodgers said, shaking his head. "This

team pushes it up relentlessly, and we have to worry about transition. Teams have been hurting us badly of late pushing it up. This team has young legs and some excellent jumpers. The frightening thing about it is that with so much youth I really don't think they care that they're playing us, or that they're playing in the Boston Garden. They just go out and play. A team with more experience might actually be more concerned playing us. This is a young team that relies on talent. If they knew any better, they might not come in here and be loosey-goosey, but I think they will."

•

As the Cavs entered the Garden, they were greeted by a man about fifty, wearing black horn-rimmed glasses, an insti- tutional-style, very short haircut, and a Shamrock Celtic coat that probably was left over from the days of Bob Cousy.

"Mr. Harper, can I have your autograph?" said the guy, holding out a pen and an autograph book.

"This dude seems all right to me," said Harper, signing his name. "I don't know, I kind of like his style."

The players and coaches all took time to sign the man's book. Then they followed Gary Briggs to the dressing room. But television broadcaster Jack Corrigan, the self-proclaimed Bird-watcher, went out to the floor.

Briggs walked into the locker room and went right for the window. "Must be ninety degrees in this place," he said. "Every damn time. They pull the same crap every damn time."

As the players started to undress, Corrigan came to the dressing room and told a few writers, "I was out there watching Bird. He made fifty-nine in a row."

"Foul shots?" asked a writer.

"No," said Corrigan. "All kinds of shots. From every- where. He was out there by himself, a ballboy rebounding for him. It was swish after swish after swish."

6:15 p.m.

John Bagley went over to Lenny Wilkens and said, "My knee is all right. I don't know what happened before, but I'm fine."

"That's good," said Wilkens, who smiled.

Maybe this will be a close game after all.

•

As Harper walked on to the court, a writer asked him, "Did you hear about Bird?"

"The fifty-nine in a row," said Harper.

The writer nodded. Harper shrugged. You could tell he had suddenly realized that Ohio U. didn't have anyone like that.

•

Wilkens was being interviewed by a couple of Boston writers. He was talking about his team's youth, the problems that come with starting three rookies. All the usual stuff.

Then Wilkens saw Earl Strom walk into the official's room. He smiled. The game was getting closer all the time.

•

Yesterday, as the Cavaliers stood around the baggage-claim area at Boston's Logan Airport, the talk turned to officiating, specifically the question: "If you could pick two guys to work the game in Boston, who would they be?"

Wilkens: "No question, my top guy would be Earl Strom. Then either Jake O'Donnell or Hugh Hollins. I know that any one of those three guys will give us a fair shot. They won't be intimidated by the crowd or being in Boston Garden."

Veteran forward Ben Poquette: "My one guy would be Earl [Strom]. He is head and shoulders above the rest. I want him any game I play on the road because I know he plays it straight. After that, I suppose Jack Madden or O'Donnell would be all right. But Earl is tops. He has been in the league for a long time. Crowds don't bother him. Coaches don't bother him. Really, nothing bothers Earl."

Joe Tait: "My choice would be Earl Strom and Hugh Hollins. Earl Strom is the greatest road ref in the history of the game. I'm not saying that Earl is corrupt or political. Rather, he's been in the league for twenty-eight years and he has the kind of demeanor where he likes the crowd to get on him. When Earl makes a call and the crowd boos, he loves it. I think he sort of revels in the attention. As for Hollins, he's very cool under fire. Not much affects his judgment."

Assistant coach Dick Helm: "No doubt about it, the one guy I want to work our game is Earl Strom. He is a great official, a man beyond reproach. When Earl works your game, you know that he will award the aggressor. The team that is working the hardest gets the calls, and that's how it should be. If your team is dogging it or a little flat, boy I'll tell you that Earl will let the aggressive team just grind you into the floor."

Strom has a quick, go-to-hell smile and an ego that means he must be at the center of the action. Supposedly, officials are doing a good job when you don't notice that they are on the court. But you always notice Strom. He doesn't just call a foul, he orchestrates it. Sometimes he blows the whistle and pauses, knowing that everyone is looking at him, waiting for a call. Other times, a play will disgust him, and he'll sort of shrug as he makes the call. But above all else, Strom is revered for his attitude.

Wilkens: "He controls the game, but he doesn't ruin it. Earl lets the guys play."

Helm: "When Earl is on the floor, you know you can't take the night off. If you do, if you want to run around out there on nothing more than your reputation, Earl will let someone knock your head off. Earl's games are always physical. He likes it when both teams are really trying, when they are fighting for rebounds and loose balls."

Tait: "Earl is the epitome of the old guard. These guys don't like to make a lot of calls, they don't worry about the crowd, and they don't call technicals every five seconds. Each team won't be shooting fifty foul shots. They know what they're doing, and when they're on the court, you can feel that confidence."

So Earl Strom was the unanimous choice, but that also means there are a lot of officials that the Cavaliers don't want to see.

"Of course there are," said Wilkens. "But only a fool would start naming names. Look, officials are quick to tell you that they go out and call the game the way they see it. They say no one gets special favors. But that's the problem. How do these guys see the game? What are they looking for?"

"Put it like this," said Joe Tait. "There is a collision at midcourt in the Garden between Larry Bird and John Bagley. Who do you think, in the situation of an either-way call, will get the advantage? You have two guys running into each other, one in a Cleveland uniform and one in a Boston uniform. I'd say it's an 80-percent chance that the call would go against the Cavs, and I know I'm being conservative."

Poquette: "Some guys just get taken care of by the officials. That's a fact. Who wants to go to a game and see Larry Bird play only twelve minutes because of foul trouble? Who wants to pay twenty bucks and watch Michael Jordan foul out? Basketball is like life—some people get more breaks than others."

Brad Daugherty: "I don't care what they say, the game isn't called the same. I just touch somebody like Moses Malone, and the whistle blows. Moses knocks me across the floor and nothing. I've gotten called for more ticky-tack fouls. The other players keep telling me it's because I'm a rookie. The veterans tell me to wait a few years and I'll get mine. It's really frustrating."

Wilkens: "Officials tell you that they make no distinction between rookies and veterans, between stars and guys off the bench. But if you analyze the film, you see there is a real difference. I don't know how many calls Daugherty has gotten because he was just standing there, hands over his head, and somebody jumped right into him. After a while, it isn't coincidence. They're making Brad pay his dues. Brad is a rookie center. We tell him to go out, play physical, and fight for position. Some guy is pushing you across the floor and nothing happens, you push back and get a foul. And in Brad's case, the officials heard that he came out of college with the rap of being soft, so when they see him try to push a little, they say he's overcompensating and hit him with a foul. In a couple of years, he won't get those fouls. The officials will be used to him, they will have seen his moves."

Helm: "Familiarity is important. The officials know the Celtics. They are a great team, a veteran team. When you're in Boston and Larry Bird gets on an official, you know whose side the crowd will take. And there's Bird, the MVP, telling the official he's wrong, the crowd is screaming, and unless the official has a very strong personality, he is liable to say to himself, 'You know, maybe I did miss that one or Bird wouldn't have said anything.' I mean, if you're an official and you're questioned by Larry Bird you will think about it a lot longer than if Johnny Newman said something to you. That's a fact of life. There was a game early in the season when Bird got thrown out. That's a very hard thing to do. It puts a lot of pressure on the official who gives Bird the two technicals. Not too many officials want that pressure."

Tait: "It isn't in the best interest of the league for Larry Bird to get thrown out of games. No one pays to see Bird sit on the bench or end up in the dressing room, and you better believe the officials know it."

Poquette: "I remember a playoff game in Boston where Bird drove the baseline, I stepped in and drew the charge. The crowd went crazy, but I got the call. A minute later, we're down at the other end of the floor and the action has stopped for a foul shot. Bird is complaining to the officials. All of a sudden, an official, I won't say who, came over to me and said, 'You deserve an Oscar for your act on the baseline.' The guy was agreeing with Bird, and telling me that the other official, the guy he's working with, was wrong. Think about that."

Wilkens: "What really drives me crazy is anticipation calls. Making a foul call as Bird drives to the basket before anyone even touches him because it looks like someone will. I mean, some guys just blow the whistle, the action stops and nothing has happened. Then they have to make up a call. Those things drive coaches insane."

Helm: "The Celtics get a lot of those calls because their players have been in the league for so long. The officials have been watching Bird, McHale, Parish, and the rest for years and they know these guys' moves even before they are made. When one of the Boston guys goes to the basket and blows a lay-up, some officials just assume there had to be a foul. Why else would the guy have missed a shot? He's too good a player just to have messed it up."

Wilkens also said that coaches also adopt a strategy for dealing with officials.

"You can't go out there screaming at everyone," said Wilkens. "In fact, I don't like to scream at officials. I prefer to talk to them, to explain my point. But how much I talk to officials varies from guy to guy. I won't say that much to Earl Strom because Earl does a very good job. That way, when I do speak up, I know Earl will listen to me because I haven't been on his case all night.

"Officials' attitudes vary so much. Some guys, you tell them something once and they've grasped it. With others, you can go on and on, say the same thing ten times, and forget it. No chance. Officials are supposed to go into the game with an open mind, but some of these guys make you wonder. You say one word, and they're all over you, like 'How dare you question me?' Or some guys act like they would like to be anywhere else in the world but on that floor. You have to pay because they had a bad day at home or something.

"After you've been in the league a while, talking about officials can make you crazy. You can't control them. The league makes it so that you don't find out until right before the game who will be working. So I try not to think about the officials until I get to the arena and see who is calling the game. Now that I've said all that, I still hope Earl Strom is there when we step on the floor."

Tonight, Wilkens has gotten his wish.

6:30 p.m.

All the Cavs were shooting around with the exception of Phil Hubbard, who was alone in the dressing room.

He was asked about covering Bird.

"It will be the same," said Hubbard. "I've been coming here for eight years, and it's always the same. The floor is the same, the dressing room is the same, and Bird is the same. What else is there to say?"

Hubbard was in the kind of mood anyone would be in if he knew that in an hour, he was supposed to guard Larry Bird.

•

On the court, Craig Ehlo was demonstrating his last playoff basket for the few players who might have missed the story the first time around. He dribbled, threw elbows, and slammed.

•

Scooter McCray came over to a writer at the press table.

"I feel like dunkin' on someone," said McCray.

"Think you'll play?" asked the writer.

"Who knows?" said McCray. "Hey babes, why don't you

go out there and I'll dunk over you. At least that way I know I get to dunk over someone."

.

Harper looked at the Boston Garden floor and was appalled by all the black scuff marks and the loose bolts.

"Man, my driveway is better than this," said Harper.

Harper bounced the ball. There was a thud as it hit the floor.

"Dead spots," said Harper. "They got a lot of those."

But Harper wasn't concerned. He jumped up and down a couple time.

"I kind of like it here," said Harper. "I've seen this floor on TV. I thought it was the greatest floor there ever was. But who wrecked it? One thing I know—I can score here. There's something about this floor. It's a jumper's floor. It's got spring, you know? Some gyms I walk into and I know I can get up, this is one."

No one had the heart to tell Harper that Boston seldom has had a great leaper on this floor. Most of the guys were like Don Nelson and Bailey Howell, getting rebounds below the rim.

"I feel so good," said Harper. "I can score in this place. I remember watching my main man, M.J. [Michael Jordan], run up sixty-three here. I saw it on television. It can be done."

6:45 p.m.

Wilkens sent a ballboy onto the floor to call the players into the dressing room. When they all had settled down in front of their lockers, Wilkens stood up and talked about the following topics:

Kevin McHale

"What we need to be very concerned about is McHale. We know they are going to run a lot of two-man games, McHale and a guard. What we will do is keep running a guard at McHale. Ron [Harper], sometimes it will be you and sometimes it will be Bags [Bagley]. We have to give Hot Rod some help."

Dennis Johnson

"Ron, you can't let D.J. take you inside and post up. He likes to do that because he figures he can jump over about anyone in the league. Let's keep him away from the basket."

Danny Ainge

"Bags, remember that Ainge is most effective when he drives to the basket. Play off him. Let him think about taking an outside shot. If he hits a three-pointer, he hits a three-pointer, okay? Look, if Ainge is shooting, that means Bird and McHale aren't, and that's what we want—keep the ball out of the hands of Bird and McHale."

Rebounding

"Everybody, crash the boards. I want to hold them to one shot. No tip-ins. And when we get the ball, run it upcourt. Push them, make them run. Listen, we can run against them better than they can run against us. Remember the game in Cleveland, how we moved the ball, making four, five, six passes. That's how we get easy shots. When we move the ball, we hit the outside shot."

Robert Parish

"Brad, make Robert go to his left on that shot. Keep your body on him, hands straight up. Block him out."

Earl Strom

"Another thing. Earl Strom is working tonight and remember that Earl lets a lot of contact go. Play strong, fight for position. Earl will give us a good game if we work hard. He's not going to be intimidated by the fans or anyone else."

Larry Bird out-of-bounds play

"Listen up, we need to pay extra attention when they take the ball out on the sidelines out of bounds. Remember, they like to put McHale alone under the basket and Bird takes the ball out. They try to pass it to McHale. If he gets it and the guy guarding Bird doubles down on McHale, McHale throws a pass back out to Bird, who takes a three-pointer. So we need the guy guarding Bird to be active, to remember that he may have to run down on McHale, and then run back up to get Bird, okay?"

See the ball

"You can't run down the court with your backs turned. See the ball, always see the ball. Be aware of who has the ball and where your man is. Take away the long pass. Make them dribble the ball."

•

That was it. There was no mention of playing in the Garden, what the Celtics had recently done, or even much talk about the first time the two teams met, in Cleveland.

"Why go into all that garbage?" asked Wilkens. "The point is tonight's game, not what happened before. The guys have enough to think about just concentrating on the next two hours. Why make it any tougher?"

6:55 p.m.

The Celtics' locker room was cleared of everyone but team personnel. The official pregame meeting had begun.

Rodgers had diagrammed eight Cleveland plays on a board in front of the room. The players took their seats in front of their respective lockers, with the exception of Bird, who stretched out on the floor. Lying on a towel, he did some loosening-up exercises for his cranky back. K.C. waited until things settled down and then said quietly, "All right, Jim," turning the session over to his chief planner.

"A couple of reminders," said Rodgers. "They will play a little 'softer' [on defense] than we've been looking at. They will try to run every time. Harper will release. Daugherty and Williams really come hard as trailers on the break. Those two will come over your back. I don't know how smart they are, but they work hard. They are scrappy."

Rodgers went over a few of the Cavaliers' plays.

"We'll try to unravel them. A lot of 'Fist' defense. We'll try to get Bagley to go one-on-one and get plays to break down. They like the secondary break for Harper. If not Harper, there's Newman, a good shooter. Dennis [Johnson], be physical with Harper. Try to cut down the curls.

"Larry: On Hubbard, step up and bump. Look for him to 'flash.' [A "curl" is when an offensive player comes off a pick, or screen, and cuts. A "flash" is a hard diagonal or lateral cut to the basket in the hopes of receiving a pass from the high-post area.]

"If we can keep the ball from reversing to Daugherty, we can throw their whole offense off. They also use a lot of cross-picks. If we go 'Fist' [a defense in which the defense plays in front of, rather than behind, the Cleveland big men], in every situation we can switch. Front low and pressure. On any cross-pick, talk and switch."

Bird started to pace the room, stretching.

"One more thing," continued Rodgers. "On sideline out-of-bounds, they want to run Harper down off a stack. They enter to pick for Harper or Newman. The other thing, they may go to a two-man game."

Ford, standing off to the right, spoke up. "We've got to be patient on the offensive end. Run plays through. . . . Use your options."

Whether or not Rodgers was done, Bird decided he was. Bird has been kvetching for two days because in the previous game Danny Ainge had taken twenty-one shots against Dallas. An incessant needler, Bird especially loves to ride Ainge, whom most of the team treats in the same disparaging manner David Nelson used on little brother Ricky.

Bird looked over at Bill Walton, the injured center who has yet to play in a game. "Hey, Bill," Bird began. "You sittin' on the bench, right? If you see Danny open, holler at his man to guard him, not me. Maybe I'll get twenty-one shots tonight."

The world champions were ready to take the floor.

7:10 p.m.

The Cavaliers went out on the floor, shooting around and nonchalantly going through a lay-up drill. Wilkens, Dick Helm, and Brian Winters remained in the Cavs' dressing room. The coaches didn't say much, just small talk.

7:20 p.m.

Officials Earl Strom and Mel Whitworth came onto the court. Whitworth stood stoically at midcourt, his arms folded across his chest, his expression blank. Strom walked up and down the press table, saying hello to people he knew.

7:25 p.m.

Wilkens and his assistants came out of the dressing room, and it was the first time that Wilkens saw that Whitworth was the official working with Strom.

"I intentionally try not to pay attention to who will be the officials," said Wilkens. "I can't control that, anyway, so why worry? But since I saw Earl Strom in the hall about an hour before the game, I was feeling good. And when I saw Whitworth . . . well, I was a little concerned about him. But I wasn't going to say anything to the players."

7:30 p.m.

The buzzer sounded and the players came to the sidelines to line up for the national anthem. During the anthem, Wilkens seemed in a good mood as he looked around, spotted some people he knew at courtside, and smiled.

Brad Daugherty stood very erect, very military. You could tell he was the son of a retired Marine sergeant.

Ron Harper bowed his head, eyes closed.

John Bagley also bowed his head, but in the middle of the song, he reached down and rubbed his left knee.

John Williams was standing on his tiptoes, leaning forward and staring at the Celtics bench.

•

At the end of the anthem, the Cavaliers' starting lineup was announced. Harper was announced first, followed by Bagley, who got a nice hand.

"These people in Boston are always nice to me," said Bagley. "Once you play here like I did for B.C. [Boston College], they never forget you. They give you respect."

The rest of the lineup followed—Hubbard, Hot Rod Williams, and Daugherty.

The players returned to the huddle, and once again Bagley rubbed his left knee.

"It felt all right, but I guess I just wanted to make sure," said Bagley. "I had spent all afternoon with ice on it. I almost felt frozen."

Williams would look down at Wilkens in the middle of the huddle, then sneak peeks at the Celtics.

Wilkens: "Remember, push the ball at them. We can run better than they can. And see the ball, guys. See the ball."

With that, the Cavaliers took the floor for the jump ball.

3

First Quarter

THE MATCHUPS

POINT GUARDS	Ainge vs. Bagley
SHOOTING GUARDS	Johnson vs. Harper
CENTERS	Parish vs. Daugherty
POWER FORWARDS	McHale vs. Williams
SMALL FORWARDS	Bird vs. Hubbard

12:00 *The jump ball; John Williams against Robert Parish. Parish easily wins the tip and taps the ball back to Bird.*

Prior to 1938, possession of the basketball was obtained following each basket by a jump ball between the respective centers. The rule was then changed to provide for jump balls only at the start of each quarter and in the event of either a held ball or a ball knocked out of bounds when the officials can't determine whose ball it should be.

A number of years ago, the NBA adopted a proposal for just one official jump ball for possession, at the start of the game. The team winning the tap then receives possession to start the fourth quarter as well. The opposing team receives possession at the start of the second and third periods.

A prime mover in the adoption of the revised jump-ball

rule was Red Auerbach, who said he had gotten tired of watching officials make a farce of the jump ball by throwing the ball up to one side or the other. The rule is a part of the NBA fabric now, and there is no agitation to restore the jump ball prior to each period.

•

Wilkens sent Williams instead of Daugherty to jump against Parish, even though Daugherty is the center and is usually the man jumping to start the game. While the seven-foot Daugherty has a one-inch height advantage over Williams, Hot Rod is a better leaper.

For all that thought, it really didn't matter much. Official Mel Whitworth threw the ball up decently, although it was closer to Parish than to Williams. One of Auerbach's prime contentions was that few officials were capable of throwing the ball up properly for a fair jump ball. It is much more difficult then it looks. Most of the time, one of the players jumps too early and "steals" the tap—tips it on the way up. That is an illegal move, although the officials sometimes ignore it. Other times, the official throws the ball too high. Then both players jump and still can't reach it. They end up back on the floor, whacking at the ball, looking like two giraffes trying to play volleyball. Few sights in sports are as ugly as that of a seven-footer whose timing is thrown off and who has become disoriented.

So the fact that Whitworth threw the ball about the right height and that neither Parish or Williams stole the tip meant it was at least a passable jump ball.

"Let's face it," said Wilkens. "Just because the ball was slightly toward Parish, I wasn't going to argue. I didn't see us winning the tap anyway. The main thing was for us to match up with Boston, to force Parish to tip the ball behind him so they couldn't get a fast break off the opening tip."

That was exactly what happened, as Parish indeed tipped the ball behind him—right into the hands of Larry Bird.

The game had begun.

11:41 *Bird sixteen-footer top of the key.*
Assist—Ainge.

BOSTON 2, CLEVELAND 0.

"The play was a 'Bull-swing,' " Rodgers explained. "Actually, a Bull-swing-swing."

This is a basic Celtic play in which Parish comes up high and two players—here Bird and Johnson—criss-cross in front of and around the seven-foot center. Meanwhile, on the left side, McHale went from the high post to down low, picking off Bagley to free Ainge for a pass from Parish. Parish then went to the low post, setting a screen for Bird. When Bird popped out, Ainge had a choice of passing targets, because McHale had excellent position inside on the lower left-hand box. Ainge pump-faked a pass inside and hit Bird for the foul-line jump shot. The shot went up and it was true, hardly touching the net.

From the bench, Wilkens yelled, "Push the ball," at about the same time the ball was going through the net.

11:26 *Bagley sixteen-footer baseline.*
Assist—Hubbard.

BOSTON 2, CLEVELAND 2.

The Cavs knew that Boston was willing to let Bagley shoot. Bagley knew that Boston wanted him to shoot, and the reason was obvious—to put it kindly, the Celtics felt that Bagley was

First Quarter

11:26   Part I

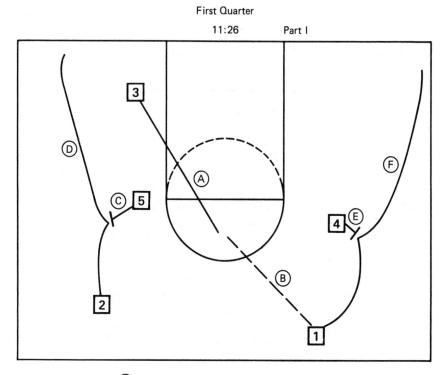

1 — Bagley   (A) Hubbard breaks up to the foul line.

2 — Harper   (B) Bagley passes to Hubbard.

3 — Hubbard   (C) Daugherty picks for Harper.

4 — Williams   (D) Harper breaks around Daugherty's pick and goes to the corner.

5 — Daugherty   (E) Williams picks for Bagley.

                  (F) Bagley breaks around Williams's pick and goes to the corner.

ILLUS. 1

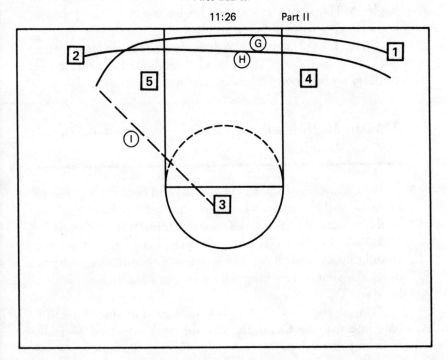

First Quarter

11:26   Part II

1 — Bagley
2 — Harper
3 — Hubbard
4 — Williams
5 — Daugherty

(G) Bagley cuts across the lane into the opposite corner.

(H) Harper cuts across the lane the same time as Bagley.

(I) Hubbard passes to Bagley, who is open for the jumper.

ILLUS. 2

the least likely Cleveland player to hurt them from the outside. To put it bluntly, the Celtics didn't think he could knock down the fifteen-to-twenty-footer, and his 43-percent mark from the field indicated that it was a safe bet to let Bags fire away. When Harper and Bagley crossed at the baseline, Ainge decided to switch from Bagley to Harper without letting his backcourt partner Johnson know. Bagley was left open, and he hit.

On the Cleveland bench, Wilkens leaned over to his assistant, Dick Helm, and said, "That's good. Bags didn't hesitate. He just went up for the shot. When he hesitates, he misses."

11:10   *McHale misses an eight-foot hook on the baseline.*

An isolated post-up, Kevin's bread and butter. Parish went up to the foul line to draw Daugherty away from the action. But Williams played textbook defense on McHale. He didn't go for McHale's shoulder fake; he just stood his ground, his arms straight up over his head. He resisted the temptation to try to block the shot by reaching out and toward McHale's shooting hand.

Despite the miss, the Celtics had a good feeling about this play because the Cavaliers had not double-teamed McHale from any direction. McHale, the Celts believe, cannot be guarded one-on-one by any forward in the league. If the Cavaliers persist in this approach, you can book McHale for thirty points right now.

10:59   *Harper drives right lane for scoop.*

CLEVELAND 4, BOSTON 2.

Daugherty rebounded McHale's missed hook, and threw a two-handed chest pass to Harper at half-court. It was the classic outlet pass, hard and well thought out. Obviously, Daugherty had learned more than good manners from Dean Smith at North Carolina.

Harper remembered what Wilkens had said in the dressing room: "Take the ball at 'em." Of course, Harper never needs to be reminded to drive to the basket and shoot. Harper had missed three weeks of training camp because of a contract dispute, and about twelve hours after signing, found himself playing in a Cavs scrimmage before a packed house of 8,200 fans at Akron University. The first time he touched the ball as a pro, he let loose with a twenty-footer. In twenty-five minutes that day, Harper took twenty shots—seven went in, four were blocked, and two were air balls. In his first regular-season weekend as a pro, Harper cut loose with forty-seven shots in back-to-back games. That was the most brash shooting debut by a rookie since that of legendary gunner John Drew.

So when Harper got the ball at half-court, he wasn't thinking about passing lanes, or passing anything except Dennis Johnson and Bird on his way to the hoop. The Celtics had been warned by Rodgers about Cleveland's immediate defense-to-offense transition, and here was the first glimpse. As soon as the rebound was thrown to Harper, the Celtics should have retreated, en masse. "But both Ainge and D.J. gambled and went for a steal in the backcourt," said Rodgers. "You give Ron Harper that type of room to operate, and you've got a problem." As he got near the basket, Harper put the ball in his right hand and held it high above his head, almost waving it for the crowd to see. Then he completed the Dr. J–like move by softly banking the ball off the boards.

"Ron is so good in the transition game, he is sometimes a one-man fast break," said Wilkens. "When he is in the open court, Ron has the green light to go to the basket. I just don't think that anyone, anywhere, can stop him."

As the ball went through the rim, Harper turned upcourt and smiled. Hey, maybe this was like playing Ohio U. after all.

Wilkens yelled, "See the ball."

10:51   *Johnson pushes the ball up and misses a floater.*

There is a firm belief in the NBA that one of the great opportunities to fast-break comes in the aftermath of an opponents' successful transition. The reason is two-fold: First, teams naturally congratulate themselves for accomplishing something good and let their guard down. Second, the average player just naturally runs the floor harder going from defense to offense than vice versa. Over the years, no team has had more success coming back at opponents who have just scored than the Boston Celtics. And it can be a devastating play, since a quick strike makes the rival feel his own efforts have, in effect, been wasted.

In this instance, Johnson did the right thing by Celtics' standards, but simply missed the shot. The rebound was knocked out of bounds to Boston, but Johnson and Robert Parish missed connections on a pick-and-roll pass and the ball was turned over to Cleveland.

10:39   *Ainge foul. First personal, first team foul (P1, T1).*

Down on the Cleveland end, Ainge and Williams became tangled on a rebound. Williams was feeling his face, checking for his right eye. Whitworth called the foul on Ainge. Ainge yelled, "Oh, come on, I barely touched him." Williams seemed relieved to find that his right eye is still in its socket.

10:20 *Harper misses underhand layup.*

Harper could still hear the words "Take it to 'em." And he still had visions of his last lay-up. But as he drove into the key, it was not a fast-break situation. And when Wilkens said, "Harper is unstoppable," the key part of the sentence was "in the open court." This court was as closed as you can get, as three guys wearing green and white were all over Harper, and they were a lot bigger and stronger than the Ohio U. Bobcats. Stuck, Harper flipped up some sort of finger-roll underhand lay-up, which might not have been the worst shot in the world except for one fact—he was ten feet from the basket. Well, the ball did hit the rim.

Ainge would later say of Harper, "Once in a while he makes a shot so spectacular that you temporarily forget he's missed his last ten." This was one of those ten.

10:12 *McHale turns for six-foot jump hook.*

CLEVELAND 4, BOSTON 4.

McHale caught the ball at the side of the lane and was in no real hurry to take a shot. Nevertheless, everyone knew what McHale would do when he was six feet from the basket. First, he faked a dribble toward the baseline. He did it with a simple move of the shoulder, not even bouncing the ball. Williams moved up to try and stop the drive. Next, McHale used a head-and-shoulder fake to make it look as if he were taking a jump shot. Williams stood there, his arms straight up. Finally, McHale shot a right-handed hook over Williams that went in.

"There is absolutely nothing you can do to stop that shot," said Wilkens to Helm. "Hot Rod played perfect defense, the ball just went in." McHale has simply reached into what Hubie Brown calls his "bank vault of moves" and made a withdrawal at the expense of the talented Cleveland rookie, one of the few players in the league whose own arm span rivals McHale's extraordinary reach. McHale is 6-11, but he is 6-11 going on about 7-5 because of his spring and his absurdly long arms. And exactly how long are those arms? "I have no idea," McHale says. "I only wear short-sleeve shirts."

McHale also benefits greatly from the team framework of the Boston Celtics. As he gained position on the lower left box, Bird saw this and backed away, toward the foul line. Johnson, meanwhile, "spotted up" (i.e., ran to a useful location on the floor, back toward the sideline, to the left as you're looking at McHale). If things got sticky for McHale, he had two available passing outlets. Either Bird or D.J. would be open should his man drop off to double-team McHale. But Cleveland isn't doing that, so Kevin took the shot.

"A good play," Rodgers said. "We have a perfect triangle here."

10:02   *Daugherty misses a hook shot.*

Ainge is in what the Celtics refer to as "Rover." He is the double-up man on the Cleveland big men, leaving Bagley open. Ainge gets to Daugherty late, but he misses the shot anyway.

9:48   *Bird misses pull-up jumper.*

9:40 *Daugherty stuffs over Bird.*
         Assist—Bagley.

Cleveland 6, Boston 4.

Off Bird's miss, Bagley rebounded near the foul line and dribbled behind his back as he drove from foul line to foul line. Fifteen feet from the Celtic basket, he threw a bounce pass to Daugherty, who caught it and slammed over Bird, who was late getting there for the block. Parish, who was covering Daugherty, was simply beaten down the floor by the Cavs' rookie.

"I keep telling Brad that he is good enough and quick enough to outrun any center in the league, not just Parish," said Wilkens. "But the key is to get your big guys to believe it. Then, when you do get them running, the other players have to reward them by getting the big guys the ball at the right moment. The Celtics do it all the time. That's why Parish runs so well. He knows if he goes, Bird or someone will hit him with a pass and he'll get a dunk. That also is why this was an important play for us early in the game. It let Brad know that we were looking for him. It was the first time during the game that he really took off, and we made the right play."

9:23 *McHale shoots two free throws. (Hubbard,*
         P1, T1.) Swish, clang.

Cleveland 6, Boston 5.

A broken play. D.J. had originally called a "Down," but Ainge broke the pattern, and the Celtics wound up with a quite acceptable two-man game involving Ainge as the feeder and McHale as the receiver.

There was no way of knowing it, but this would be Boston's only miss from the free-throw line during the game. The Celtics would go forty-seven minutes and thirty-seven seconds—and thirty-seven straight shots—without a miss.

Just as McHale was to take his second foul shot, Cavs broadcaster Joe Tait said, "The Celtics are shooting 80 percent as a team from the line." As usually happens when an announcer praises a free-thrower, the guy missed.

"So far," Rodgers said, "we've established (1) Cleveland wants to run; (2) Boston is not getting back; and (3) Boston can post up at will."

9:08   *Bird steals Daugherty pass.*

As the Celtics headed back upcourt following McHale's missed free throw, Rodgers jumped up and yelled, "Fist!" He was setting the Celtics' defense.

"In 'Fist,' " Rodgers explained, "you want to front the low post and exert great pressure on the ball." So Parish played in front of Daugherty and Ainge got up tight on Bagley. Cleveland's play eventually broke down because Ainge would not allow a swing pass back to Bagley. "We made them do something they didn't want to do," said Rodgers.

Bird wound up stealing a pass from the confused Daugherty. But Hubbard reached in and knocked the ball loose. Hubbard and Bird both dove for the loose ball. Hubbard sort of knocked Bird out of the way with his hip as both players hit the floor. Bird asked Earl Strom for a foul call. Strom shrugged as the ball rolled off Hubbard's hands out of bounds.

"Who said no one dives for a loose ball in the NBA?" asked Wilkens.

The play showed why Hubbard has the reputation of being

physical and not backing down from anyone, even Bird. And he had an official in Strom who respected that reputation.

8:56 *Johnson misses jump shot.*

"Bull," the play that began the game, was called again. The free man was Johnson, who then took the ball low but missed the jumper. This time, the Celtics retreated back on defense properly.

8:48 *Hubbard travels.*

8:30 *Bird misses twenty-one-foot jumper after popping out behind a screen.*

"We ran 'Motion' and both options were there," Rodgers explained. Bird could have either taken a jumper or dumped it in to a posting McHale. Hubbard came flying at Bird and Larry missed the shot. "See Hubbard jumping at Larry?" inquired Rodgers. "Hopefully, we can make him pay for that."
Daugherty pulled in the rebound, his fourth.

8:15 *Williams misses turnaround.*

8:10

As the Celtics worked the ball around the key, Cavs trainer Gary Briggs yelled, "Three seconds." It wouldn't be the last time he offered this bit of advice to the officials.

8:05   *McHale misses teeny-weeny jump hook.*

Again, a very good shot off the secondary break: not a fast break, not a set play, just five veteran players pushing the ball up the court and free-lancing. McHale found himself one-on-one with Williams. McHale and the Celtics' staff were still drooling over that, confident that his time will come before this game is over.

Daugherty rebounded again—his fifth.

8:00

Wilkens got out of his chair for the first time in the game. With Strom officiating, he saw no reason to be up and yelling at the officials early. If Strom wouldn't be influenced by a packed house at the Garden, he certainly wasn't going to think much of a coach griping, unless that coach picked his spots and only spoke when he had a legitimate point. What got Wilkens up was Daugherty's tough play on the boards, and he yelled, "Push the ball."

7:56   *Harper floats in lane for runner.*

CLEVELAND 8, BOSTON 5.

As Daugherty rebounded McHale's shot, he uncorked an outlet pass to Hubbard, who was at midcourt on the wing. Harper was also at midcourt, near the center circle. Harper called for the ball. Hubbard looked at Harper but didn't throw the ball. You could almost hear what was going through Harper's head: "Take it to 'em." You can't take it to 'em unless you have the ball. Harper ran to Hubbard, who flipped about a five-foot pass to Harper as both players reached the three-point arch. Then Harper took it to 'em. As he approached Johnson, D.J. tried to take the easy way out by reaching in and trying to "poke-check" the ball away in the manner of an NHL defenseman. It is one of his favorite tricks, and no one in the league is better at the maneuver. But Harper blew past Johnson with one dribble and split McHale and Parish by simply jumping and floating through the big men for a lay-up.

7:50 *Bird at foul line. (Bagley, P1, T2.) Swish, swish.*

Cleveland 8, Boston 7.

A classic "Right-Back" response to a rival fast break. McHale took the ball inbounds and passed it to Johnson, who then threw a long lob to Bird under the Cavs' basket. Bird pump-faked and Daugherty flew by. Bird went up for the shot and was whacked from behind by Bagley. Thus far, the Celtics have run twice in ten possessions; each one has sprung from a Harper fast-break basket.

Wilkens registered his first complaint: "He traveled." There was no response from Mel Whitworth.

"Bird switched pivot feet," said Wilkens later. "This was a case of a young official getting mesmerized by Bird and so he calls the foul instead of seeing the travel first."

7:25 *Daugherty misses follow-up.*

After Bird made his two free throws, the Cavs ran the same play they opened the game with, but this time Ainge and Johnson stayed with their men, so no one was open. With the shot clock down to five, Hubbard forced a jumper over Bird.

The rebound ended up in Daugherty's hands, but he missed the four-foot banker.

7:09 *Parish six-foot lane rainbow.*

BOSTON 9, CLEVELAND 8.

The rebound nearly bounced off a couple Celtic players and out of bounds, but Johnson came over, jumped, and caught it with one hand. While in the air and flying over the end line, he flipped the ball back inbounds to McHale. McHale drove coast-to-coast as the Cavaliers seemed stunned to see the big guy bringing the ball all the way down the court himself. McHale missed a five-footer, but Parish rebounded the ball and shot a soft six-footer that bounced around the rim several times before it fell in.

6:52 *Hubbard fourteen-footer, right baseline.*
Assist—Harper.

CLEVELAND 10, BOSTON 9.

Harper drove baseline with Johnson guarding him. Hubbard set a pick on Johnson, and both Johnson and Bird continued to chase Harper. Harper spotted Hubbard open and delivered the ball, Hubbard hitting the baseline jumper.

"The play was designed to get Hubbard open," said Wilkens. "We wanted to get him the ball and have him score so Bird would be forced to pay attention to Phil and stop roaming so much on defense."

6:40   *Bird misses from top of key.*

Bird and Parish ran a basic pick-and-roll play from the top of the key. Bird got open but missed the running one-hander; the ball bounced off Daugherty's hands, but Bagley picked it up off the floor.

6:30   *Bagley drives middle for banker.*

CLEVELAND 12, BOSTON 9.

Getting the rebound at his own foul line, Bagley drove the length of the floor and when he reached the Celtic foul line, he was confronted with McHale and Johnson. Harper was breaking down the left wing, and Bagley looked in his direction as if he might pass, but he never picked up his dribble. The look was enough to freeze both McHale and Johnson, who thought Bagley was giving up the ball to Harper. Bagley just kept going and made what looked like an easy lay-up. Bagley also dragged his foot in a clear travel, and this would hardly be the last missed call of the evening. But this was Bagley doing what Bagley does best: taking it to the hoop.

"The interplay between Bags and Harper set up the play," said Wilkens. "If Harper doesn't run to fill the lane, the defense would have converged on Bags. If Bags didn't bother to look at Harper and at least think about passing him the ball, he still would have been in trouble. But the guys worked together even though no pass was made."

6:19   *Parish misses short jumper.*

6:21   *Harper at foul line. (Johnson, P1, T2.) First shot crawls over the front of the rim and in. Second shot, swish.*

CLEVELAND 14, BOSTON 9.

Parish's miss was rebounded by Bagley. One thing often overlooked about the 5-10 Bagley is that he is a very opportunistic rebounder who excels at getting the balls that bounce off the big men's hands, or those rebounds that are banged around until they hit the floor. This was Bagley's fourth rebound of the game. Bagley dribbled the ball up the court and passed to Harper on the wing. Harper dribbled through his legs twice and then took Johnson one-on-one, driving to the baseline. After trying for the steal last time he was caught in the open floor with Harper, Johnson was ready to get serious this time. "D.J. got down and dirty," said Rodgers. "He dug in. He knew where the help was—Danny was on his right—and he didn't get lost when Harper dribbled between his legs. He forced Harper to the baseline but he didn't get the call from Whitworth." Harper went up for a shot while behind the backboard, about eight feet from the rim. It was not a thing of beauty, but the move was enough to draw a foul.

K. C. Jones called timeout.

•

In the Cavs' huddle, Wilkens said, "Good job, guys. Listen, when we drive to the basket, we also should be aware of guys who might be open under the basket. Ron, that last time you had Hot Rod [open for a pass]. All right, great job. Let's just keep moving the ball. Don't hold it and don't dribble it in one spot, pass, keep it moving around. One more thing. When Parish sets up at the foul line, watch him rolling down the middle for a pass. We have to cut him off."

After the timeout, Harper went to the foul line and hit his shots. The first one resembled a football spiral more than anything else, but it fell in. Harper's form on the second shot was perfect.

Wilkens yelled, "See the ball."

5:50   *Parish drives to middle for six-foot hook.*

CLEVELAND 14, BOSTON 11.

Parish caught the ball on the right side of the lane. Ainge ran around behind him. Parish faked a pass to Ainge, which caused Bagley and Daugherty both to react to Ainge, leaving Parish open for a left-handed hook.

"That was a helluva play by Parish," said Wilkens. "We'll let him take left-handed hooks all night. If he beats us going to his left like that, then he beats us, but he'll be doing it by going against his strength."

But Parish has been making that shot in the last two seasons. The Celtics were very patient in exploring their offensive options. The Celtics are delighted, because, once again, the Cavaliers have not double-teamed one of their prime inside scoring threats.

5:30   *Williams misses.*

Williams shot an air ball from ten feet as his jumper was tipped by McHale. Bird caught the shot and then threw a sixty-five-foot baseball pass down the floor intended for Ainge, but Bagley intercepted.

Bagley played it perfectly, just like a free safety, as he

remembered Wilkens saying, "We have to guard against their long passes as if they are wide receivers."

5:20 *Hubbard lay-up on left baseline.*

CLEVELAND 16, BOSTON 11.

Hubbard drove the baseline, guarded first just by Bird and then also by Johnson. Hubbard gave a pump fake, causing both Bird and Johnson to jump. As they came down, he banked the ball in.

"I know it looks like Phil should never make that shot," said Wilkens. "He barely leaves his feet, but some guys have a knack of scoring inside. It all comes in knowing when to fake and when to shoot."

5:00 *Ainge misses three-pointer.*

4:51 *Hubbard left lane lay-up. Assist—Bagley.*

CLEVELAND 18, BOSTON 11.

The play began on the Boston end when Ainge took a twenty-two-footer that was too strong and too long. Bagley let Ainge go up with the shot, remembering that Wilkens had said: "If Ainge wants to shoot three-pointers, fine. That means McHale and Bird aren't shooting the ball."

Bagley picked up the rebound near the foul line and drove down the middle of the floor. Harper filled the right lane, Hubbard the left, with Dennis Johnson back on defense. Bagley gave Harper a quick look, Johnson leaned in that direction, then Bagley threw a bounce pass to Hubbard, who put in a grade-school, one-handed underhand lay-up.

First Quarter

4:51

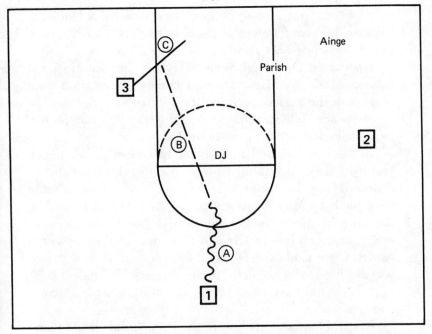

1 — Bagley	Ⓐ Bagley starts the fast break by dribbling down the middle of the floor.
2 — Harper	
3 — Hubbard	Ⓑ Bagley looks toward Harper, freezing the defense, and then passes to Hubbard.
4 — Williams	
5 — Daugherty	Ⓒ Hubbard catches the pass and drives for a lay-up.

ILLUS. 3

"Bagley made the play by looking to Harper," said Wilkens. "Harper is so talented that he demands attention. If you're on defense, you can't help but think the pass would be going his way. As for Hubbard, he is just amazing. The guy has bad knees, he really can't jump, but he was able to fill the lane on the break."

Wilkens is not the only one who has marveled at Hubbard, because Hubbard is one of the few players who has completely revamped his game.

He was the Ohio High School Player of the Year in 1975 at Canton McKinley High. He was one of the top ten prep players in the nation, recruited by virtually every school of consequence. When Hubbard signed with Michigan, he was being talked about as the next Dr. J.

In high school and in his first two years at Michigan, Hubbard was everything he was not this Friday night in Boston. He was a sprinter, a leaper, a scorer. He made the Olympic team after his freshman season at Michigan, and he had a gold medal before he turned twenty-one. Former Michigan coach Johnny Orr said, "Phil was the best player in America. He made the Olympic team as a freshman and he was destined to be one of the all-time greats. If he hadn't been hurt, he would have been Michigan's all-time leading scorer and rebounder."

But Hubbard did get hurt in the 1977 World Games when he fell down and a member of the Russian national team fell on his leg, ripping up his left knee. He sat out what would have been his junior year at Michigan because of knee surgery. Hubbard came back to play one more season in college, but his scoring average dropped from 19.6 to 14.8 and his rebounds from 13.2 to 8.5. Nonetheless, he was drafted in the first round by the Detroit Pistons and was traded to Cleveland in 1982.

With the Cavs, Hubbard became a tenacious, fingernails-under-the-skin defender. He no longer could jump, but he could push and shove. He is 6-7, 210 pounds, and seldom as big, as fast, or able to leap as high as the small forwards he covers.

World B. Free once said, "I'll tell you about Hub and dunking. The man can't even get up high enough to dunk a letter in a mailbox."

"But Phil is so determined," said Wilkens. "He is so smart. He gets rebounds under the rim, he takes balls out of opponents' hands, and he seldom gets faked out or is out of position."

Before the knee injury, Hubbard's game was one of pure ability. After, it is pure basketball intelligence.

"Phil has a move where he gets a rebound on the left side of the basket and then he puts it in with his right hand," said Wilkens. "It's a right-handed lay-up from the left side of the basket while surrounded by a couple of seven-footers. I have no idea why he doesn't get it blocked, but he doesn't."

Larry Bird once said, "Hubbard was about the toughest guy I ever faced when I played in college. I hate to think what he might have done if he hadn't gotten the knee injury. He still is one of the toughest guys in the league when it comes to guarding me."

At this point, Hubbard has outscored Bird, 6–4.

"We wanted to get Phil into the game on offense," said Wilkens. "If he is looking to score, Bird has to guard him. That does two things: First, Bird can't wander so much on defense and double-team Hot Rod or Daugherty. Second, Bird has to use up some energy guarding Hubbard, and that might take something out of Bird's offense."

4:38 *McHale lay-up. Assist—Ainge.*

CLEVELAND 18, BOSTON 13.

The Celtics set up perfect triangle situations on both sides of the lane with Johnson high and Parish low on the right,

Ainge high and McHale low on the left, and Bird at the top of the key. Bird swung the pass to Ainge, who fed McHale in the lane. Williams was overplaying McHale, and Hot Rod went for the steal. He didn't get the ball and kept going out of bounds, seemingly not stopping until he got to Quincy Market.

"When McHale is that close to the basket, you can't overplay him and go for the steal unless you know you're going to get it or you know there's a teammate behind to help," said Wilkens. "But Boston does such a good job of isolating McHale. There was no way we could set up a double-team, so Hot Rod was on his own."

As the Cavs ran up the court on offense, Wilkens yelled, "Hot Rod, don't gamble for the steal unless you have help." Williams nodded.

4:23 *Bagley nineteen-footer from the right wing. Assist—Hubbard.*

CLEVELAND 20, BOSTON 13.

This time, the Cavs ran a variation off their opening play. While Harper cut across the baseline from left to right, Bagley started across from right to left around a Williams pick. But instead of continuing through, Bagley popped back out to the right, losing Ainge, who now had to fight through the same screen twice on one play. He couldn't get there in time, and Bagley hit the open jumper.

4:14 *Parish offensive foul (P1).*

After Bagley's basket, Johnson brought the ball down the court, guarded by Harper. Parish came up to the top of the key to set a pick on Harper; Daugherty followed Parish. "Offensive," yelled Wilkens.

Official Mel Whitworth agreed and called Parish for an illegal pick, saying he was still moving when he put his body on Harper. But it looked like Daugherty gave Parish a slight push, and he sort of stumbled into Harper. Daugherty got away with the push, and Parish got the foul.

4:05   *Harper alley-oop dunk on lob from Hubbard, foul by Ainge (P2, T3). Harper's foul shot goes in, bounces out and up and back in.*

CLEVELAND 23, BOSTON 13.

Harper walked the ball up the court. When he reached the three-point line at the top of the key, Harper passed to Hubbard on the right side. Then Harper broke down the middle of the lane, caught a lob pass from Hubbard, jumped over Ainge and Johnson to grab the ball with two hands, and kind of shoved it around the rim before getting it in.

"Ainge saw it coming," said Rodgers, "but he couldn't stop it." Indeed it was an extraordinary athletic feat by Harper, except for one thing: Replays revealed unquestionably that he never actually made the basket, that, in fact, the ball rattled around the rim and fell in while he had both hands on the rim. Bird complained right away to Earl Strom, but Strom had no interest in Bird's protest, and he dramatically indicated that the basket was good with a wide sweep of his right arm. The play should have been called offensive interference and the basket negated, but since it took about three freeze-frame viewings to determine exactly what had happened, Messrs. Strom and Whitworth can be forgiven for missing the call.

Harper, meanwhile, should be signed up as the seventh Flying Karamazov Brother.

"Take that, Ainge," yelled Cavs trainer Gary Briggs. "God, I love when we do something like that on Ainge."

Harper had lulled the Celtics into believing he was doing nothing more than walking the ball up the floor. It was only after he passed that Harper ran, and his burst of speed around a Daugherty screen left Johnson no chance to catch up. The lob pass was not perfect, but it was up there near the rim and Harper got more hang time than a Ray Guy punt as he simply floated in the air, catching the ball and scoring, Ainge tapping him on the wrist for the foul.

"How many guards in the league can make a play like that?" asked Wilkens. Then Wilkens answered his own question.

"Michael Jordan, Julius Erving in his prime. Maybe Michael Cooper. Who else?"

This was a move of sheer talent. Either you can jump that high or you can't. Either you can hang in the air for that long or you can't. And either you have good enough hands to handle the pass and fight the ball over a couple of Boston defenders or you don't. None of it can be taught, and Harper has it all.

At this point, the Cavs were ten for seventeen from the field, and Harper had nine points.

3:50 *Johnson turns for nine-foot fallaway over Harper.*

Cleveland 23, Boston 15.

Bird had the ball on the right wing.

"Ron, watch out for D.J. posting," yelled Wilkens from the bench.

Wilkens has read the Celtics' minds perfectly. From the

moment Harper walked to the foul line after his high-wire act, every Celtic knew that the only appropriate teammate to take the next shot was Dennis Johnson. It's the way the game is played, whether it's on an asphalt court in Greenwich Village, a court next to the Pacific Ocean in Laguna Beach, California, or the Boston Garden on the third Friday in January, 1987. Dennis Johnson must demonstrate to the kid that he's got some shit in his bag of tricks, too.

The play is "21 G," and its objective is to have D.J. post up his man. Johnson, a 44-percent career shooter, is more like a 55-percent shooter when he takes a turnaround rather than a face-up jumper. The only reason he doesn't do this more often is that he currently ranks fifth on the list of Celtics' offensive priorities. Until this year, he was fourth, but Ainge is now regarded as a more significant offensive threat. In this instance, however, it is necessary to relay a message to the frisky pup, Harper. D.J. gets the ball, takes his favorite shot, and scores.

"The Celtics came right back at Harper after he got the dunk," said Wilkens. "They put D.J. in position where he could do the most damage on Ron, by posting him up. It is a psychological move more than anything else. You scored on us, we'll score on you and make you think about defense.

"Another factor is that after making a great basket, a player sometimes is still thinking about that play instead of concentrating on defense. With some guys, the best time to go at them is right after they've scored."

3:27 *Daugherty drives left baseline for lay-up.*

CLEVELAND 25, BOSTON 15.

Daugherty got the ball on the baseline and drove right around Parish for an easy lay-up. It is the same kind of move

Parish had been doing to other centers for years, but this was a game where Parish ran into a big man who has as much quickness as he does.

Cavs broadcaster Joe Tait said, "When Brad made that move on Parish, it was the first time I thought Lenny might be right and this would be a close game. There was something about the way Daugherty took that ball at Parish that really impressed me. He did it with such confidence."

3:16   *Parish fouled by Daugherty (P1, T3).*
Swish, swish.

CLEVELAND 25, BOSTON 17.

Did somebody say "retaliation"? Daugherty has just put a strong move on Parish. It's automatic: This Boston possession will have the same basic theme as the last ones.

Parish posted up, took a pass from Johnson, and took it extremely hard to the basket, drawing a foul on Daugherty. "An experienced ball team like ours has a sense of that," explained Rodgers. "You go from being the 'usee' to the 'user.' And the guy who orchestrates that so well is D.J. He saw what happened to Parish at the other end and he went right back at Daugherty."

•

Dennis Johnson is a very intriguing player, and not just because he's got enough freckles to be first runner-up in the Eddie Hodges Look-alike Contest. There really isn't another NBA guard quite like him.

He is very likely the only contemporary NBA player who drove a forklift for a year and a half before attending college. He was a classic late bloomer: Nobody wanted him when he came out of Dominguez High School in Compton, California.

In this case "nobody" means *"nobody,"* not "Division I nobody," but "nobody nobody." He eventually enrolled at Los Angeles Harbor College in San Pedro, and wound up at Pepperdine. After his junior year there he decided it was time to earn some money. He put his name into the "Hardship Draft" pool and was selected in the second round by the Seattle Supersonics, the twenty-ninth man chosen in the 1976 draft.

In college he had played mostly forward. Now he had to learn what being a guard in the NBA was all about. Bill Russell was then in his fourth and final season as the Sonics' coach, and he had a reputation for employing people he thought could play, not necessarily the collegians with press clippings. Johnson wasn't even a household name in Malibu, let alone Seattle; he was just a 6-4 kid with long legs, a high-rising butt, reddish hair, plenty of freckles, and a hard-nosed attitude. He feared no one. He could not be intimidated. He also couldn't shoot very well, but that didn't concern Russell, who saw in Johnson a young man who had enormous defensive potential.

Russell gave this "Who's He?" twenty minutes a game, and Johnson responded with 9.2 points a game and an honest effort on defense. Under Russell's successor, Bob Hopkins, and his successor, Lenny Wilkens—the name should be familiar—Johnson became a major contributor to a Seattle team that went all the way to the NBA finals in 1978. Johnson became something of a star in the playoffs, but in the final game he shot a horrifying 0-for-14.

Dennis Johnson had the last laugh, however, returning in 1979 with his Seattle team for a rematch with the champion Washington Bullets. This time D.J. walked off with the playoff MVP award as the Sonics won the championship.

By now he had a big name and a bad reputation. He was viewed as a great player—he had secured his first All-Defensive citation in that second year—but an even bigger headache. He was said to be arrogant and selfish. Insiders said he wasn't satisfied to be hailed as a great defender, that he was in competition with backcourt mate Gus Williams, an explosive scorer, and wanted to be known as a great offensive player, too. After he hit a game-winning basket one night, a teammate said, "Too bad it couldn't have been someone other than *that* asshole." Another said, "Watch the box scores. If Gus gets thirty one night, D.J. will try like hell to get thirty the next night."

On June 4, 1980, the Sonics traded him to Phoenix for All-Pro guard Paul Westphal, who, at thirty, was four years older. Lenny Wilkens was widely quoted to the effect that Dennis Johnson was "a cancer" on the ball club.

He spent three full seasons in Phoenix playing for John MacLeod, a demanding coach who favors a highly structured style of offense. People kept waiting for D.J. (so dubbed to distinguish him from Seattle teammate John Johnson, "J.J.") to cause problems, but to this day the people in Phoenix say he was never a bother to them, that he had matured by the time he came to their ball club. In his first year in Phoenix he made the All-League first team. He was first team All-Defensive all three years. He was everything they expected.

Why trade him, then? Because the Suns felt that a Dennis Johnson–Walter Davis backcourt was topheavy, that the team needed a more classic playmaker to pair with a scoring guard. The Suns had long coveted rugged Rick Robey, the Celtics' backup center. Walter Davis had begun his career in Phoenix and was something of a civic institution. Dennis Johnson was sacrificed to the cause. The trade was made on June 27, 1983.

Dennis Johnson has brought nothing but joy and happiness to the Boston Celtics, who feel he has continually broadened the scope of his game. They knew they were getting a man who, while not a pure shooter, was a scorer. They knew they were getting a man who could defend. But there turned out to be a bonus: Dennis Johnson can run a ball club. And so can Danny Ainge. Just about every other NBA team has a clearly defined backcourt in which there is a "one guard," or "lead guard" who calls the plays and initiates the offense, and a "two guard," or "off guard" who is primarily a scorer (like Bagley and Harper, respectively on the Cavaliers). With Johnson and Ainge, the Celtics had plain old "guard guards," well-rounded players who can both make a play and score.

But the leader back there is Dennis Johnson, simply by the force of his personality. He is a player who commands tremendous respect. He has earned a reputation throughout his career as a player who excels in "big" games. Larry Bird continually refers to Dennis Johnson as "the best player I've ever played with." He has his idiosyncracies, to be sure, but without them he wouldn't be D.J.

Once or twice a season, D.J. becomes irritated about something or other and essentially absents himself from the offense. These snits don't last longer than one game, and they've decreased in number over the years. But he is capable of such numbers as 5 shots attempted in 30 minutes (1983), 7 shots attempted in 42 minutes, 7 shots attempted in 36 minutes (1984), 4 shots attempted in 46 minutes (1986), or even the ultimate: zero shots attempted in 26 minutes (1985) or in 27 minutes (1986).

In these games D.J. basically stands off to one side and observes. He offers no apology, and the team knows he will return to normal by the next game.

The Celtics feel very comfortable with Dennis Johnson on their team. They like the way he thinks and acts, and right now Robert Parish likes the way D.J. has just given him the ball and a chance to get even with Brad Daugherty.

3:00   *Bagley misses a three-pointer from the right wing.*

Harper drove to the basket and attracted attention from several Celtic players. Harper spotted Bagley wide open, and

Bagley missed his first three-point attempt. He would try seven more three-pointers, making only one.

"I told Bags several times to move in a few steps when he sees that he is open for a shot," said Wilkens. "A three-pointer is a very tough shot, a 30-percent or worse shot for most guys. In the case of Bagley with Harper driving to the basket, he would be just as open from eighteen feet as he was open from twenty-three feet. But some guys get mesmerized by the three-point line and they want to keep shooting from behind it."

2:50   *Johnson fouled by Harper (P1 T4). Swish, swish.*

CLEVELAND 25, BOSTON 19.

Johnson rebounded Bagley's shot and drove all the way down the court, around a Parish pick, and was fouled by Harper as he took a six-foot jumper. The Cavs were then charged with a television timeout.

"Okay, guys, way to move the ball," said Wilkens in the huddle. "Any time we penetrate to the basket, look for the open man. [This is directed at Harper.] You draw a lot of attention, sometimes that leaves somebody open underneath."

Wilkens to Bagley: "When we set up for the outside shot, don't be afraid to step in. It doesn't always have to be a three-pointer."

Wilkens to Harper: "In that last situation with D.J. bringing the ball up, you have to stick with him close. He's trying to draw Brad away from Parish. We don't want to make that switch."

Assistant Dick Helm: "Any time we're stuck, just move the

ball. Keep the ball moving, don't stand there dribbling or holding it."

As the Cavs leave the huddle, a note on the scoreboard read: "Brad Daugherty was twelve years old the last time the Cavs won a game in Boston."

2:34 *Bagley misses wild scoop.*

2:18 *Williams blocks Bird.*

Celtics got the ball to Bird at the right low post. Bird was guarded by Hubbard. He gave Hubbard a shoulder fake to the right and turned to his left, taking an underhand shot with his right hand. Williams left McHale alone on the left side of the key and broke across the lane, just in time to block Bird's shot. Bird never saw Hot Rod coming. Bird will file this in the computer chip in his brain marked "post-up situations."

"That was a purely instinctual play," said Wilkens. "Hot Rod just knew Bird was going up with the shot and he went for the block."

Gary Briggs put it in more elementary terms: "Hot Rod told Bird to get that weak shit outta there."

2:12 *Harper reverse banker.*

Cleveland 27, Boston 19.

Harper picked up Bird's blocked shot and drove the length of the floor. Parish challenged him, cutting off his route to the basket. But Harper leaped across the lane past Parish and shot a spinning lay-up off the glass. That gave Harper eleven points.

2:01   *Bird six-foot baseline turnaround.*

CLEVELAND 27, BOSTON 21.

Though the average fan would not recognize it as such, the Celtics consider this a fast-break basket because it emanated from what they call the secondary break. The Cavalier defense was not completely set when Bird received the ball. After having had his shot blocked in the Celtics' last possession, Bird once again posted under the basket and got the ball from Johnson, but instead of going for a shoulder fake or hesitating in any fashion, Bird let the ball go with a release that would have impressed Bill Mazeroski.

"Larry got the shot off before Hot Rod or anyone else had a chance to double-team him," said Wilkens.

1:50   *Daugherty drives lane for lay-up.*

CLEVELAND 29, BOSTON 21.

Bagley passed to Daugherty at the top of the key. Parish went for the steal but didn't get it, and as Parish continued to run away from the basket, Daugherty drove down the middle of the lane for a lay-up. This is a move Wilkens had been encouraging Daugherty to make; he tended to catch the ball at the top of the key and look for the pass.

"Brad is unselfish, sometimes too unselfish," said Wilkens. "But this time, he was smart enough to see that Parish had taken himself out of the play by going for the steal and Brad made the good move by taking it to the basket."

1:37 *McHale lay-up. Assist—Ainge.*

CLEVELAND 29, BOSTON 23.

A play simply called "Iso-Kevin," the "iso" part, of course, standing for "isolation." Once again, this was a two-man game with McHale and Ainge. Williams played in front of McHale to cut off the usual bounce pass, but Ainge simply lobbed the ball over William's arms, and McHale caught it on the way to the basket for an easy lay-up.

"That was inexperience on Hot Rod's part," said Wilkens. "He needed to remember that you can't play in front of McHale like that unless he had help behind, and he didn't."

Still no double-team?

1:30 *Harper signals that he is tired.*

Harper raised his hand as he ran up the court past Wilkens. Wilkens saw it and sent Johnny Newman to the scorer's table.

"That was a smart move by Ron," said Wilkens. "He had been all over the court, and the effort had to take something out of him. I try to watch and see if a guy is getting fatigued, but the best way to let the coach know you need a rest is to tell him."

1:20 *Bagley drives line for seven-footer.*

CLEVELAND 31, BOSTON 23.

After McHale's basket, Bagley walked the ball up the floor. He noticed that Ainge was guarding him sort of flat-footed.

First Quarter

1:37

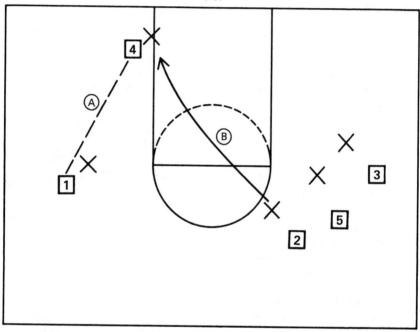

1 — Ainge
2 — Johnson
3 — Bird
4 — McHale
5 — Parish

Basic two-man game set-up, with Ainge passing down low to McHale (A). Wilkens is looking for Johnson's man—usually Harper, sometimes Newman—to double-team McHale when he gets the ball (B).

Illus. 4

Bagley gave Ainge a fake to his right with a strong dribble of the right hand, then dribbled the ball directly in front of the back-pedaling Ainge, switched the ball from his right to his left hand, and dribbled past Ainge to drop in a short flip shot from the middle of the lane. Ainge was trying to play Bagley toward some defensive help rather than thinking about individual defense. Bagley now had eight points. What knee injury?

1:10 *Bird misses an open eighteen-footer from the top of the key.*

Bird got himself so wide open that there was no rebound action. Though three Cavs were in better position, Parish was able to slip through the middle and grab the rebound. "The only one moving was Robert [Parish]," Rodgers said. "The other eight people must have figured that Larry would never miss that shot."

Parish went up for the right-handed slam, but he banged the ball off the back of the rim. The key was Daugherty's getting a hand on the ball as Parish brought it back for the dunk. That was just enough to alter his shot, even though Daugherty did not get enough of the ball for it to be considered a blocked shot.

Newman remained at the scorer's table, waiting to get in for Harper during the next stop in action.

:56 *Williams right lane lay-up. Assist—Harper.*

CLEVELAND 33, BOSTON 23.

Williams picked up Parish's rebound. He passed to Bagley, who passed the ball up the floor to Harper. Harper drove into the lane and went up in the air, not sure what he was going to do. That's a mortal sin in basketball—leaving your feet when you don't know what you'll do with the ball. But Harper is so talented that even his mistakes sometimes turn into great plays. As he was hanging in the air, he spotted Williams wide open under the basket. Harper flipped the ball to Williams, who caught it and gave a pump fake, getting McHale off his feet. As McHale came down, Williams went up for a lay-up. These were Williams's first points of the game.

Newman remained at the scorer's table, which was fortunate for the Cavs since he could hardly have thrown the kind of improvised pass that Harper just made.

:45   *McHale nine-foot hook. Assist—Ainge.*

CLEVELAND 33, BOSTON 25.

After Hot Rod's basket, Ainge dribbled the ball up the court. He spotted McHale alone under the basket. This time, Williams did not front McHale, as he had the last time the Celtics looked to McHale. Since Ainge couldn't lob the ball over Williams to McHale, he simply threw a bounce pass to McHale, who flipped in a hook shot over Williams.

"Retaliation again," declared Rodgers. And the Cavaliers stubbornly refused to help the by-now defensively hapless rookie Williams.

"I figured I was playing Kevin real good," said Williams. "I was behind him, I had my body on him. But he just made the shot. What is anybody supposed to do?"

:43   *Daugherty slam on lob. Assist—Harper.*

CLEVELAND 35, BOSTON 25.

Sometime, perhaps before the 11:00 news, the Celtics will realize that the Cavaliers will push the ball upcourt as quickly as possible. Daugherty simply beat Parish down the floor. Harper spotted Daugherty open and threw him the lob, Daugherty grabbed it and jammed it. As Daugherty ran back down the court, he gave Harper a high five. Parish stared first at Daugherty, then at Harper.

Standing on the sidelines, Wilkens nodded. "That is exactly what we've been preaching to the kids. Reward your big men. When they run down the floor, give them the ball. That kind of play will keep Daugherty running down the floor all night."

:35   *McHale baby jump hook. Assist—Johnson.*

CLEVELAND 35, BOSTON 27.

See :45. Also 1:37. Celtics aficionados refer to Williams's sorry predicament as being in "the McHale Torture Chamber." Given this type of receiving room on the floor, and with the Cavs *still* not double-teaming, McHale can rebook the thirty points. He could break his career scoring high, which, Wilkens and Williams should be informed, is fifty-six.

•

The basic rules of the game have changed in Boston. Larry Bird is no longer automatically the focus of the Boston attack. Sometimes he is, and sometimes, as is happening right here, he isn't.

Kevin McHale is just too great a weapon not to exploit. If a team is going to play him in a conventional one-on-one manner, the Celtics have no choice but to go to him, because throwing the ball to Kevin McHale has become the surest way any team has to get two points at any given moment in the NBA.

That's gospel. When this game begins he is fourth in the

league in field-goal percentage (he will go on to lead the league in this category), and he is making 84 percent of his free throws, a new personal high. Those who are shooting anything near his percentage neither take as many shots nor derive as much benefit from the free-throw line. He is the most efficient scorer in the league. He will become the first man *ever* to shoot 60 percent from the floor and 80 percent from the foul line in the same season.

He broke in as a sixth man, scoring ten points a game for the 1980–81 championship team. He has increased his production each season since, raising his scoring to 13.6, 14.1, 18.4, 19.8, 21.3, and, entering this game, 26.1 points a game. The increased scoring is the dual reflection of an ever-increasing shots-per-game total (from thirteen a game in '84–85, for example, to seventeen a game in this season), as well as his basic improvement as a player.

Remember that McHale spent the first four and a half years of his Boston career as a substitute, albeit a high-class one. The other starting forward was Cedric Maxwell, a tremendous inside scoring threat himself and a man who had changed his game greatly in order to accommodate Bird. McHale got his minutes, to the point where such luminaries as Kevin Loughery were hailing him as one of the top ten players in the league, even though he was a sixth man for the Celtics. He might have remained in that capacity for years to come had Maxwell not injured his knee in the 1984–85 season. McHale became a starter, a situation most teams in the league had secretly feared.

He has refined every move he had when he came into the league while adding new ones. He is a consummate scorer, capable of picking up points in a variety of ways. He can run the floor, and he's had a great many baskets as a fast-break finisher, in addition to all of his turnaround jumpers, his jump hooks, his dip-in moves, his offensive rebound baskets, and assorted other so-called garbage points.

Bird has been the leading scorer on the team since his

rookie season, and always by at least three points a game. In Bird's first six seasons, no other Celtic player had even scored 20 points a game; in his seventh, 1985–86, McHale averaged 21.3 in his first full season as a starter following the trade of Cedric Maxwell to the Los Angeles Clippers. Things are different now. McHale started the season with 22 points on 8-for-11 shooting on opening night and has challenged Bird for the team scoring title ever since. He scored 20 or more in each of his first twenty-eight games. In his entire career, the most times in succession Bird has ever scored 20 is seventeen games.

As Bird struggled with assorted injuries (ankle, achilles tendon, back, etc.) in the first seven weeks of the season, McHale became the primary offensive threat in many games. The more they went to him, the more his confidence soared. The word was out that McHale was at the peak of his career, that he couldn't be guarded one-on-one, that perhaps he, not Bird, was now the team's most valuable player. In sixteen of the first thirty-five games this season, he has been the Celtics' high scorer. In eighteen he has been the high rebounder. At this point in his career he believes that if given the ball in the low post he can do anything he wants to do.

The Cavaliers have thus far done nothing to disprove that notion.

:25   *Daugherty leaner in middle.*
     Assist—Harper.

CLEVELAND 37, BOSTON 27.

Harper drove the baseline past Johnson. He went up for the shot and was flying under the backboard, once again seemingly not sure exactly what he would do with the ball. Before he touched down, Harper spotted Daugherty wide open in the lane. Harper hit him with the pass and Daugherty had the easy basket.

Johnny Newman remained at the scorer's table waiting to get into the game to replace Harper, who now had three assists during the time he was supposed to be out of the game in favor of Newman.

"I guess Ron wasn't as tired as he thought," said Wilkens. "Actually, it was adrenaline. This was his first game in Boston Garden and Ron was just pushing so hard, he forgot he was tired when he had the ball."

:05   *McHale hook in middle of lane. Assist—Johnson.*

CLEVELAND 37, BOSTON 29.

How high is up? Will McHale ever miss again? He has now scored on the last four Celtic possessions, each shot seemingly easier than the last. The Celts have put aside the rest of their offense in favor of the two-man game featuring their one-man gang, McHale.

:01   *Bagley misses from half-court.*

As the Cavaliers brought the ball upcourt for a final shot, assistant coach Chris Ford yelled to Ainge, "We've got one to waste!" The Celtics have only committed three team fouls, and if they foul a Cavalier before he can shoot, the ball will be taken out on the side. But when trainer Ray Melchiorre heard this, he quickly said, "He can't take it; he's got two." Bagley shot from half-court and missed. The issue is moot.

First quarter ends: Cleveland 37, Boston 29.

McHale led the Celtics with 13 points.

The Celtics were 11 for 24 from the field (46 percent) and 7 for 8 at the foul line.

Cleveland was 17 for 27 from the field (63 percent) and 3 for 3 at the foul line. Harper had 11 points, Daugherty 10. Daugherty led everyone with 6 rebounds. Both teams had 11 rebounds.

Cleveland has attempted 11 fast breaks and converted each for 22 points.

The only four Boston fast-break points have been two pairs of free throws after Cleveland scored on a fast break.

The Celtics have posted up various people (everyone but Ainge, in fact) 11 times and scored on 9 of the possessions.

Boston had 28 offensive possessions and scored on 15.

Elapsed time of first period: 20 minutes.

4

Second Quarter

In the huddle between quarters, Wilkens said, "What we have to do with McHale is give some help. Okay, we have McHale and either D.J. or Ainge on one side of the court and everyone else on the other side. For example, Ainge is in the two-man game with McHale. That means D.J. is on the other side of the floor. The man guarding D.J.—Ron [Harper], Johnny [Newman], or whoever—can break down and try and put the double-team on McHale as soon as Ainge passes to McHale. [See Ill. 4.] Look how the court is spread. We don't need three guys to guard their three guys, who are just standing out of the way and watching the play. Let's force them to react to us."

Dick Helm said, "They are starting to pressure us on the perimeter a little more, trying to take away some of the outside shots. So guards, if they run at you, look inside to make the pass. This is the best we've moved the ball all year, just keep it up."

Wilkens said, "Okay, guys, keep pushing the ball at them. On defense, see the ball."

•

At the start of the second quarter, both coaches finally went to their bench. Of course, Johnny Newman had spent the last 1:30 of the first quarter waiting at the scorer's table to go in for Harper.

So Newman was the Cavs' first substitution, and he was

another rookie. At Richmond, Newman was a 6-6 small forward. "In college, pretty much all the plays were run to me," he said. "If someone was getting a screen to shoot the ball from the perimeter, it was me. If someone was getting the ball inside to post up, it was me. I seldom had to pass." Or bring the ball up the floor for that matter. But with the Cavaliers, Newman's size meant he had to switch from forward to shooting guard, and that meant dribbling, passing, and creating shots for himself and other players. In other words, he had to do sort of what Harper was doing—setting up everyone on the floor, including himself. But Newman hadn't quite made that adjustment. He had a fine long-range jumper, and he occasionally displayed remarkable leaping ability, but the guard position was foreign. And of the Cavs' five rookies, he was the most likely to feel the awe factor of his first game in Boston Garden. He had played the least of the five rookies, and he was from the smallest college.

Wilkens's other move was to replace Hot Rod Williams at power forward with Mark West.

"Hot Rod needed some rest," said Wilkens. "The Celtics kept going down low to McHale under the basket, and that's a tough position for anyone to be in, especially a rookie. I don't like to put a whole new five on the floor to start a quarter, but it was obvious we had to make some moves, so I decided to rest Harper and Hot Rod because they were the most active. Also, I thought West's bigger and stronger body [6-10, 230 pounds] would give McHale a different look."

The Celtics replaced Ainge with Jerry Sichting and Bird with Fred Roberts. Sichting is a veteran six-foot guard, "a good outside shooter," Wilkens told Bagley. "You have to play up on Sichting more than you did on Ainge."

As for Roberts, "He's a right-handed player," Wilkens told Hubbard. "Force him to his left. He doesn't have much of a shot, but he likes to go to the boards, so block him out."

Sichting entered the game averaging six points, Roberts seven points.

SECOND-QUARTER MATCHUPS

POINT GUARDS	Sichting vs. Bagley
SHOOTING GUARDS	Johnson vs. Newman
CENTERS	Parish vs. Daugherty
POWER FORWARDS	McHale vs. West
SMALL FORWARDS	Roberts vs. Hubbard

11:44   *Bagley leaner in lane. Plus foul, Sichting (P1, T1). Foul shot, swish.*

CLEVELAND 40, BOSTON 29.

To start the quarter, the Cavs took the ball out of bounds under their own basket. Daugherty passed to Bagley, who drove all the way up the court. Bagley wanted to establish his dominance over Sichting, who is a weaker and far more passive defender than Ainge. Bagley just took the ball to the basket, using a couple of shake-and-bake spin moves off the dribble to get free of Sichting in the lane and hit the short shot; Sichting fouled Bagley on the arm. This gave Bagley eleven points, which not-so-incidentally was the difference in the game. Bagley went into the evening averaging only eleven points.

11:29   *McHale four-foot jump hook. Assist—Johnson.*

CLEVELAND 40, BOSTON 31.

Déjà vu, and recently, too. This time Johnson made a dribble entry while Jerry Sichting set a cross-pick (criss-crossing through the lane with McHale to set a pick on McHale's man) on burly Mark West, who has replaced John Williams in the Torture Chamber. West fought through the pick, but McHale posted him, anyway. When he received Johnson's pass, he shot an instantaneous jump hook—so quick that West has no chance to react. McHale is so nonrhythmic in his basic shooting pattern that it is impossible to time his shot. He now has Boston's last ten points, and fifteen for the game.

11:07 *West five-foot baseline hook.*
       Assist—Newman.

CLEVELAND 42, BOSTON 31.

Lenny Wilkens called for a two-man game with Newman and West, being guarded by Johnson and McHale. West caught the pass from Newman and made a short hook over McHale, who stood staring at West wondering where that left-handed shot came from. Until this season, West barely had any right-handed moves, and he certainly didn't have any with his left. But he spent the off-season developing his weaker side and he came up with this little hook shot. The book on West was that he had no offense, and the book on Newman was that he couldn't make even the most elementary pass into a player at the post. This was only Newman's fourth assist of the year, and he was averaging an assist every forty-two minutes, which didn't exactly make him the second coming of Magic Johnson.

"But Johnny did get the ball into West," said Wilkens. "And West scored, which was a way of letting McHale know he would have to play some defense, that he couldn't just coast out there and think only about his offense."

What about going at the fresh players? Bagley did it to Sichting. Then Johnson and McHale did it to Newman and West.

"If you've been on the floor a while, you're loose and into

the game," said Wilkens. "Coming off the bench, you're going to need a few trips up and down the floor to get into the floor and get loose. That is why I tell our guys to try to run a little instead of taking a shot the first time you touch the ball after coming off the bench. Defensively, sometimes a guy coming off the bench can be caught flat-footed."

10:57   *Bagley fouls Fred Roberts (P2, T1).*

10:50   *McHale misses a hook over West.*

Once again, it was a Celtic two-man game with Johnson and McHale against Newman and West. McHale banged and smacked with West and attained the position he wanted. But there must have been a sudden realignment of celestial bodies because the shot wouldn't drop. The Celtics had no chance for the offensive rebound. "One bad thing about isolations," Rodgers said. "If you don't hit it, the chance for a second shot are not too good."

"McHale loves to get you on his back and then he starts backing you towards the basket," said Wilkens. "He keeps pushing and pushing with his body. I've told our guys that when McHale does that, step out of the way and Kevin will just fall on his ass. But they never do it. The natural inclination is when someone leans on you, you should lean back."

10:24   *Daugherty hook in middle. Foul by Parish (P2, T2). Foul shot clanged off back rim.*

CLEVELAND 44, BOSTON 31.

Hubbard rebounded McHale's missed hook shot. Bagley brought the ball up the court, and the Cavs threw five passes with four different players touching the ball before Bagley unloaded a three-pointer from twenty-three feet on the right wing.

"Our ball movement was so good," said Wilkens. "I just wish Bags would remember to take a few steps in; he'd still be open for the shot."

Daugherty and Parish went up for Bagley's missed shot. Parish got to the ball first, holding it with two hands above his head. But Daugherty got only his right hand on the ball, and with that one hand he ripped it away from Parish, getting control of the ball and then going up for the little hook, Parish fouling as the shot went in.

"Break his arm," yelled an excited Gary Briggs on the Cavs' bench.

If any one play alerted the smug Boston Garden crowd that the conventional wisdom concerning Daugherty—too soft, too mushy, or too something-they-wouldn't-want-around—was inaccurate, it was this one. There was definite murmuring among the nightly gathering of 14,890 when he embarrassed Parish, the proud Chief.

•

When Daugherty was at the foul line, Wilkens yelled, "Fingers."

Daugherty said later, "Lenny wanted me to remember to get my fingers into the shot, not to shoot it off my palm."

No luck, as Daugherty's foul shot hit the rim hard enough to be heard in Brookline.

10:10

As the Celtics worked the ball around, Briggs yelled, "Three seconds on McHale." No response from the officials.

10:02 *McHale leaner in lane.*

CLEVELAND 44, BOSTON 33.

The Celtics went to what they call "Mix," a sequence
featuring simultaneous cross-picks (side to side) and up-picks
(up and down). The end result was the same as it's been since
the final two minutes of the first period. McHale got it down
low. To this point he had settled for variations on hooks and
jump hooks. Now he faked West off his feet and threw in a half
one-hander, half jump hook. He now has scored twelve
straight Boston points.

But relief is in sight for the Cavaliers. McHale is going out.
Oops. He's replaced by Bird.

9:52 *Rebound of Hubbard miss out of bounds.*
Ben Poquette came in for Hubbard, Bird
for McHale.

"It was time for me to get Hubbard out," said Wilkens.
"He had played the whole first quarter and he needed a rest.
Normally, I like to get Phil out at the end of the first quarter,
but I didn't want to take out three guys at once and take a
chance on disrupting our flow, not with us playing so well in
Boston."

Wilkens decided to have Ben play Roberts, "Because I
thought West's big body would give Bird a little different look.
Ben is a smart player, and I knew he would come into a game
like this and help us maintain what we were doing."

9:30 *Newman travels.*

The Cavs got the ball out of bounds and they set up a double pick at the foul line with West and Daugherty, their two biggest bodies on the court. Johnny Newman ran around the double pick, rubbing off Johnson on to West's back. No Celtic switched to Newman, and he was wide open in the middle of the lane. Bagley hit Newman with a pass, but Newman was either nervous or was *trying* to catch the pass with his elbows. He sort of stumbled as he made the lay-up, but Earl Strom called Newman for traveling, taking away the basket.

"Johnny looked awkward in the way he caught the ball," said Wilkens. "But he didn't shuffle his feet. They called that one on him because Johnny was a rookie, pure and simple."

That's one explanation. Another is that in pro basketball the flow of the game is so important. When a player clumsily makes a move to the basket, he's often called for walking even if he didn't shuffle his feet, because he *looks* like he was walking. That was the case with Newman on this play.

9:16 *Johnson fouled by Newman (P1, T2).*
Swish, swish.

CLEVELAND 44, BOSTON 35.

After Newman's turnover, the Celtics brought the ball up the court.

"Johnny, watch out for D.J. posting up," Wilkens yelled to Newman.

Too late. There are two types of mismatches in the NBA. The first is a size mismatch, such as when a small guard gets caught in a pick and winds up guarding a seven-foot center. That is mismatch A. The second kind is when a wily veteran winds up in a one-on-one situation with a kid. That is mismatch B, and a textbook example is when eleven-year veteran Dennis Johnson gets isolated on the low right box with rookie Johnny Newman. Johnson got a lob from Bird, turned, and went up for the shot. Newman made his best defensive move of the sequence—he jumped on Johnson. The ball didn't get anywhere near the basket, and Johnson checked his nose to see if it was still on his face.

"We tell our guys, if you're going to foul, really foul. Don't let them get off a shot," said Wilkens.

8:50 *Daugherty misses ten-footer.*

The Cavaliers worked their way to a classic mismatch A, but six-foot Jerry Sichting battled seven-foot Brad Daugherty so long and so hard that the Cavaliers didn't get the ball to Daugherty where and when he wanted it, and he missed the turnaround jumper.

8:43 *Sichting eighteen-footer left lane on break.*

CLEVELAND 44, BOSTON 37.

Bird rebounded Daugherty's miss and threw a bounce pass to Jerry Sichting near half-court.

•

Jerry Sichting is what is known in the trade as a "role player." His role on the Celtics is to make open jump shots, both in the half-court offense and in situations exactly like this one.

He had spent five seasons playing for the Indiana Pacers, for whom he started on many occasions, twice averaging double figures. A free agent at the conclusion of the 1984–85 season, he attracted some interest because he was known as one of the great open shooters in the league. The Celtics, desperate for a third guard, signed him to back up Ainge and Johnson. After the usual posturing that dominates such situations in the league, Sichting was obtained for two future draft choices.

Sichting gave the Celtics precisely what they were looking for in 1985–86, shooting an eye-opening 57 percent from the floor as he took advantage of the incessant double-teaming that stymies the Boston big men. His repertoire is limited. He shoots jump shots and little else, as befits a loyal Hoosier from Martinsville, Indiana.

Indeed, Sichting is the embodiment of every Indiana kid who has ever come into the NBA. Martinsville is a town straight out of the film *Hoosiers*. It is the birthplace of the sainted John Wooden, and Sichting grew up right next to a playground and played his high school ball for a certified Indiana legend, Sam (father of Steve) Alford. He matriculated at Purdue, where he knocked home jumper after jumper during a glittering four-year career for the Boilermakers.

At 6-1 (his program height) or so, Sichting is no burner, although he has adequate speed. He can pass, but he's not a floor leader as such. He seldom goes to the basket, and later in the 1986–87 season would have a stretch of twenty-two games and 389 minutes of game time without going to the free-throw line. In his entire NBA career he has averaged one trip to the line approximately every forty minutes on the floor. Leigh Montville of the *Boston Globe* quips that the title of Sichting's autobiography should be *I've Never Been to the Paint*.

He did a decent job filling in for Ainge when the latter

started the regular season on the injured list due to a back injury. Inserted in the starting lineup when rookie Sam Vincent played his way out of a job, Sichting was averaging twelve points a game during a six-game stretch in November when he was suddenly taken ill. His condition was originally diagnosed as a stomach virus, but it turns out that his system was attacked by an intestinal parasite that robbed him of strength and made him extremely nauseated. For the next three and a half weeks he was useless, although he tried to play.

When he came back he discovered that coach Jones was determined to stick with Ainge and Johnson to the death. His playing time did not approach that of his first season in Boston, in part because the staff had lost a little confidence in him and in part because Ainge had raised his game to such a high level that there was little reason to take him out, other than for the traditional second-quarter rest.

Sichting was finding it difficult to get into his shooting rhythm playing such drastically reduced minutes. The Saturday previous to this game, Sichting had started in Pontiac against the Pistons when Ainge re-injured his back. Sichting shot five for eight in that game, scoring eleven points and handing out seven assists. It was his best performance since playing unwilling host to the parasite six weeks earlier.

In '85–86, getting the ball to Sichting on a fast break like this one was one of Boston's best percentage moves. This year? No one knew. But as Sichting advanced on the left wing he was clearly into his rhythm.

"I love to look at Jerry when he's getting his steps down," Rodgers said. "Da-da-da, da-da-dah, Dah!" Yup, Sichting pulled up at eighteen feet, bounced it hard one last time, a la Jerry West, and swished the jumper. The Celtics have now scored six straight since the Daugherty display of muscle and will and Wilkens wants to quiet the suddenly raucous Garden crowd. Timeout, Cleveland.

8:39   *Second Cavs timeout of the game.*

"Let's see if we can get the ball down low to Brad," Wilkins said in the Cavs huddle. "Okay, let's just keep moving the ball. Don't hold it. We're starting to walk the ball up the court. Keep pushing them. If we get a chance to run, let's run."

Wilkins made several moves. First, he took out Newman and brought back Harper at the shooting guard. "I thought Newman did all right," said Wilkins. "He helped us maintain what we had going." The Cavs had an eight-point lead at the start of the second quarter when Newman replaced Harper. The lead was seven at this timeout.

Wilkens also replaced Bagley with Craig Ehlo. "First time I ever got into a game in the second quarter in Boston Garden," said Ehlo. "In fact, it was the first time in a long time I got into any game in the second quarter." And this was the guy Wilkens had said would give him experience and stability.

"I had to get Ehlo in the game for Bags," said Wilkens. "Craig could handle the ball well enough, and I knew Boston would not press or use any trapping defenses on him. I played Bagley long enough. When you think about how his knee was bothering him earlier in the day, we had already gotten a lot out of Bags." Wilkens also saw that Sichting had simply beaten Bagley down the floor in Boston's last possession.

Boston brought in Ainge for Johnson.

NEW MATCHUPS

POINT GUARDS	Sichting vs. Ehlo
SHOOTING GUARDS	Ainge vs. Harper
CENTERS	Parish vs. Daugherty
POWER FORWARDS	Bird vs. West
SMALL FORWARDS	Roberts vs. Poquette

8:33 *Daugherty eight-footer baseline turnaround. Sichting foul (P2, T3). Foul shot goes in on a line drive.*

CLEVELAND 47, BOSTON 37.

The Cavs took the ball out on the sideline just inside midcourt. Poquette threw a pass directly to Daugherty on the baseline, who had caught Parish napping by making a smart cut to the basket. Daugherty caught the pass, went up for the turnaround. The eight-footer banged against the side of the rim, bounced straight up and fell clean through the rim. Daugherty flipped his wrist a second time as a pantomime to help get the ball into the basket. As Daugherty went up, the whistle blew for a foul on Parish. At least, that's what Wilkens thought. "Who else could it be besides Parish?" asked Wilkens.

How about Jerry Sichting?

The moment the whistle blew, Sichting raised his hand, trying to get the foul instead of Parish. "That was a smart play on Sichting's part," said Wilkens. "He can play for five years without fouling out. This way, he keeps Parish in the game. I just can't believe that Whitworth went for it."

Wilkens paced the sidelines, yelling at Whitworth, "Mel, Parish pushed him."

Whitworth looked away from Wilkens to the scorer's table, holding up one finger on his left hand and two on his right to indicate that the foul was on number 12, Sichting.

"Parish pushed him in the back, not Sichting," yelled Wilkens. "Come on, quit protecting those guys."

On the play-by-play sheet, Parish's name was typed in as fouling Daugherty. Only later was it scratched out and replaced by Sichting's name.

"That should have been three fouls on Parish and it probably would have gotten him out of the game for the rest of the half," said Wilkens. "Sighting wasn't within five feet of Daugherty. Stuff like that drives you crazy and it can change the whole game around."

As Wilkens pointed out, with Bill Walton hurt, the Celtics weren't quite the same when Greg Kite came off the bench to replace Parish in the middle.

Even though Parish didn't get a foul, Jones took him out of the game and put McHale in as center.

"Because Parish avoided that third foul, K.C. only needed to get him a couple minutes of rest," said Wilkens. "That's why he could use McHale at center instead of Kite."

And the funny thing about the play is that *nobody* fouled Daugherty—not Sighting, not Parish, not Bird, not K. C. Jones, not Red Auerbach, not Ron Hary the organist, not Ray Flynn the mayor of Boston—nobody. But of all the potentially guilty parties, Sighting is about the least culpable. "You could drive a compact car between the distance Sighting is from Parish," Celtics' TV announcer Mike Gorman is telling his audience.

As the Celtics see it, Daugherty ought to have his basket, as lucky a shot as it was, and the game should proceed. Keep in mind that the call was made by Mel Whitworth, a man widely considered a substandard NBA ref, a man the Celtic staff derisively refers to as "Mr. CBA," since he splits his duty between the NBA and the minor-league circuit.

Whitworth. Remember the name.

8:23   *Gary Briggs yells, "Three seconds."*

8:20   *Bird twenty-footer left sideline.*

CLEVELAND 47, BOSTON 39.

Larry Bird, realizing that he was covered by the much bigger (and slower) Mark West, drifted alone along the left wing, waiting for a pass. McHale got the ball to Bird, he gave West a pump fake and lost him. Is there a moral to all this? Yes: Mark West was never meant to cover Larry Bird. But remember the first period, when Bird missed a twenty-one-footer from the right with Hubbard flying at him? "Hopefully," said Rodgers, "we can make him pay for that."

Hubbard didn't pay the price, but Ben Poquette did. Emulating his teammate's action in the first quarter, Poquette came roaring at Bird, who held his shot, faked, waited until Poquette was by him, and then drilled the jumper. "Daylight shooting," said Rodgers.

8:15   *Daugherty misses lay-up.*

Daugherty again took off, hoping to sneak away for an easy two. He missed the shot, and the Celtics got control of the loose ball on the rebound.

8:08   *Bird lookaway pass on the fast break stolen by Craig Ehlo.*

7:59   *West lay-up on break.*

CLEVELAND 49, BOSTON 39.

West caught a long pass from Ehlo, but West was still about thirty feet from the basket. Bear in mind the following about Mark West:

1. As stated before, he was never meant to guard Larry Bird.
2. He would never make anyone forget Magic Johnson, or even Dennis Johnson or Vinnie Johnson, when it came to handling a ball.

3. He has two favorite moves—getting the ball under the basket and dunking it with his right hand and getting the ball under the basket and dunking it with his left hand.
4. Until this season, when Wilkens went to work on West's confidence, he had never scored more than fifteen points in a pro game in his three-year career.
5. No one works harder or ever experienced more sheer frustration when it came to trying to catch the ball and score. One NBA broadcaster put it this way: "West plays the game as if he were wearing mittens."
6. Even though he had scored twenty-seven points in a game under Wilkens, he still had the nickname "Hammer." That was for the strength of his dunks, the intensity of his fouls, and the speed of his shots from the foul line.

Keeping all this in mind, you know why Wilkens yelled, "Slow the ball up, Mark." when West caught Ehlo's pass in the middle of the floor about thirty feet from the basket. "Get it to a guard," yelled Wilkens.

But West was still thinking about how easily Bird had scored on him. And who knows what else he was thinking, but he put the ball down and was rambling toward the basket. A couple of Celtics simply got out of his way figuring that the 6-10, 230-pound West would probably dribble the ball off his foot and lose it, so why stand in his way and take a chance of getting run over and ending up with tennis shoe prints on your chest?

Well, West just kept going to the basket and he more or less kept control of the dribble. As he got near the rim, West did a bizarre-looking scoop shot that went in.

"Nice shot, Mark," yelled Wilkens.

Later, Wilkens would look at the tape of that shot, shake his head and say, "I've never seen Mark do anything like that."

Conclusion: Not only was Mark West never meant to guard

Larry Bird, he was never meant to make scoop shots. But he was doing both this night in Boston.

7:40   *Bird loses ball out of bounds.*

7:29   *McHale loose-ball foul (P1, T4).*

After Bird's turnover, Ehlo inbounded to Harper, who dribbled up the floor and drove down the middle of the lane, heaving a ten-footer off the back of the rim. McHale, Bird, and West were under the basket. As the shot went up, West cleared Bird out of the way with a left elbow. Bird ended up on his hands and knees, and West fell down on top of him.

"He pushed me," yelled West, pointed at McHale. "He got me from behind."

Earl Strom blew the whistle when the bodies started falling, but he had yet to make a call when Wilkens yelled from the bench, "McHale got him from behind."

Strom nodded and pointed at McHale, nailing him with the call. McHale disgustedly shook his head.

"A call like that is why I wanted Earl to work the game," said Wilkens. "It's a tough call for an official in the Garden, especially when you have Mark West surrounded by Bird and McHale."

This call also shows why every team on the road prays that Earl Strom will show up. True, the call took guts, but that doesn't mean it's right. West pushed Bird completely off the court, yet the call went against McHale. Earl may be the greatest referee who has ever lived, but he does have a tendency to go against the grain to demonstrate his refusal to orchestrate a home crowd. Earl may be the only referee on the planet who would have decided that McHale was at fault here. Of course Lenny is happy Earl has shown up.

7:29   *Lee in for Daugherty.*

"I had to get Brad some rest," said Wilkens. "I waited this long to take him out because he was playing so well and so strong. Also, he had stayed out of foul trouble. In a number of games, he got in early foul trouble, and I had to take him out. But this time, he was in such a good flow, I wanted to stay with him."

Wilkens had two backup centers on the roster—Mel Turpin and Lee. But Turpin wasn't at the game because he had to attend the funeral of his grandmother-in-law.

"That's what he said," said Wilkens. "His wife's grandmother died. Look, it's a death in the family."

Turpin had been playing so little and so ineffectively that he was not about to be missed, anyway.

7:15   *Poquette loose-ball foul (P1, T3).*

When play resumed Harper went funky again, moving into the lane with no clear purpose. Fred Roberts switched on him and Harper went left-to-right, taking a weird left-handed shot that refused to drop. In the rebound battle, Whitworth, very likely deciding that he had to undo the injustice his partner has just perpetrated, called a very dubious loose-ball foul on poor Ben Poquette, an unfortunate victim of circumstance who has made the mistake of battling Larry Bird for the ball rather than an ordinary player.

NBA referees swear to the death there is no such thing as a

make-up call; experienced observers rely on what their eyes, not their ears, tell them in these matters.

7:06 *McHale short jump hook. Foul on Lee (P1, T4). Foul shot, swish.*

Cleveland 49, Boston 42.

There is only one way McHale could have gotten easier and better position to receive Ainge's entry pass. That is if McHale had gone up to Keith Lee, the man who is guarding him, and said, "Excuse me, Keith, but I'd sure appreciate it if you'd allow me to take this spot right here. Do you mind?"

"Not at all, Kev. You're the boss."

Keith Lee has about as much chance of stopping Kevin McHale as he has of relieving Wilkens as coach. He probably didn't deserve a foul on this play, but he should be sent to bed without his supper when the game is over for allowing McHale such a ridiculously lush position on the floor.

7:06 *Hubbard in for Poquette.*

"I wanted to get Phil back on Bird," said Wilkens. "I didn't like that matchup with West guarding Bird."

6:50 *West fouled by Bird (P1, T5). First foul shot, lined in. Second foul shot, lined off back of rim.*

Cleveland 50, Boston 42.

Ehlo drove to the basket and put up a scoop shot that was too hard. West crashed the boards from the right wing and cupped the ball with his right hand. Bird was on West's back, and West's feet flew out from under him. West fell, Bird becoming a sandwich between West and the floor. Bird yelled for a foul, but Strom pointed at Bird, hitting him with the foul. Wilkens nodded from the bench.

This call is another reason Wilkens loves to see Strom at the Garden. Very few officials would call Bird for an over-the-back foul such as this one, especially in Boston. The Garden crowd booed. Joe Tait said, "It was a foul. Bird undercut West and put him on the deck."

It would be interesting to let Lenny Wilkens and K. C. Jones watch the tape of this play together and then record their comments. What the *Celtics* saw was Mark West hooking Larry Bird with a massive left forearm, yanking him to the floor, and then getting the call! They would agree, however, that Earl Strom is nothing if not fearless.

West is a 52-percent foul shooter this season, which is better than his 49-percent career mark. And remember that his nickname is the Hammer.

"Get the ball up," Wilkens yells from the bench, reminding West to try and get a little arch on his shot.

He gets very little and is lucky to make one of the two free throws.

6:32 *Johnson drives left lane for lay-up.*

CLEVELAND 50, BOSTON 44.

McHale rebounded West's missed free throw and handed it to Johnson. Johnson brought the ball up the court, guarded by Harper. McHale set up at the high post for the first time in the game. Johnson passed to McHale and then cut off McHale, taking a handoff as if McHale were a quarterback and D.J. a running back. Lee and Harper both stayed with McHale, and Johnson was wide open to drive in for a lay-up.

The play is called "Thumbs Up," and this was the first option, which is seldom utilized. Then again, the Celtics don't play against Keith Lee very often. Johnson was able to take the simple give-and-go handoff and drive to the basket because (a) Harper, guarding Johnson, was caught napping and (b) Lee, guarding McHale, is in a permanent defensive coma. Lee never acknowledged Johnson and D.J. just took it to the hoop for a nice left-handed lay-up. This is basic New York City basketball, circa 1925.

5:55 *Hubbard lay-up on baseline. Assist—Harper.*

CLEVELAND 52, BOSTON 44.

Harper passed the ball to Hubbard on the left baseline. Hubbard had Roberts on his back. Hubbard gave Roberts a head and pump fake, and Roberts went up too soon. As Roberts came down, Hubbard went up for the easy lay-up. It is the same move Hubbard has been using for seven years, and the same move he has scored on twice already in this game.

"I'll just keep making that move until they stop it," said Hubbard. "The key is varying your fakes. When you fake, you have to make sure that it looks like you're really going to shoot the ball."

Hubbard has ten points, only two under his season's average.

Prior to this shot, Cleveland had two cracks at the basket: Harper began the possession with a shot in the lane, and the ball was kept alive by West, who certainly knows how to use that monstrous body. "Mark West," said Rodgers, "is in the game for one reason—physicality. He can hurt you physically."

The Celtics have been unusually vulnerable on the boards all season, anyway. Boston has the image of being a rugged rebounding team over the years, and the presence of the Bird-Parish-McHale front line would seem to perpetuate that tradition. But in truth, the '86–87 Celtics were, at best, an indifferent rebounding team, especially on the offensive boards, where they were twenty-third and last all season long in percentage of their own misses retrieved. But their biggest problem was their inability to keep teams from getting damaging second shots. During the course of the regular season, the Celtics would surrender twenty or more offensive rebounds a total of eighteen times while managing the feat themselves on just three occasions.

With regard to their defensive rebound deficiency, there were three possible explanations:

1. Because they do so much double-teaming defensively, they left rebound lanes available to unguarded men.
2. They were simply being beaten to the ball by stronger legs belonging to eager young men who were quicker, more explosive jumpers than the thirty-year-old Bird, the twenty-nine-year-old McHale, and the thirty-three-year-old Parish.
3. They were so confident of their own ability to score at the other end that they subconsciously adopted a "what-the-hell, we'll-get-it-back" philosophy on the glass. In other words, they reasoned it really wasn't worth working all that hard.

5:39 *Bird thirteen-footer. Assist—Johnson.*

CLEVELAND 52, BOSTON 46.

Johnson brought the ball up the court and passed to Bird, who shot it over Hubbard for the basket. Nothing tricky; just a pass, a shot, and a basket. Simple free-lance basketball. This may get Bird going, and the Celtics can use an offensive lift right now because the Cavaliers are still controlling the game.

5:34 *McHale blocks Harper's shot.*

Ehlo brought the ball up the court and drove the right lane before handing off to Harper. But McHale blocked Harper's shot and the ball went out of bounds.

Boston brought in Parish for Roberts.

•

The Celtics are the talk of the league when it comes to their substitution patterns. They have no Vinnie Johnson, no Ricky Pierce, no Michael Cooper. No player on their bench challenges a starter for his job. The five starters expect very little relief and are quite willing to assume all the responsibility for winning the game.

A year ago, K. C. Jones had the option of putting in Scott Wedman if Bird was tired, fully expecting that Wedman might hit two or three jump shots while Bird was resting. If Robert Parish was having one of the walkabout nights that have dotted his Celtics career, K.C. had the very pleasant opportunity to insert Bill Walton.

But Walton has yet to play a game in the '86–87 season. He somehow or other managed to injure his right ankle while riding a stationary bicycle during the first week in October. Surgery was performed on the ankle on December 17, 1986, and the Celtics are now patiently awaiting his recovery. K.C. has two options if he needs to replace Parish. He can bring in Roberts, who is 6-10, but who plays as if he is 6-7, and let McHale play center. Or he can go with Greg Kite, his backup center. Kite is currently playing about as poorly as he can play, and with Kite, that is a horrifying statement.

Wedman had heel surgery in June 1986, and has never recuperated. He was activated on November 25, 1986, and played in six games between that day and December 5 before going back on the injured list on December 11. The Celtics miss his scoring punch. Roberts has been the first forward substitute all season, but he is having a very difficult time tonight.

Jerry Sichting was the primary guard substitute throughout the 1985–86 season, and the Celtics were quite pleased with his overall performance. He did, however, play fewer average minutes in the '86 playoffs (15.2) than he did in the regular season (19.5).

The reason for the decline in minutes was the increased confidence in Ainge, and that reasoning carried over into the '86–87 season. K.C. was more reluctant to replace Ainge with Sichting than he had been the year before. Sichting was still the third guard, but he wound up playing less quality time. His actual minutes and average playing time were up, but 31 percent of his 1,566 minutes were picked up in fifteen starts he was given when Ainge or Johnson were out of the lineup.

Behind Sichting, the Celtics had a haphazard substitution system that could not accurately be termed a "pattern." At various times, Sam Vincent, Darren Daye, or even Rick Carlisle were employed as backcourt reserves, with minimal distinction.

5:25   *Lee offensive foul (P2).*

Poor Keith Lee. He's not playing well, but he can't get a break, either. As he made a spin move to his left, K. C. Jones yelled out "Offensive!" Perhaps that influenced the call, because the flustered Lee didn't create much contact.

5:08   *Bird twenty-footer from the left.*
Assist—Johnson.

CLEVELAND 52, BOSTON 48.

Look out, world, Bird appears to be heating up. This was a "20-Bump," in which McHale picks off Hubbard, Bird takes the entry pass from Johnson and swishes the twenty-footer while drifting slightly to the left. The shot was so soft that if a dozen eggs had been placed in the bottom of the net, none would have been cracked.

4:52   *Hubbard misses seventeen-footer.*

After Bird's basket, the Cavs worked the ball around the perimeter but were unable to get the ball inside. With five seconds left on the shot clock, Hubbard got the ball in the corner and took a seventeen-footer, a shot he normally doesn't take, much less make. Parish rebounded Hubbard's miss and handed the ball to Johnson.

4:43   *Johnson shot blocked by Harper.*

Johnson brought the ball up the court and drove to the baseline. Then he took a jumper that Harper swatted out of his hands from behind.

The Celtics took a twenty-second timeout.

In the Cleveland huddle, Wilkens told West that he did a good job and that Williams was going back into the game.

"Boston has the ball out on the side," said Wilkens. "Remember their out-of-bounds play. Hot Rod, remember that McHale is probably going to set up under the basket. Phil, watch Bird after he takes the ball out of bounds. Remember, guys, see the ball."

At this point in the second quarter, the Celtics were eight for ten from the field and the Cavs were six for seventeen.

4:33 *Gary Briggs yells, "Three seconds."*

4:29 *Bird right lane for banker.*

CLEVELAND 52, BOSTON 50.

The Celtics adopted a different tactic than Wilkens expected. Bird inbounded to Johnson on the side, who then threw the ball to Bird at the foul line. Ehlo and Hubbard both jumped out to double-team Bird. First, Bird dribbled right past Ehlo, then Harper jumped out, joining Hubbard to throw a second double-team at Bird. Bird then split Hubbard and Harper with another dribble, freeing himself for an easy bank shot. It took Bird only two dribbles to shake three Cavaliers.

Joe Tait said, "Larry Bird has decided to take charge of this one." Bird has scored on his last three possessions, and the Celtics have scored twenty-one points on thirteen second-quarter possessions. It is now 19–8, Boston, since Daugherty's monster follow-up gave Cleveland a 44–31 lead nearly six minutes earlier.

4:16 *Williams ten-footer from baseline.*
       Assist—Harper.

CLEVELAND 54, BOSTON 50.

Harper and Williams set up their own two-man game on the right wing, with Johnson on Harper and McHale on

Williams. Harper drove toward the foul line, and McHale left Williams to help Johnson form a double-team on Harper. Harper spotted Williams open under the basket and hit him with a bounce pass; Hot Rod scored on a rainbow jumper.

"Like so many young players with great talent, Harper tends to want to do everything himself," said Wilkens. "But he's learning that when he's double-teamed, someone has to be open. It sounds simple, but the natural inclination of most scorers is to try and get to the basket no matter how many guys are covering them. That comes from being a great player in college, where you can usually beat a couple of guys and score."

The other aspect of this play was Williams's jumper.

"Hot Rod is 6-11, but he has a lot of moves like a small forward," said Wilkens. "I remember scouting him during his senior season at Tulane. He was only 6-9. When I got the Cleveland job, I had heard stories that Hot Rod had grown and was almost seven feet, but I didn't believe it; you hear stuff like that about players' heights all the time, and it's seldom true. But when I walked into rookie camp and saw Hot Rod for the first time, I about fell over. He really was almost seven feet, yet he still has the quickness and agility of a guy who is smaller."

What made Williams grow between his twenty-third and twenty-fourth years? For the first time in his life, he was eating regularly and was on a concentrated weight program. At least, that's the logical explanation. But another possibility is that he might be younger than that. When Williams's stepmother, Barbara Colar, went down to the Sorrento, Louisiana, town hall to get his birth certificate, there was nothing on file for John Washington, Jr., which was his name. So Barbara Colar asked about a John Williams, since Williams was his mother's maiden name. There was a John Williams on file who was born about the time Barbara Colar thought her stepson was born, so she took the certificate. But she has no way of knowing for sure if the date on that certificate, August 9, 1963, is the birthdate of *her* John Williams.

4:11   *Gary Briggs yells, "Three seconds."*

The officials didn't listen. The ball had just crossed half-court.

4:01   *Bird misses twenty-footer.*

Back to "Bull-swing-swing," the play with which the Celtics opened the game. They have now gone to Bird four straight times. Earlier they milked McHale. The Celtics aren't embarrassed to exploit certain players when they appear to be hot. They are the leading NBA proponents of the "If-it-ain't-broke-don't-fix-it" theory.

3:49   *Harper pass off Lee's hands and out of bounds.*

Williams rebounded Bird's missed jumper. He got the ball to Harper, who once again drove into the lane and drew a crowd. He tried to get the ball to Lee under the basket, but Parish deflected the ball, which rolled up Lee's arm and out of bounds. Wilkens then sent in Bagley and Daugherty for Ehlo and Lee, giving the Cavs their original starting team on the floor.

While Bagley was out of the game, the Cavs were outscored 13–10. Without Daugherty, they were outscored 11–5. That's why Daugherty's rest was cut short after four minutes. Ehlo and Lee did not score. The Cavs' bench (West) has outscored the Celtic bench (Sichting) 5–2.

"The main thing was that our bench didn't kill us," said

Wilkens. "That could have happened since Boston was playing its starters so much."

NEW MATCHUPS

POINT GUARDS	Sichting vs. Bagley
SHOOTING GUARDS	Johnson vs. Harper
CENTERS	Parish vs. Daugherty
POWER FORWARDS	McHale vs. Williams
SMALL FORWARDS	Bird vs. Hubbard

3:40   *McHale misses hook.*

Sichting brought the ball up the court, guarded by Bagley. McHale was the only Boston player on the left side of the floor; everyone else was on the right and at least thirty feet from the basket. A classic two-man-game set-up. As Sichting went to pass, Wilkens yelled, "Ron, now!"

Just as Wilkens had outlined before the start of the quarter, Harper bolted from the right side of the court, where he was guarding Johnson, down low to help Williams double-team McHale. McHale seemed surprised by Harper's presence and he missed the hook shot. The Celtics had been wondering if the Cavs were *ever* going to double-team McHale.

3:16   *McHale blocks Daugherty.*

Bagley rebounded McHale's shot and dribbled up the floor. The Cavs moved the ball around the perimeter until Hubbard spotted Daugherty at the low post. Hubbard lobbed the ball to Daugherty, who caught it, turned, and went right up with a jumper. Under ordinary circumstances, it's a good play since Daughtery is seven feet tall. But when he turned, there was McHale, standing straight, arms up.

"Man, that guy has some long arms," said Daugherty.

Daugherty found out just how long as his jumper was easily blocked by McHale.

•

McHale was the greatest white shot blocker of all time until Mark Eaton came along. Eaton is 7-feet-4. McHale is 6-feet-11. So McHale remains the best sub-seven-foot white shot blocker of all-time.

It's doubtful that some opponents will ever reconcile themselves to McHale's greatness, solely because he is such a weird-looking player. He has a skinny barrel chest and a short neck. When University of Minnesota teammate Mychal Thompson took one look at McHale, he immediately dubbed him "Herman Munster."

The Celtics worked an elaborate draft-day deal in 1980 in order to bring him to Boston. Boston had gone from twenty-nine victories in 1978–79 to sixty-one in 1979–80, primarily due to Bird, but when they were wiped out in five games by the 76ers during the playoffs, coach Bill Fitch decided he had to get bigger up front. Fitch and Red Auerbach began to maneuver, and they had some good bargaining chips. An old deal with Detroit had brought them the number-one pick in the draft, and they also owned the thirteenth spot. The two prime players that year were Purdue's 7-foot-1-inch center Joe Barry Carroll and Louisville's 6-foot-2-inch guard Darrell Griffith.

The Celtics needed a shooting guard, but they also let on that they were very interested in Carroll, a talented but unfathomable pseudo-intellectual whose work habits and desire were questionable. Lurking on the fringe was McHale, who intrigued many scouts and general managers with his scoring and rebounding potential, but whose strange body frightened off others.

On draft day the Celtics traded the first and thirteenth picks to Golden State for the Warriors' number-three pick and for seven-foot center Robert Parish, a perplexing underachiever. Immediately, the Celtics went from being one of the smallest teams in the league to one of the biggest.

McHale wasn't easy to sign, however. He even went so far as to travel to Milan to listen to an Italian League offer. Finally, a deal was struck, and McHale signed with the Celtics. Arriving in Boston after a lengthy flight from Milan, he headed straight to Hellenic College, where the Celtics were conducting their training camp. Despite rubbery legs from his intercontinental journey, McHale walked onto the floor and immediately started blocking shots.

Moreover, he was instinctively blocking the shots of right-handed opponents with his left hand even though he himself is right-handed. Here was a man standing 6-11, with a phenomenal reach and good jumping ability. Those three attributes alone would have enabled him to be a superior shot blocker. But perhaps one player out of a thousand can automatically use his off hand to block shots. When a right-handed player goes up to contest the shot of a right-handed player, he often reaches across his body and creates contact. A righty can bother a lefty easier than he can a righty, and vice versa. The truly gifted can use the off hand, whichever one that might be, to block shots.

It was Brad Daugherty's misfortune to run into that one player in a thousand as he put up his shot on this particular evening.

•

The phrase very carefully used above was "*white* shot blocker." The NBA is perhaps the only arena of American life where to be white is to be immediately judged inferior. Just as Bob Dylan said, "You don't need a weatherman to know which way the wind blows," so, too, is it unnecessary to have a Ph.D. in kinesiology to realize that the average black player can jump higher and run faster than the average white player.

People in basketball don't really care *why* that is. They just know it's so, and they act accordingly. When a scout turns in a report saying that so-and-so, a Caucasian, is a "white leaper," the general manager receiving the report has an immediate frame of reference. "Ah-ha," he'll say. "Another Billy Cunningham." Or Dave Cowens. Or Tom Chambers. He'll know the prospect jumps far better than the run-of-the-mill white player, perhaps even close to a level of the better black players. And he'll know they're talking about an exceptional physical prospect.

It takes far more than just exceptional running and jumping ability to become a top-level ballplayer, of course. Blacks bristle when white commentators routinely imply that black players rely solely on physical ability and something vaguely referred to as "instinct," while white players are often cited for their sagacity. The implication is that hard work and/or brainpower had nothing to do with the career development of the black player, but everything to do with the success of the white player.

People seldom stop to think that no one learns how to dribble the basketball between his or her legs in five minutes. The moves black players unveil on the court are the product of work. In order for any black player to reach the pinnacle of his profession, thousands of hours have been spent practicing, learning, and experimenting. What good does sheer jumping ability do if the person doesn't know what to do with the ball once he gets it? Speed is nice to have, but speed without purpose is irrelevant to the essence of the game.

Speed, even more than jumping, is a problem for whites in the NBA. White guards are usually shooting guards who struggle on defense to stay with the swifter black players. That's why Danny Ainge is such an anomaly. He is not only fast *for a white guy* (a compliment in and of itself in this world), but he's also considered to be fast, period. He is, without question, the fastest white man to enter the NBA since Doug Collins was a rookie in the 1973–74 season. And

Fred Roberts may very well be the fastest white forward in the league, for whatever that's worth.

Nevertheless, the average black player does have an advantage in running and jumping, and it is harder for the average white player to succeed as a result. It is practically a given that white players must work incredibly hard to succeed, because they are starting with a physical handicap compared to their black brethren. It's no accident that many white players make it a point to play as often as possible with black players during their adolescence in order to enhance their own development.

The overwhelming superiority of blacks is borne out by the roster numbers. In any given year, the NBA is composed of approximately 70–75 percent blacks and 25–30 percent whites. Moreover, blacks are usually 85–90 percent of the starters in the league (a tally at the conclusion of the 1986–87 season revealed 15 white starters out of 115 players, a total of 13 percent).

In such circumstances, whites are deferential in a way they are not in most areas of American life (a possible exception being the world of jazz, and that doesn't mean the professional team in Salt Lake City). It's a black world, and whites are happy to be a part of it. The problem comes when the white-dominated media either overpraises white players or fails to give sufficient credit to black players for triumphs of the mind and work ethic, or when blacks aren't gracious enough to acknowledge when a white player has actually risen to the level of the best blacks, as in the case of Larry Bird. Then people get angry, and with reason.

The Celtics are particularly sensitive about the black-white issue, for despite the most exemplary record of any team in any sport in employing black athletes and coaches, they are continually subjected to the irrelevant scrutiny of amateur social scientists who are upset because they seem to have a disproportionate number of white players.

It's true that the Celtics have always seemed to have more white players than almost any team, the only annual challengers being the Phoenix Suns and Utah Jazz. Some people interpret this as a clear indication of some devious management intent to placate their white clientele. It would be one thing if the Celtics were employing white players at the expense of black players, and losing. But is there anything wrong with utilizing Larry Bird, Kevin McHale, and Danny Ainge, not to mention (if healthy) Bill Walton and Scott Wedman? You *win* with players like that. The Celtics need apologize to no one, especially to latecomers who have never even heard of Chuck Cooper.

Was it OK with the overreactors when the Celtics ran eighteen people through the locker room in the dismal '78–79 season, twelve of whom were black? That team went 29-53, but it had a coloration acceptable to the watchdogs.

Since then there has been a clear imbalance on the Boston roster. They have had a disproportionate number of *great* players, both black and white.

3:09 *Hubbard steals Bird pass.*

Bird got the ball low in the lane with good position on Hubbard, but Hubbard got a hand on the ball and Bagley grabbed it.

2:55 *Harper misses a jumper.*

Daugherty kept the ball alive, but Williams's follow-up was no good and Bird picked the ball up in the right corner.

2:33   *Johnson drives to the basket and is fouled by Daugherty (P2, T5). Cleveland timeout. First foul shot, swish. Second foul shot, swish.*

CLEVELAND 54, BOSTON 52.

This was an improvised secondary-break play. Johnson threw the ball in to a posting-up McHale, and when Harper went low to double on McHale, Kevin returned the ball to Johnson, his first inside-out pass of the game. Johnson looked back in at McHale and then decided he had an avenue to the hoop. Johnson drove past Harper down the lane and was picked up by Daugherty, who made sure Johnson didn't make a lay-up.

The Cavs called timeout.

"All right, we gotta show some patience on offense," Wilkens said in the huddle. "Early in the game, we were moving the ball around, making them move and work on defense. We gotta stay out of that pass-and-shot thing. Let's get back to moving the ball.

"Now, two other things. First, if we double down to help on McHale, the rest of us have to drift toward the middle. We have to cut off the middle. Make them kick the ball back outside and take the jumper. We can live with their guards taking the outside shot. Let's make them move the ball."

Wilkens never got to his second point as the buzzer sounded and the players returned to the court.

At this point, the Cavs have been outscored 23–17 in the second quarter. Boston was nine for twelve from the field, Cleveland seven for twenty-two.

2:12 *Bagley nineteen-footer, top of key.*
Assist—Williams.

CLEVELAND 56, BOSTON 52.

This time, the Cavs moved the ball: Bagley to Hubbard to Daugherty to Harper to Williams at the low post. Boston was in a "Rover" defense. The Celtics released Sichting from his Bagley duty; the only way they get burned is if an unlikely suspect—someone like John Williams, for example—makes a good read of the situation and delivers the right pass. Even then, Bagley, a noted erratic shooter, must hit a shot that isn't exactly a gimme.

Win some, lose some. Williams made the pass, to Bagley at the top of the key, and he buried the 19-footer. Six passes, two dribbles, and two points.

"Way to move the ball," yelled Wilkens.

"When Bags saw Sichting go down on Hot Rod, Bags moved in closer so if he got a pass, he'd be at the top of the key instead of at the 3-point line," said Wilkens later. "Those two steps in really help your shooting percentage."

1:31 *Parish spins for five-footer. Foul by*
Williams (Pl, T6). Foul shot, swish.

CLEVELAND 56, BOSTON 55.

When the Celtics defeated the Lakers to win the 1984 championship, one of their major offensive weapons was the missed shot. Parish, McHale, Bird, and Cedric Maxwell were all way above average on the offensive boards, and the Lakers couldn't cope.

Two and a half seasons later, the Celtics are the most ineffective offensive rebounding team in the league, even worse, if it's possible to imagine, than the New York Knicks. Since the first week of the season the Celtics have been twenty-third and last in percentage of potential offensive rebounds recovered.

This is not as big a problem as it might appear, since the Celtics have less need of offensive rebounds than most teams. They have been one-two with Los Angeles all season long in team field-goal percentage, and number one all season in free-throw percentage. The oldest team in the league, they lack the strong young legs that characterize such aggressive offensive-rebounding teams as Atlanta and, yes, Cleveland. Still, the Celtics could get more second shots if they wanted to. Offensive rebounding is often a simple child of desire, and the truth of the matter is that the Celtics have become very lax parents.

So when the 1986–87 Celtics get four shots in one possession, it's news. First an isolated Bird let fly and missed. There's one. Parish rebounded and his jumper wouldn't fall. That's two. Parish got the long rebound and pitched it out to Sichting, whose fifteen-footer wouldn't go, either. Bird hauled in the miss and set up a little two-man game with Parish on the left side. Robert turned, up-faked Williams, laid it in, and drew the foul.

1:16 *Daugherty fouled by Parish (P3, T6).*
Swish, swish.

CLEVELAND 58, BOSTON 55.

The Cavs got the ball down low to Daugherty, who drove around Parish and was bumped. Daugherty made the basket, but Strom ruled that the foul was before the shot. Since the Celtics were in the penalty, Daugherty went to the foul line for two shots.

"Fingers," yelled Wilkens.

Whether it is more concentration, more fingers, or his hands finally stopped growing, no one can say, but Daugherty swished both free throws. As Parish went to the bench for his third foul, Greg Kite replaced him.

Daugherty had sixteen points and seven rebounds.

1:01 *Bird twenty-one-footer left sideline.*
Assist—McHale.

Cleveland 58, Boston 57.

A nice little cat-and-mouse game with Bird working Hubbard over behind a pick. Bird and McHale were stacked on the left side of the lane. McHale set a pick, and Hubbard guessed that Bird was coming up to the foul line. Uh-uh. Larry quickly popped out on the left side and hit the jumper. The name of the play is "Cleveland."

Incidentally, the official score sheet showed McHale receiving an assist on Bird's basket. McHale set the pick on Hubbard that freed Bird for the pass from Johnson, but, it was Johnson who deserved the assist.

:50 *Williams spinner in middle.*
Assist—Daugherty.

Cleveland 60, Boston 57.

Harper brought the ball up the court and drove to the baseline, running into several Celtics. He passed back to the top of the key to Daugherty, who spotted Williams cutting across the lane. Daugherty passed to Williams, who hit a spinning lay-up over Bird.

Passes like that are the reason Daugherty went into the game leading all NBA centers in assists. Daugherty is the smartest, most offensively alert rookie center to hit the NBA since Bill Walton came in twelve years earlier. No first-year center in recent memory makes this play; it's that simple.

"Not only does Brad see the court like a point guard, he thinks like one," said Wilkens. "He is so unselfish, it almost is a fault. I want him to shoot more, but at North Carolina, he was always taught to think pass. That is great training."

:40   *Harper blocks McHale.*

The Celtics set up a two-man game with Johnson and McHale. Harper was guarding Johnson, Williams was on McHale. Johnson lobbed the ball under to McHale, and Harper remembered what Wilkens said during the last time-out: "Let's make them move the ball."

Harper left Johnson to double-team McHale. McHale caught the pass, turned for his shot, and never saw Harper coming. Actually, soaring is more like it, as Harper blocked McHale's shot from behind.

:35   *McHale travels.*

After Harper's block, the Celtics took the ball out of bounds. Johnson passed to McHale under the basket, who turned and seemed to hesitate. Was he looking for Harper? Wilkens would like to think so. Anyway, the hesitation caused McHale to shuffle his feet. Harper made no attempt to double-team McHale, the thought that he might was enough to throw off McHale's rhythm on this play. At last, the Cavs' defense is having an effect on McHale. This is the fourth straight low-post opportunity in which Cleveland has kept McHale from scoring.

:15   *Williams follow-up jump hook.*

CLEVELAND 62, BOSTON 57.

The running sheet and the scorebook will indicate that Williams scored the basket and that Bagley missed the original shot, but the man who triggered what could only be described as a breakdown in the Celtics defenses was Mr. Brad Daugherty.

As a rule, seven-foot rookie centers do not command attention once they stray from the basket. But Daugherty has already shown on several occasions that he can put the ball on the floor and do some damage. Accordingly, when Daugherty started moving from right to left, he attracted a convention of white-shirted tall people. In this case, we are talking about McHale, who recognized that Daugherty is far too mobile for the ponderous Greg Kite to contain on the open floor, and Bird, who simply decided that his presence was needed. When these two left their men, the remaining Celtics started rotating toward the most dangerous shooters, leaving, once again, John Bagley alone behind the three-point line.

Bagley shot and missed, but the Celtics' big people were no longer matched up with anybody. Three-point shots are very unpredictable rebound missiles in any circumstance. They normally bounce out farther than the average shot, making a fundamental such as positioning irrelevant. But the Celtics cannot out-jump the Cavaliers up front; they need to execute the basics.

But this play has broken down. No Celtic has been able to put a body on anybody, and when the rebound became a struggle between the athletic Williams and the willing but limited Kite, it was lights out for Boston—and it's all due to the sudden respect the Celtics have for Brad Daugherty.

:03 *Bird nine-foot fallaway.*

CLEVELAND 62, BOSTON 59.

In Bird's first year the Celtics were captained by Dave Cowens, and Bird was the first to accord his leader the proper respect. Big shots and most end-of-the-period shots were taken by the veteran. Bird, while recognizing his own talent, had no problem with this. Such respect fit into his general sense of world order.

But for the past seven years the man to whom the Celtics turn when they positively, absolutely *need* a basket is Larry Bird. The surest lock in the course of any Celtics' game is that whenever there is enough time at the end of the period to set up a proper shot, the man who will take that shot is Larry Bird.

In his early years, this wasn't always as good an idea as the outside world might think. Bird would have to have a set play, because he wasn't much of a one-on-one player. Sometimes he wouldn't be able to get free. But that's no longer true. In the past two years Bird has worked hard at his one-on-one game, however philosophically opposed to that style of play he happens to be.

There were fifteen seconds left after the John Williams basket, and everyone in the building knew where the ball was going. The Celtics went to what they call "Hawk." All this means is that the entire right side of the floor is cleared, except for Bird, who posts up as deeply as possible on the right box, and the feeder. The ball was thrown into Bird. The clock wound down. Bird maneuvered himself along the baseline. Harper made a half-hearted attempt to help out Hubbard, but Bird ignored him. Finally, Bird turned and shot. Swish.

:01 *Bagley misses a sixty-footer as the half ends.*

In the second period the Celtics have had 21 possessions and have scored on 14. They have posted up 8 times and have been successful in 7.

In the first half Kevin McHale has posted up 12 times and has scored on 9. The Celtics as a team posted up 19 times in 49 possessions.

In the second quarter the Cavaliers, who had successfully executed 11 fast breaks in 11 tries in the first quarter, had no fast-break attempts whatsoever.

5

Halftime

Halftime, and you don't need to see the scoreboard to know that the Cavaliers are doing something special in Boston Garden. All you have to do is watch how they walk off the floor and into the runway that leads to the dressing room.

There are three ways that teams leave the court:

1. Angry. In this case, the coach is the key. He tends to stay behind, letting the players leave the floor first. He is looking for the officials, who usually are the last to leave the floor. Sometimes the coach just stares, but if the first twenty-four minutes were really bad, he just might start shouting, not caring if the officials are by themselves, guarded by two policemen (as is usually the case) or so far away that they can't hear the coach. All the coach really wants is for the officials to see him yelling. They don't have to hear to get his message.

2. Depressed. The score is something like 55–37 and your team is shooting 51 percent at the line, 35 percent from the field, and hasn't gotten a rebound since Harding was president. No one even bothers to glance up at the scoreboard. Keep the head down and the feet moving. Get out before a fan throws a chair at you. On these nights, the trainer makes sure to have all the sharp objects locked up and a bottle of aspirin near the blackboard in easy reach of the coach.

3. Content. The players and the coaches glance at the scoreboard and sort of nod. The game is well played and going
   just as they imagined. It's close and it's probably going to
   remain so. The players and coach walk off the floor con-
   fidently, heads up, staring straight, and the sweat pouring
   off their faces feels good. The team and coach want to get
   off the floor soon so that a few strategic adjustments can be
   made in the dressing room, the moves that could make a
   difference in the game.

For the Cavaliers, the walk off the floor this Friday night in
Boston Garden was one of contentment. Wilkens did glance at
the scoreboard and nod. Ron Harper and Brad Daugherty
were smiling. Hot Rod Williams was still stealing looks at the
Celtics, but he no longer seemed in awe. Rather, Hot Rod
wanted just one more peek at the guys who are supposed to be
legends, but who are sweating and just as tired as he.

"When we walked off the floor, we knew we were in the
game with Boston," said Wilkens. "And the Celtics knew it,
too."

In the dressing room, Wilkens is not prone to dramatic
gestures. There is no throwing Coke cans at the blackboard,
no insulting his players' manhood, no emotional demands.

"I ask the guys to be realistic, to give what they know they
can," said Wilkens. "If I suddenly yelled and screamed all the
time, it wouldn't be me. The players would see it was phony.
And when things are going well, I don't get too high, either.
Primarily, I want us to keep in mind what we were doing to
get this far. The idea is to reinforce what the guys are doing
right and correct what they did wrong."

As the Cavs entered the squashed, steamy dressing room,
Wilkens started with the positive.

1. "I love the ball movement. See how much better we shoot
   from the outside when we throw three-four passes and

keep the ball moving? That's the key. Keep the ball moving, make them play defense on us."

The Cavs are hitting 50 percent from the field and they have more assists than Boston, 15-14.

2. "Keep pushing the ball. We got a lot of fast breaks in the first quarter, but we didn't run as well in the second quarter. We can make them tired. They've hardly gone to their bench, and if we can keep pushing the ball at them, fatigue can become a factor and work for us."

The Cavs had twenty-two transition points in the first quarter, two in the second quarter.

3. "Stay on the boards. Rebound. Get the ball out and up the court fast."

The Cavs and Boston each have twenty rebounds.

4. "On defense, always see the ball. And when they get a rebound, guard your man so he can't get a long pass."

The Celtics have not scored off one of their famed court-length baseball passes.

The negative:

1. "We've got to get Hot Rod some help on McHale. When we decide to double-team, do it quickly. Guards, don't hesitate. Get down there and make McHale give up the ball."

McHale has 20 points on 9 for 15 from the field.

2. "Too many three-pointers. Don't be afraid to take a step or two in. There is nothing wrong with an 18- or 20-footer."

Bagley has taken all four of the Cavs' three-pointers, and he missed them all. He is 6 for 9 from two-point range and 0 for 4 from three-point range. Wilkens did not look at Bagley or even give any hint that he was talking about Bagley, but everyone in the dressing room knew who was supposed to get this message.

3. "Let's stay aggressive, but no silly fouls. We don't want to put these guys on the line."

The Celtics are 13 for 14 at the foul line. The Cavs are holding their own, as they are 8 for 10. It looks as if Wilkens's foul-shooting lessons have worked.

•

Before Wayne Embry became the Cavaliers' general manager in June of 1986, the franchise had made the playoffs only once in the last eight years. It had the worst record of any team in the first half of the 1980s, and it had traded away all of its first-round draft picks from 1980 to 1986.

Those picks became James Worthy for Los Angeles; Detlef Schrempf, Roy Tarpley, Sam Perkins, and Derek Harper for Dallas; Rodney McCray for Houston. All of those deals were made under the ownership of Ted Stepien (1980–84), and none of the players the Cavs received in those transactions were with the team or had been dealt for anyone else who was on the roster at the start of the 1986–87 season.

Or how about this? The Cavs had nine coaches in the last seven years before Embry took the job, and that includes Bill Musselman—twice.

There are hundreds of Stepien stories. Under his ownership, the Cavs had a mascot dubbed "Fat Guy Eating Beer Cans," appropriately enough, because he was a fat guy who ate beer cans. Well, he didn't actually eat them, but during the first timeout of the opening game of Stepien's regime, Fat Guy Eating Beer Cans walked to midcourt, can in hand. Then he took a bite, his teeth ripping a hunk of metal out of the can. In one hand, he held up the can, in the other hand, he held the piece of metal and he raised his hands above his head. The crowd booed. Fat Guy Eating Beer Cans also was at various times Fat Guy Eating Raw Eggs and Fat Guy Eating Glass.

Stepien also owned a bar where he had a special form of female entertainment, the show hosted by Stepien himself. "I may not be able to run a basketball team, but I sure can run a lingerie show," Stepien once said.

The Celtics had championship banners hanging from the ceiling; it was suggested that the Cavs put up a Peek-a-boo nightie leftover from Stepien's reign.

By the time Stepien sold the team to the Gunds, it was amazing that the Cavs were still in Cleveland. Things got better, and the Cavs even made the playoffs in 1985–86, but there remained a certain degree of turmoil under general manager Harry Weltman.

In April of 1986, the Cavs were paying George Karl, Tom Nissalke, and former assistant Mo McHone all *not* to coach the team, and that happened after Stepien had sold the team to George and Gordon Gund.

"There were problems with the Cleveland situation," said Embry. "I knew and everyone in the league knew. But I also saw possibilities and great potential. Despite a bad year (in 1985–86), the team drew very well (9,300 per game), and we have a great building. We also have owners in George and Gordan Gund who own the building and are financially committed to winning. That's why I took the job."

Embry told the Cavs he would build through the draft and with the accent on young players. He talked about a team with character, not one made up of characters. He also told them he was going to take out the broom and clean house. He is an impressive-looking man, 6-foot-8 and close to 300 pounds. He is reportedly a millionaire, thanks to several shrewd business investments in the fast-food and auto-parts businesses. Embry was an NBA center for eleven years, and the general manager and later a vice-president for the Milwaukee Bucks from 1972–85. He then was hired as a basketball consultant by the Indiana Pacers for the 1985–86 season.

Gordon Gund said, "We were looking for a man who was well-grounded in the NBA, a man with experience in running a team, and a man who was willing to build a winner the right way."

In other words, Gund was tired of headcases in Cleveland uniforms.

Embry told the Gund Organization this: "This just isn't a very good team, and some of the people on it . . . well . . . they weren't the kind of players I like."

The Cavs finished the 1985–86 season with a 29-53 record. In March of 1986, Harry Weltman fired George Karl as coach. A month later, the Gund brothers fired Weltman and started a two-month search for a general manager, with the team left in the hands of a former high school basketball coach from Bangor, Maine, by the name of Thaxter Trafton. Trafton's title was president of the Cavaliers, but his main responsibility was running the building, not the team.

Under Trafton was Gene Littles, a Cavs assistant coach who took over for Karl during the last month of the season. But two days before the draft, Littles, frustrated because the Cavs had not offered him any guarantees about remaining with the organization in some capacity, quit and took an assistant's job with the Chicago Bulls. That made Barry Hecker the ranking basketball man for the June 1986 draft. Hecker was the player personnel director under Weltman. Before he joined the Cavs, Hecker had been a high school junior-varsity basketball coach in Salt Lake City. He had virtually no professional experience—unless you count working at Adrian Dantley's basketball camp—until he was hired by the Cavs in 1984.

On the surface, this meant the Cavs went into the 1986 draft with no general manager, no coach, and no assistants in place. Everyone knew that Hecker would be out once the new front office team was assembled, and the Cavs had the eighth pick in the draft.

"Even though I had not been officially hired, I had been talking to Cleveland for about a month before the draft and it was evident that I was going to get the Cleveland job," said Embry. "I was working for the Indiana Pacers as a consultant at the time, and they gave me permission to talk to Cleveland about the draft."

Nonetheless, the draft preparation fell into the hands of Gordon Gund, team legal counsel Richard Watson, and Trafton. Gund was a former hockey player, Watson a former 105-pound high school wrestler, and Trafton the former Bangor high school coach. In four days, those men changed the face and the direction of the franchise.

The day before the 1986 draft, the Cavs received the news that John Williams had been acquitted of sports bribery charges in the Tulane point-shaving case. Williams was charged with three counts of conspiring to fix games and shave points in three games. The penalty could have been up to seventeen years in prison (with or without hard labor) and up to $10,000 in fines. The prosecutors insisted that Williams actually shaved points in games against Mississippi State and Memphis State, and discussed the possibility but did not actually follow up on the plan in a game against Virginia Tech.

Williams was a 6-11, 220-pound forward who would have been among the top ten players selected in the 1985 draft if he had not been indicted in the Tulane case. Weltman selected Williams in the second round with the forty-fifth pick.

"In my four years with the Cavaliers, nothing has made me prouder than taking John Williams," said Weltman. "The point is not that John has become a very good player. Rather, we knew he was a good kid, a kid who was far more of a victim than a criminal. I remember how we got killed in the media when we selected John. One columnist called me 'morally reprehensible.' Now that the kid was found innocent, you don't hear much from those people today."

Weltman and the Gund Organization stood behind Williams as he missed the entire 1985–86 season because of court cases and appeals. Williams was found innocent because of the excellent defense by his attorney, Mike Green, who explained the case like this:

"John was born in Sorrento, Louisiana, which is as poor

and as rural and as deep Southern as you can get. His mother died soon after he was born, and one day John's father took his infant son to his grandfather's house. John's father said he was going to a funeral and would be back in a few hours. He never returned, leaving John to be raised by a seventy-eight-year-old blind man. John use to stand on his grandfather's porch, crying. One day, a women named Barbara Colar got tired of hearing the baby cry, so she simply took him. Barbara Colar had three children of her own in addition to John. She worked two jobs—as a short order cook and a janitor at a school—and the family lived in a trailer."

Williams's background was crucial to his case.

"It was unfortunate that he got the name Hot Rod," said Green. "It makes John sound like some guy who works angles. He's just the opposite. In fact, he got the name from Barbara Colar, who said that John loved toy cars and always made engine sounds while playing with them in the trailer."

By the time Williams was a senior in high school, he was 6-10 and being recruited. Tulane signed him after a recruiter left a shoebox at Williams's trailer. When Williams opened it, he found $10,000.

"John called his uncle when he saw all the bills in that shoebox," said Green. "He couldn't believe the money was real. He used it to buy a used car and gave the rest of the money to Barbara Colar."

Williams graduated 181st out of a high school class of 262. He scored 490 on the Scholastic Aptitude Test. The minimum score is 400 for signing your name. Williams got the lowest possible total of 200 on the verbal and he scored 290 on the math. A member of the Tulane admissions department wrote "The pits" on his application to the school.

"Tulane was everything John Williams was not," said Green. "It was an urban university in New Orleans. The average Tulane student scored 1,100 on the SAT. Tulane bills itself as the Harvard of the South. Kids get new cars for Christmas. They start the year off with $15,000 in their checking accounts."

Tulane somehow kept Williams eligible for four years.

Williams also said he received $100 a week during basketball season from Tulane basketball boosters.

"Sure, I saw the money coming in," said Williams. "I used to find it on my dresser. But I never threw no games and I never thought the money was for throwin' no games. I just figured they were givin' it to me like they always done."

When Williams's case went to court and when a variety of coaches testified that it didn't look like Williams had done anything different in the games that were fixed, the jury believed Hot Rod's story. Since then, Williams has become Harry Weltman's legacy with the Cavaliers.

"It came down to this," said Weltman. "We took John when no one else would touch him for one reason: He looked me in the eye and said he didn't do it. This kid was so naive and so scared when the scandal broke, I just didn't think he could lie."

With Williams in place, the Cavaliers suddenly found themselves with a dubious center (Mel Turpin) and four power forwards (Roy Hinson, Keith Lee, Mark West, and Williams) on their roster. Meanwhile, the phone was constantly ringing at the Coliseum as other teams were hoping to work a trade with the GM-less Cavs.

During his interview with the Cavs, Embry continually talked of North Carolina seven-footer Brad Daugherty.

"The Cavaliers have never had an respectable center for any length of time," Embry told the Cavaliers. "Daugherty is the kind of player you need. He's played four years at North Carolina, but he's only twenty. He's 250 pounds and going to get bigger and stronger. What's more, he's the kind of kid you want to build your team around."

So the Cavs decided to do more than just answer the phone. They called Philadelphia and asked about trading for the Sixers' number-one pick in the draft. The Cavs found out that Philadelphia was willing to move its pick. Watson and Trafton called Embry and said Philadelphia had an interest in Roy Hinson.

Watson said, "Wayne, if you had the number-one pick in the draft, who would you take?"

Embry said, "Daugherty."

Trafton said, "What about Lenny Bias?"

Embry said, "Absolutely not. The guy you'd want is Daugherty."

Watson said, "What do you think of Roy Hinson?"

Embry said, "In my opinion, Hinson is a 6-9 small forward who is not a good outside shooter. I really don't know if he can play power forward in the league, considering how it keeps getting bigger and bigger. With Daugherty, you're going to get a center for many, many years to come. He's tall, he's got a center's skill and a center's mentality. I don't care what some guys said about not being sure what Daugherty's position is. He's a center, and that is the hardest position on the court to fill."

So the Cavs put together a package of Hinson and $800,000 for the rights to Daugherty.

"It's funny. The Cavs told me that I was the cornerstone of the team," said Hinson, who had averaged 19 points and 7.2 rebounds. "Then I get a call at two in the morning saying I was traded to Philadelphia. So much for being the cornerstone."

From the moment the Cavs started negotiating for the first pick, Daugherty was their man. "No one else was even considered," said Embry. "There was no reason to trade a quality player like Hinson unless it was to get a center."

That was lucky for the Cavaliers, as cocaine wiped out the second and third picks in the draft. Celtics' pick Lenny Bias died from the drug and Golden State's Chris Washburn was hospitalized because of it.

In addition to owning the first pick in the draft, the Cavaliers had the eighth selection. They were stunned when 6-6 Ron Harper, a guard billed as the next Dr. J, was available. They jumped at the chance to pick him.

"I make no pretense of knowing anything about basketball," said Cavs legal counsel Dick Watson. "But even I knew we had to take Harper."

But the real surprise came when Trafton and Watson pulled a trade on their own, without consulting Embry. They sent the Cavs' second-round pick in 1989 and $50,000 to Dallas for Mark Price, who had just been taken in the second round by the Mavericks.

"Dick [Watson] and I just liked Price," said Trafton. "We felt he'd make a good backup point guard."

"I was absolutely floored when I heard about the Price deal," said Embry. "I guess they just thought it was a good idea. I liked it after I thought about it, but it caught me completely by surprise."

The Cavs used their regular pick in the second round to take 6-6 guard Johnny Newman from Richmond University.

Two days after the draft, Embry was officially hired. He had a roster that included five rookies—Daugherty, Williams, Harper, Price, and Newman. And two weeks after he got the job, Embry hired Lenny Wilkens as coach.

Wilkens said, "During the college all-star games in Hawaii, Harry Weltman sort of talked to me about coaching for him," said Wilkens. "Then Harry was fired, so I stopped thinking about Cleveland. When it became obvious that Wayne was going to get the Cleveland job, I did mention to him that I really wanted to get back in coaching and to keep me in mind. After the draft and when I saw all the young talent Cleveland had so quickly assembled, I was intrigued by the job and glad that Wayne wanted to talk to me."

At the press conference to announce his hiring, Wilkens mentioned that he liked a guard named World B. Free.

"He could be the next Fred Brown," said Wilkens. "I can see him coming off the bench and scoring big numbers in a short time."

Free had spent four years with the Cavaliers. In that time, he *was* the Cavaliers. Thirty-three, balding, and built more like a 6-2 linebacker than a greyhound guard, Free was the classic scorer, the guy whose attitude was, "If I score 25 and the man I cover scores 20, I've outscored him by five and done my job. If everyone else on the court did the same, we'd win by 25."

Embry didn't want to keep Free. He worried that he was too selfish, too set in his ways to help a young team. In a sense, Free was a guard of the past, the product of the New York playgrounds. He was what remained of the one-on-one, winner's out, half-court game. "When the ball would go to World, it would just stop," said George Karl. "That would be the end of our offense."

Yes, Free loved to pound the ball and pound the ball as he either backed his way to the basket or tried to get in position to take a twenty-two-footer. But the current trend is for a tall, sleek guard, the 6-5 to 6-7 model that once played small forward. This guard is more of a sprinter and a leaper than a shooter. He is an athlete, the guy who fills the lanes, scores off the fast break, a guy who considers a pass almost as important as a shot. He is a product of the Julius Erving generation. He is Michael Jordan or Magic Johnson or even Ron Harper, not George Gervin or World B. Free.

But the fact remained that the Cavs were a much better team with Free shooting than with Free on the bench. He could be counted on to score, "and creating your shot and putting the ball in the basket remains the hardest part of the pro game," said Harry Weltman, who traded for Free. "World brought talent and charisma to a franchise that had been devastated and desperately needed him. I don't care what did or didn't happen to World in Philadelphia, with the Clippers, or with Golden State. All I know is that he may be the best player in the history of the Cavaliers."

Free certainly was the one player the public could identify with. "I'm the guy they see in the airport and ask for my autograph," said Free. "When people in Cleveland see me, they think pro basketball."

Wilkens said, "I looked at films of World and I saw a guy who can still shoot and a guard who played hard. I had a meeting with him and he said he was willing to back up

Harper. I didn't care what other coaches said or if people thought he was a gunner or whatever. I wanted World."

Free averaged twenty-three points and shot 45 percent in his four years with the Cavaliers. He had altered his game and made some concessions to passing and at least token defense. And he was a superstar, always willing to sign autographs and pose for pictures. If a fan called his name when Free stepped on the court after a timeout, he'd turn and wave.

"Cleveland and World were a perfect match," said Joe Tait. "World found a town that loved him as much as he loved himself. I don't mean that as a knock. Rather, that part of World's personality that bothered some people in other cities really appealed to the fans here."

Embry wasn't so sure.

"I don't want to denounce the player," said Embry. "But we had an age factor. World would be thirty-three at the start of the season, and once guards get over thirty they're pretty much on borrowed time. And obviously, he had had some character problems in the past. I know what Free meant to the franchise and how the fans loved him, but I felt we needed to change the personality of the team."

Nonetheless, Embry did offer Free a one-year deal worth $400,000, only half of which was guaranteed. Free's agent was Ron Grinker, who had just been hired by Free four months before Embry took the Cleveland job. Free had earned $675,000 in his last season with Cleveland.

"From the moment we began talking until the end of the negotiations at the start of the regular season, Wayne never changed his offer," said Grinker.

The talks went something like this:

Grinker: "Wayne, why don't you just guarantee him the $400,000."

Embry: "Grinks, it's four and two. That's how the contract has to be, that's how we want it."

Grinker: "Why don't you do this? Sign him for $400,000 this season and $1 million for next year. Only guarantee

$100,000 of that $1 million. Then, if you don't sign him, you're creating an extra $1 million for yourself on next year's salary cap."

Embry: "Four and two."

Grinker: "What about this? We'll take your offer, but at the end of the year you should have a day for World, retire his number, the whole bit. Take your average crowd for that night. Suppose it's a Wednesday and you usually draw nine thousand. You keep the gate for the first nine thousand fans and give World the receipts from the rest of the fans."

Embry: "Grinks, we can't do something like that."

Grinker: "Why not?"

Embry: "It's just not done."

Grinker: "Be creative. Let's get this thing done."

Embry: "We can get it done. Take the offer, four and two."

Grinker: "World means a lot to the fans."

Embry: "I'm aware of that, but I'm prepared to take the heat. In Milwaukee, I was the guy who had to convince Oscar Robertson to retire. The World thing isn't nearly as difficult as Oscar's situation. So Grinks, it's four and two."

This went on for months, with Grinker making various proposals and Embry sticking to his original offer.

"I really respect Wayne, but I think he was awful stubborn on the World issue," said Grinker after it was over.

Embry said, "I love to talk to Grinks, but he can get so damn stubborn."

When two sides are stubborn, in Grinker's words, "You get a classic stalemate." That's why Free did not sign with the Cavs.

"I thought our offer was fair," said Embry. "All World had to do was what we asked and he would have gotten $400,000 for coming off the bench. No one else was making him offers. In retrospect, you'll see that we were fair."

Free ended up signing with Philadelphia in December of 1986 for $250,000, and he ended up on the bench as one of the Sixers' four shooting guards and was released after six weeks.

"This was the toughest, most unpopular decision I had to make after taking over the team," said Embry. "If this had been a team with a .500 record, a team with a legitimate chance to contend for a championship, I'd have made more of an effort to keep World. But we were building for three years from now, and we want Ron Harper, Johnny Newman, and Mark Price to be the core of our backcourt. I also don't know if World's pride could have handled coming off the bench, playing behind the kids. It's funny, I thought Boston would have been an ideal place for World. I even called Red Auerbach about him, but I guess they didn't want to go in that direction."

When the regular season opened, the Cavaliers had three rookies in the starting lineup: Harper at shooting guard, Williams at forward, and Daugherty at center. Two weeks into the season, a fourth rookie, Price, had become the sixth man.

From the opening tap, the Cavs' top three scorers were rookies. The last team with that distinction was the 1955–56 Rochester Royals.

"I really believe what we're doing is unprecedented," said Wilkens. "I've been in the pro game all my life and I've never seen a team go this young."

When they faced the Celtics, the Cavs had only one legitimate veteran in the lineup—thirty-year-old small forward Phil Hubbard, who had averaged 11.7 points in seven seasons. The point guard was twenty-six-year-old John Bagley, but he had spent more of his time as a reserve guard than a starter.

"If someone had told me that four of my six top players would be rookies, I never would have believed it," said Wilkens. "It's a shock to some people in the league that we have been able to get the kids playing as well as we have. Sometimes, there is a temptation to bring in a guy for the short run, but we're committed to youth. And if that means playing the Boston Celtics with three rookies, that's what we'll do."

•

Those Cleveland rookies were wreaking havoc with the more experienced Celtics and their much vaunted Celtic pride. The prevailing wisdom holds that when the Boston Celtics have lost on the road to an opponent, that club can forget about matching that feat when the clubs meet in Boston. This is even more likely to be the case when the foe is a team in the lower echelon of the NBA.

When the Cavaliers knocked off the Celtics by that 88–86 score on December 6, the Celtics had several handy excuses:

1. Larry Bird wasn't there.

Bird had missed the two previous games due to a strained right achilles tendon. The Celtics had won both at home, trampling Denver, a team with a gross inability to win on the road, and defeating Philadelphia the night before in a tense, extremely taut game in which the Celtics committed but one hotly disputed turnover in the entire second half (a tap-in by Greg Kite disallowed on the grounds of offensive interference; even Philadelphia coach Matt Guokas said it was an invalid officiating judgment, and he's capable of phrasing it in just that manner).

But not having Larry Bird at home was one thing, and not having Larry Bird on the road was another. The Celtics were clearly at a disadvantage playing on the road without the three-time league Most Valuable Player. They still had people named McHale, Parish, Johnson, and Ainge in the lineup, however, and if any sympathy cards were forthcoming from league rivals, they were thus far lost in the mail.

2. It was the second game in two nights, and the third in four.

Playing back-to-back games really does bother some teams. But everybody has to do it, and the Celtics have been on an autumn Wednesday-Friday-Saturday regimen since the Truman administration. A team capable of winning the

NBA championship is quite capable of winning games on successive nights in December.

3. They underestimated the Cavaliers.

Quite possible. The Celtics are as interested in the whys and wherefores of the NBA as most teams, and they were well aware that in Brad Daugherty, Ron Harper, and John Williams, the Cavaliers had an unusually talented trio of rookies. But reading and hearing about people is not the same as seeing them. The Celtics, being as cocky as they are, had to be shown. Not until Harper had gone by everyone, Williams had scored inside, and Daugherty had beaten Boston's big people to the boards, perhaps, were the Celtics prepared to acknowledge the real ability of the young Cavaliers. And once they saw what the kids could do, they might very well have said, "Oh, yeah? Lemme see that again."

4. The lid was on.

Boston shot .402 (33 for 82) from the floor that night, their worst figure of the year. Johnson and Ainge combined to shoot 8 for 26. The bench shot 2 for 12. The easiest rationalization in the NBA is the one in which a player or a team says, "I'm/We're just cold."

5. We never really lose, anyway. Sometimes we just don't win.

Conner Henry, the rookie who had been picked up by the Celtics the week before, noticed this right away. "It's an amazing team," he observed after he'd been around a while. "If we lose, it's because we feel we've given the game away, or because we didn't get the calls."

The truth is that the December 6 game was a very poor NBA contest. The winner had very little to be proud of, although when a team like the Cavaliers defeats the reigning world champions, the temptation is to take out full-page ads in *Pravda* and the *International Herald Tribune*.

It is also quite true that the Celtics were blistered by Harper in the first two and a half periods. His innate athleticism was too much for the older Johnson to contend with. Harper, who had distinguished himself as a far better driver and penetrator than pure shooter, was hitting jump shots as if he had worked a talent exchange with Jeff Malone. He had twenty-six by the midway point of the third period, and never scored again.

Cleveland ultimately won the game because John Williams got a key offensive rebound and sank two big free throws. There was a vital rebound to be had and Williams, not McHale and not Parish, grabbed it. He finished with twenty-six points and nine rebounds, and the Celtics had every reason to be impressed with his total game.

In theory, therefore, the Celtics should have been up for the rematch in Boston. They went into the game with fifty-three victories in their last fifty-four Boston Garden appearances. The only loss had come at the hands of the Los Angeles Lakers six nights after the first Cleveland game. The Celtics could somehow stomach losing to a class team like Los Angeles, but losing at home to the Cavaliers before the 288th consecutive sellout crowd at the Boston Garden would be humiliating.

The Celtics had experienced the physical talent of the Cavaliers. They knew the Cavs could rebound. They knew the Cavs could run. They knew the Cavs were surprisingly advanced in executing their half-court offense. And yet the world champions had performed in stretches of the first half as if they were playing the Clippers, or somebody.

"We talked about their running before the game," Rodgers said, "but sometimes you go out on the court and say, 'Show me. Let's see if you can really do these things. Let's see how good you are.'"

This is especially true when the Celtics are home, where the line between pride and hubris has been worn thin by success. How could they help feeling invincible at home when their only defeat in well over a season had come at the hands of the Lakers? They had faced many seemingly difficult situations in the Boston Garden, the score close at half and maybe even close at the three-quarter mark. But they had always been able to do what was necessary to win in the fourth quarter, and the crowd also knew what its job was. This was a veteran crowd which knew better than to expend its energy in the first half. The Boston Garden crowd is a fourth-quarter crowd. The Cavaliers would find out.

So what if Harper was as big an athletic puzzle in this game as in the other? So what if Daugherty was scoring inside, rebounding, running the floor, passing, helping out on defense, salvaging broken plays with his great sense of the game, and generally putting on a pivot clinic? So what if John Williams was using those long arms to great advantage in three categories—scoring, rebounding, and shot blocking? So what if John Bagley was shooting better than he usually does from the outside? So what if the Cavaliers as a unit were executing their half-court offense in a manner that belied their collective inexperience? So what if they had survived a very substantial Celtic run from the ten-and-a-half-minute mark of the second quarter (Daugherty's memorable follow-up basket) till the four-and-a-half-minute mark of the quarter?

We are the Celtics, they felt. We are not going to lose to the Cleveland Cavaliers. We own the Boston Garden. We, the Celtics, are invincible.

•

A look at the halftime statistics:

The Celtics had shot 11 for 24 in the first period and 12 for 19 in the second, making them 23 for 43 (.535) from the floor. The Cavaliers had shot 17 for 27 in the first period and 10 for 27 in the second period.

The Celtics had 6 offensive rebounds and 14 defensive rebounds for 20 total rebounds. The Cavaliers had 7 offensive rebounds and 13 defensive rebounds for 20 total rebounds.

Cleveland had 8 points on second shots. Boston had 4.

Cleveland had 22 points in transition. Boston had 6.

Boston had 6 turnovers, good for 9 Cleveland points. Cleveland had 6 turnovers, good for 4 Boston points.

Neither team made a three-point field goal. Boston was 0-0, Cleveland 0-4.

The two standout factors were Cleveland's 22 first-quarter points in transition and Boston's 38 halftime points derived directly from post-up situations.

Conclusions from the above: (1) The Celtics had made a commitment to getting back on defense in the second quarter after being embarrassed in the first. (2) The Cavaliers had better give serious consideration to double-teaming Kevin McHale (20 first-half points, including 9 successful post-up hoops in 12 attempts) in the second half.

•

As skilled as the players are, as exciting as the game is, and as popular as the NBA is in some locales, the sport still has a long way to go before it can rate with major-league baseball and professional football in the American sporting consciousness.

But it's getting there.

The biggest advances in recent years have been off the court. There was a dip in play at the end of the seventies, but starting with the entrance of Larry Bird and Magic Johnson into the league in 1979, the league has received a steady infusion of glamour players.

Dominique Wilkins, Isiah Thomas, Mark Aguirre, Ralph Sampson, Akeem Olajuwon, Kevin McHale, Alex English, Kiki Vandeweghe, James Worthy, Terry Cummings, Buck Williams, Patrick Ewing, Charles Barkley, Xavier McDaniel, and, of course, Michael Jordan—all these people have come into the league in the eighties and have made it a better place.

But great players aren't enough, not when the majority of players, outstanding and otherwise, are black, and the clientele is predominantly white. The NBA needed to be marketed, needed to be packaged, needed to be *sold* if it was to get its proper due as a major sports league. In the regime of David Stern, it has been.

Four years earlier, the league was in trouble, with several franchises up for sale. But at the outset of the 1986–87 season commissioner Stern said there was legitimate hope that twenty of the league's twenty-three teams would make money. That's an amazing turnaround.

The league has clearly benefited from the advent of cable television. People who formerly had to be satisfied with the weekly CBS offering have now had several years of regular cable viewing, first on the USA and ESPN networks and currently on WTBS.

Marketing was another success story. The sale of NBA paraphernalia has increased dramatically, for one thing, and the amount of national corporate involvement in many areas is vast. Just about everything connected with the NBA has a sponsor, each of whom does its bit to advance the stature of the league.

Because the NBA appears to be such an attractive entertainment vehicle, the value of franchises has skyrocketed. Both Stern and the twenty-three owners were pleasantly surprised at the level of interest among prospective franchise owners in non-NBA cities. The league had last expanded in 1980, when Dallas made the NBA a twenty-two team league. But by the fall of 1986 several cities had expressed great interest in hosting expansion teams.

At first the expansion committee announced that no more than three teams would be taken in over a three-year period beginning in 1989. But when the formal announcement of expansion plans was made on April 23, 1987, the committee revealed that four teams would be formed, representing Minneapolis, Charlotte, Miami, and Orlando.

The big item, however, was money. Each new team would be charged an entrance fee of $32.5 million dollars, thereby providing the league with a quick $130 million in found revenue.

It's a safe statement that the NBA never looked brighter, nor felt better about itself, than in the winter of 1986–87.

•

One piece of evidence that the league had not been selling itself properly is the lingering notion that the college game is even remotely comparable to the pro version. All reasonable people who have had equal exposure to the two levels of basketball come away raving about the grandeur of the NBA.

There is much to like about college basketball. The excitement is infectious. The bands are fun. The cheerleaders are enthusiastic and good-looking. The entire atmosphere is energizing. And the games can be highly entertaining.

On the court, the college game is eternally appealing because people who would be too short or too slow for the same position in the pros can operate quite effectively as collegians. There are any number of clever 5-9 guards, 6-2 or 6-3 forwards, and 6-6 centers who really know how to play the game, but who would be simply overmatched in the pros, for obvious physical reasons. These people are often a joy to watch, and the only way you're ever going to see them is while they are playing for the old alma mater.

But the truth is that the quality of professional basketball is markedly superior to that in the colleges. The ultimate trump card in college basketball in most cases is atmosphere, not the level of play. In any given NBA season there are at least one hundred games played which, had they been staged in Chapel Hill, North Carolina, Lawrence, Kansas, or Albuquerque, New Mexico, would have had people streaming out of the gymnasium saying, "That was the greatest game I've ever seen in my life!" College fans are overly swayed by the trappings. There has *never* been a college game played to equal the best several hundred pro games.

Among the myths perpetrated by the college people is that the pros are always in cruise gear, that they only play hard in spurts, usually in the final two or three minutes of a game. Another persistent myth involves the absense of defense in the pro game. Don't believe it: The level of professional defense is astonishingly high. It's got to be, otherwise, given the individual offensive abilities of the players, there would be a two-hundred-point game.

The pro game is governed by the twenty-four-second clock. This gives rise to action college basketball can't hope to match. There is often great tension developed, especially in the late stages of close games, as the clock winds down. The clock tests the will and patience of an offensive team. Decisions must be made based on its presence. Most of all, the clock permits teams the opportunity for tremendous comebacks, comebacks that just aren't possible with the forty-five-second clock used in college.

Some college people believe they have a monopoly on strategy, which is preposterous, particularly when "strategy" turns out to be holding the ball. True, college coaches have the option of switching defenses from zone to man-to-man, or vice versa, but pro teams have endless variations of their basic man-to-man (and near-zone) defenses. Which way do we want to steer people? How high do we want to pick up the point guard? Do we front the low post? Do we double-team from the top down or from the side? Offensively, do we push the ball at every opportunity and take our chances in transition situations, or do we pick our spots? Do we pound it low or run a motion offense?

The pro game has become increasingly sophisticated. Years ago teams practiced for an hour and a half or two on the days they didn't play, and they showed up for the games that were scheduled. Now teams scour videotapes, practice the same amount, and then come in on the day of the game for what is commonly referred to as a "shootaround" but which is often a true practice, minus scrimmaging. There is more preparation, more thought, more dedication than ever before, and the time and effort spent trying to polish the product is truly impressive. Year after year, college coaches enter the NBA as assistant coaches and are blown away by the tremendously intense life coaches and players lead.

Yet the biggest thing that separates the pros from the collegians is the simple talent gap. The NBA players can perform some truly amazing physical feats. In the course of the average NBA game there are more spectacular shots, more artful passes, more man-sized powerhouse rebounds, and more dazzling hustle plays than in any ten college games. Coaches design plays to get guys shots college coaches would reject as ridiculous. In the NBA those shots go down every night. Very often in the NBA there are sequences in which one great play is immediately followed by another great play that negates the first one.

The NBA is the end product of a marriage between the greatest athletes the game of basketball has to offer with the best coaching and training methods. To see a well-played NBA game is to see basketball as far removed from the level of the average college game as a $100-a-plate gourmet meal is from a soup kitchen lunch. And make no mistake about it—the game being played this night between the Cavaliers and the Celtics is a gourmet's delight.

•

The Celtics were back on the floor with 6:49 left in the halftime, the Cavs with 4:10. Wilkens remained in the dressing room until there was a minute left, discussing the first half with his assistants, Dick Helm and Brian Winters.

Wilkens said he liked the way West and Ehlo played coming off the bench. "They can help," said Wilkens. "I'll go to them early. Ehlo will be the first guard to come in, West the first big man."

Ben Poquette and Keith Lee also received passing grades. "They really didn't hurt us," said Wilkens. But Johnny Newman had struggled. "You could just see his inexperience," said Wilkens. "He was nervous."

That would be the substitution pattern for the second half.

•

Some random remarks from guys in the men's room line during the half at the Garden:

"McHale can score sixty tonight, easy. No one can stop him."

"Robert Parish, I'm tellin' ya . . . Robert Parish . . . the Chief, you just never know from one night to the next if he'll show up."

"The Celts'll get 'em. Pound the ball inside, that's all they gotta do."

"Those Cleveland kids got young legs, you know?"

"Whatever happened to that fat guy that Cleveland had? Turpin? Ain't he with them no more?"

"Wait until Bird gets going. Larry'll take care of 'em."

6

Third Quarter

The Cavs had the ball to start the second half. Wilkens drew up a play for Williams to drive to the basket.

"Hot Rod, if the shot isn't there, you've got Brad on one wing, Hubbard on the other," said Wilkens.

Wilkens wanted to get Williams into the offense. He was four for seven from the field in the first half, but that was the fewest field goal attempts taken by any Cavs starter.

"Also, Hot Rod is a better rebounder when he feels he is a part of the offense," said Wilkens. "That's just human nature, especially for a young player."

As the Cavs walked on to the floor, Wilkens yelled, "Guys, see the ball. Okay? See the ball on the defense."

Wilkens went with the same lineup that started the game for three reasons:

1. "These are our best players."
2. "We were playing well, so why change?"
3. "Generally, I don't like to change a lineup to start the second half unless things are really going bad. I prefer to give my starters a chance to establish themselves right away in the second half."

There are only four reasons why K. C. Jones would start anyone other than Robert Parish at center, Larry Bird and Kevin McHale at forward, and Dennis Johnson and Danny Ainge at guard at the beginning of the second half. Those reasons are individual foul trouble, injury, death, and halftime defection to the Soviet Union. In the world of the 1986–87 Boston Celtics, everyone knows who the best five players are.

THIRD-QUARTER MATCHUPS

POINT GUARDS	Ainge vs. Bagley
SHOOTING GUARDS	Johnson vs. Harper
CENTERS	Parish vs. Daugherty
POWER FORWARDS	McHale vs. Williams
SMALL FORWARDS	Bird vs. Hubbard

11:43   *Hubbard air ball.*

Lenny Wilkens got everything he wanted except the basket. To start the second half, the Cavaliers took the ball out of bounds, Bagley bringing it up the court. As Wilkens wanted, John Williams popped out on the right wing and caught a pass from Bagley. As Wilkens wanted, Williams drove the lane, getting past McHale. On one side of the lane Parish was guarding Daugherty and on the other side Bird was guarding Hubbard. Someone had to make a decision, leave his man, and step in front of the driving Williams. That someone was Bird, who slowed down Williams, giving McHale time to drop back and set up a double-team. And as Wilkens wanted, Williams recognized that Bird had left Hubbard wide open. Hot Rod passed to Hubbard, who was ten feet from the basket. He took a peculiar-looking shot that went twelve feet, an air ball that came down on the other side of the basket. It was a completely inexplicable phenomenon. Phil Hubbard throwing a twelve-foot airball? Greg Kite, yes. Mark West, maybe. Phil Hubbard? Nah. But it happened.

On the sidelines, Wilkens winced as if someone had stepped on his foot.

While the Boston bench was relieved at the end result of the Cleveland possession, K.C., Jimmy, and Chris were irked that a Boston Celtic had once again given a Cleveland Cavalier a path along the baseline.

11:29   *Parish drives middle for banker. Foul by Harper (P2, T1). Foul shot, swish.*

CLEVELAND 62, BOSTON 62.

Immediately the crowd is into the game, because there is always something electrifying about Parish when he makes a superior offensive play. Moreover, scoring three in the first possession to tie the game has the crowd more than a little excited. They are already thinking that the Cavaliers are finished, that the Celtics, a noted third-quarter team, are about to flex their muscles and slap the impudent youngsters around. An air ball followed by *this* move is all the proof anyone would need.

McHale has done most of the Boston posting in the first half, but Robert Parish is quite capable of inflicting equal damage. When he first came to Boston he was the second offensive look, right after Bird. He averaged 19, 20, 19, and 19 points a game in his first four years as a Celtic. He has been a starter since his first game with Boston. McHale didn't become a full-time starter until the second half of the 1984–85 season, so in the Celtics' pecking order, Parish ranked ahead of McHale for a long time.

He came to Boston with a reputation as a slothful, uncaring player. He had spent the first four years of his career with Golden State, a team that made the playoffs once in that time and would not do so again until the 1986–87 season. Parish was branded as a loser.

Part of the problem was his demeanor. If Walt Frazier is cool, Robert Parish is positively frigid. Note that it's "Robert," not "Bob" or "Bobby," not ever. Robert. He is a shade over seven feet tall, and he has the posture of a West Point general. He never displays public emotion, and it's easy to understand why he was long ago nicknamed "The Chief." It's easy to picture him as a Watusi warrior in full regalia. He never complains about a bad call, and seldom even stares at an official. He can be aloof and unapproachable with the media. Fans perceive him as a totally unfeeling person. Only teammates and those close to the team are aware that off the court he loves to laugh and enjoys making his teammates smile. But once he steps onto the court, he is as single-minded as a Supreme Court justice.

His unemotional approach led many people in the Bay Area to conclude that he simply didn't care. Those in the Eastern Conference really didn't know what to think; you'd go into the Oakland Coliseum Arena, watch Parish throw up a few looping jumpers, block a shot or two, grab a few rebounds, and then you'd go out and beat the Warriors by twenty.

There were always a few people intrigued with him, however, and one of those people was Bill Fitch. He remarked on more than one occasion during the 1979–80 season, his first in Boston, that he'd love to get his hands on Robert Parish. He remembered Parish's grace and running ability when he played on the 1975 Pan-American Games team, and he believed that, with all due respect to Golden State coach Alvin Attles, a very likeable man, perhaps Parish wasn't being utilized properly by the Warriors. When the chance came to grab Parish, Fitch was ecstatic. The trade was the draft day deal in 1980 that also brought Kevin McHale.

Parish came to a Celtics team that still had Dave Cowens and had another promising center, Rick Robey. His first month as a Celtic was quite likely the most miserable experience of his life. Fitch ran a training camp straight out of Parris Island, and Parish was physically unprepared for such rigorous activity. It was run, run, run—even for the seven-footers—and Parish couldn't take it. When the exhibition games began, Parish's play was several notches below "atrocious."

On the afternoon of October 1, 1980, Cowens stunned the Celtics' organization by announcing his retirement. He could no longer jump, because of persistent foot and ankle problems. The team was in Terre Haute, Indiana. That night there was an exhibition game in Evansville against the Chicago Bulls. The squad was sitting on the bus awaiting a two-hour ride to Evansville when Cowens walked onto the bus and said good-bye. When he was done, he walked up to Parish and said that one reason he felt comfortable quitting was that he knew Parish could do the job.

Fitch started Parish in that game. Robert played about the same way he'd been playing, only worse. He picked up one quick personal. Then a second. And a third. And a fourth. The press wondered what was going on. Why was Parish still in and Robey still out? Before long, Robert Parish had picked up a fifth personal. They were still in the first quarter.

Fitch left him in. By now, the message was quite clear. *Look, buddy. I'm going to leave you out here to die. The time has come for you to start playing.*

Parish started to play a little better. He started the opener against Cleveland. He got the tap and trotted down into position. He was thrown the ball. He turned and shot. The ball went in. The crowd cheered. Robert Parish was ready to play ball.

Fitch pushed Parish as he had never been pushed before. He stressed to him that he could disrupt rival centers by running the floor at every opportunity. With teammates like Bird and Tiny Archibald, Parish got his reward when he did run. He became a much better team defensive player. He could always block shots, but in Boston he learned what being the backbone of the team defense really meant.

Not all Boston fans took to Parish; they sometimes longed for the days of Bill Russell and Dave Cowens. His hands are just fair, and he is sometimes turnover-prone. There have been some afternoons and nights when he just can't do *anything*. He goes through stretches where he refuses to dunk, and as a result he misses some very easy lay-ups.

But there were many thousands who grew to admire Robert Parish's game. No center in the NBA has a prettier or more reliable jump shot than the basic Robert Parish turnaround. He shoots it with a majestic arc, and he has amazing range. He once defeated the Denver Nuggets with a twenty-foot moon shot that just beat the twenty-four-second clock with one second left in the game. He has a nice hook shot, and he possesses truly acrobatic moves when he goes to the basket. He is especially graceful at the end of a fast break.

There has been no more consistent shooter in the NBA over the past seven years. Since coming to Boston, his field-goal percentage has always been between .542 and .550. He came into this game with the Cavaliers shooting his customary .550 from the floor.

Robert Parish may very likely be the most underrated, underappreciated player in the storied history of the Boston Celtics. He would be viewed not only as the best center but quite likely the best player, period, on a number of NBA franchises.

He is no longer the number-two offensive threat, because McHale has that honor. As reliable as Parish is offensively, McHale has become even better. As McHale's per-game shot totals increase (from 8.1 in 1980–81 to 17 when this game begins), Parish's decrease (from 15.4 in 1981–82 to 12.0 in 1985–86).

Opponents know that Parish can still score, however, and they are becoming increasingly aware that he has gotten craftier in his old age (thirty-three at game time). Once upon a time, if Parish received the ball in the low or medium post, a defender had two things to worry about: There was a 90-percent chance Parish would take a turnaround jumper, and there was a 10-percent chance he would roll in for a hook. But now Parish has added a facing move. He will catch the ball, turn, and square off against an opponent, show his man the ball with an excellent pump fake, and then put the ball on the floor and go hard to the basket while his foe comes back to terra firma—as Brad Daugherty would learn on the first Boston possession of the second half.

Bird, who is very protective of Parish (Larry feels Robert is a brilliant defensive player and an irreplaceable man on the squad), made the entry pass. Robert turned on Daugherty and simply devoured him with his best move, beating him to the basket and powering the ball in off the glass while apparently drawing the third personal on Daugherty. Quietly, Parish had twelve points after making the foul shot, and the game had been tied for the first time since it was 4–4.

Oh yes, on the foul call, Strom walked over to the scorer's table; Wilkens went with him.

"That foul I gave to Daugherty, it is Harper's," said Strom.

"That's good," said Wilkens.

No one on the Cavs' bench is quite sure what Harper did to get the foul, but no one is about to ask. Daugherty has spent much of his rookie season in foul trouble, while a basketball game could last twenty-four hours and Harper still wouldn't foul out.

11:04 *Harper left lane lay-up on offensive rebound.*

CLEVELAND 64, BOSTON 62.

Harper tried to drive the lane but was stopped twelve feet from the basket by the collapsing Boston defense. Harper went up with a rock that banged off the rim and was grabbed by Parish. Parish held the ball over his head, but Williams knocked it loose.

Actually, Williams said he wasn't going for the steal. Not at first. He remembered Wilkens saying to jump up on the Celtics when they get a rebound so they couldn't throw a long pass to start the break. But when he got to Parish and saw the ball being held out, Hot Rod knocked it loose.

Harper picked it up at the foul line and drove to the basket, dropping in a left-handed finger roll.

"We have to stay aggressive, guys," Wilkens yells as the Cavs go down the court to play defense. "See what happens when we're active?"

Give Williams credit and give Harper credit, but the Celtics were wondering, just perhaps, wasn't Parish fouled after he rebounded the ball?

10:41 *Parish eleven-foot right lane turnaround.*

Cleveland 64, Boston 64.

Ainge brought the ball up the court and passed to Johnson. The Celtics cleared out the right side of the court, so once again Parish could take Daugherty one-on-one. Johnson passed to Parish, about eleven feet from the basket on the right wing. Parish went up with the quick turnaround jumper and scored.

First McHale . . . then Bird . . . now it's Parish's turn.

Parish has just scored. Parish is still angry because he couldn't get a foul call. The Celtics don't need a basketball weatherman to know which way the wind is blowing. They are now going to the Chief.

"Robert just holds the ball so high over his head that it's almost impossible to block it," said Wilkens. "Again, the thing to do is bump him before he gets the ball, push him a little farther from the basket so when he does get the pass, he has fewer options. If you try to bump Parish when he takes the shot, it's too late because it will be a foul."

As the team went back the other way, K. C. Jones jumped up and yelled "Five on the boards! Five on the boards!"

10:20   *Ainge steals from Daugherty.*

The Cavaliers thought they had a mismatch, as a series of picks forced Bird to guard Daugherty under the basket. Hot Rod passed to Daugherty, but Daugherty committed the mortal sin of any big man: He took a needless dribble before shooting. Ainge, who had already left Bagley, flashed over and took the ball from Daugherty, who never saw him coming.

Usually, Daugherty is immune to the one-dribble disease that so many young big men bring into the league, but even he sometimes seems to want to dribble, and stops just short of putting the ball down as if he could hear Dean Smith whispering in his ear, "Don't!"

Daugherty has very little to apologize for. Being pickpocketed by Danny Ainge does not make him a member of a particularly exclusive fraternity. It's a big chapter, and it's growing all the time.

Ainge is a Professional Pest on defense. Capital "P" and Capital "P." He plays defense in basketball like the outstanding baseball infielder he was before coming into the NBA (let's leave his bat out of the discussion). "Danny has extraordinary defensive range," Rodgers pointed out. The Celtics have given Ainge great leeway to roam the full expanse of the 94-by-50-foot floor. When Ainge sees a situation like this one develop, he takes off.

For several years the standard of excellence among gambling guards has been Philadelphia's Maurice Cheeks. Ainge now is challenging Cheeks for that distinction. He is the the best athlete on the Celtics, the only man who can consistently make these harrassment-type plays. They could not function nearly as well without him.

But why do so many big men want to put the ball on the floor before they shoot?

"Some guys do it to get their balance and their shooting

rhythm," said Wilkens. "But you just can't. Good defensive guards like Ainge are like vultures. They see a big guy dribble, and they swoop down and take it."

Another theory is that taking that extra (and needless) dribble before you shoot comes from the playgrounds. There is a city game called "33" or "Scuttle" or "Cutthroat," depending upon where it is being played. It is a half-court game with an odd number of players, usually three. One guy shoots, and the others play defense and rebound. It is basketball's version of anarchy, every man for himself. In this game, a guy misses a shot and the other player who gets the rebound just needs to put the ball back up, and he usually dribbles first because he is alone under the basket and doesn't have to worry about a vulture guard making a steal.

While it is true that so many players developed their games on the playgrounds, they also developed a lot of bad habits, and this is one.

10:06.   *McHale fast break layup. Assist—Bird.*

BOSTON 66, CLEVELAND 64.
CROWD NOW AUDIBLE IN CHEEKTOWAGA, N.Y.

When Ainge came up with the ball, McHale put his head down and took off. After all, this was only the fourth Boston fast-break attempt all night, and Kevin didn't want to miss out on the fun.

By the time Ainge passed to Bird, McHale was running the left side of the floor with his hand up, calling for the ball. Bird might have noted this, and then again he might not have, because he loves pulling up in situations like these and trying three-pointers, which he views as great psychological weapons.

Bird sure looked as if he was thinking three. Hubbard

thought so. John Williams thought so, and turned his head to see, leaving McHale open. The crowd thought so. McHale, who loves two points even more than he loves his favorite fishing holes in Minnesota, was afraid Bird would want the three. But after teasing the entire building, Bird deftly dropped the ball down to McHale for the easy go-ahead lay-up. There is no other 6-9 player who has ever lived who could have terrified people in this manner, but that's why he's Larry Bird.

Anyway, the Celtics now led for the first time since 2–0, and Lenny Wilkens did the prudent thing. He called timeout.

"People use a lot of timeouts in the Garden," noted Rodgers.

10:06 *Cavs timeout.*

Before Wilkens signaled for the timeout, he said to assistant Dick Helm, "We gotta stop 'em right here."

In the huddle, Wilkens said, "We want to get the ball to Brad down low. We need a basket and we need to take a good shot. Remember, move the ball. Don't hold it, don't stand there."

Helm added, "On defense, we gotta stop them now. Be aggressive."

9:40 *Daugherty misses eight-footer.*

The Cavs did get the ball low to Daugherty, who caught it about eight feet from the hoop in the middle of the key. But the shot went off the backrim, and the rebound went off Williams's hands and out of bounds.

9:26 *Bird twenty-two-footer from the left. Assist—Ainge.*

BOSTON 68, CLEVELAND 64.
CROWD CAN NOW BE HEARD IN ASHTABULA, OHIO.

Johnson brought the ball up the court for Boston. Parish posted at the foul line. Bird casually jogged down the court, seemingly unaware and unconcerned where the ball was.

"The thing you always have to remember about Bird is that he loves to fake you," said Phil Hubbard. "He acts like he has nothing to do with the play they're running, then boom! He takes off and you're left standing there, wondering where he went and what happened."

Hubbard stayed close as Bird sauntered down the court. Bird jogged to the baseline, Hubbard behind him. Then Bird sprinted to the foul line, Hubbard in determined pursuit. Bird ran Hubbard right into Parish's pick at the foul line. The play is called "20-Bump", with Bird popping out for a jump.

"No one yelled pick or switch or anything," said Wilkens. "We forgot to talk. A big part of defense is communication"

Parish's pick set Bird free, and he sank a 22-footer. The Celtics have now opened the period with a 9–2 run, and the crowd believes this one will be over soon.

"One of the most critical parts of the game is the first five minutes of the second half," said Wilkens. "That is especially true when a young team like Cleveland is playing Boston in the Garden. The Celtics wanted to take control of the game right here, set the tone for the second half and get the crowd into the game. They wanted to get the win right now, in the third quarter."

Bird's basket gave him twenty points, and the Celtics had their biggest lead of the game. Boston was four for four to start the second half while the Cavs were one for three.

After making the basket, Bird ran down the court rubbing his shoulder. That is one thing several of the Cavs rookies noticed—a Boston player would score a basket and then he would act as if he was ready for an ambulance. There was a lot of rubbing allegedly sore shoulders, turning of supposedly stiff backs, and running strangely on ankles that seemed to be sprained.

"Then the ball comes to them and they get healthy on you real fast," said Daugherty.

9:05 *Harper miracle invention.*

BOSTON 68, CLEVELAND 66.

Desperately needing a basket, the Cavs ran a clear-out for Harper, who got the ball at the right low post. Johnson guarded Harper closely. Harper turned and faced Johnson, giving him a fake with his left shoulder. Harper drove right along the baseline past Johnson. He went up for what seemed to be an open finger-roll lay-up, but Parish came from nowhere to go for the block. Harper and Parish went up at the same time and Harper knew he was in trouble.

"It's shots like these when I gotta do something," said Harper. "I call them 'Invent-something-on-the-way-up shots.' When I jump, I don't know what I'm gonna do. I just know I'll think of it when I'm in the air."

This time, Harper decided to just stay in the air. He seemed suspended above ground as Parish went up and then came down. Finally, Harper did have to return to earth. As he floated down, he pulled the ball back behind his head with his right hand and arched his arms, flipping the ball up toward the basket. The ball went high in the air and through the rim from four feet away, Harper ending up on his rear as he watched the ball drop into the net.

You can only imagine one other player in the league seriously hoping to make that shot. His last name is Jordan, and he wears ugly, ugly sneakers. Harper should never have been allowed to extricate himself from the mess he was in when he slithered along the baseline. But he did. It's shots like this that serve as a reminder you're not watching the Cornell-Columbia game.

"I used to watch the Doctor [Julius Erving] do his thing on television," said Harper. "Then I'd go out and practice the same moves. When I was growing up [in a Dayton ghetto], there was a court behind our house and I'd play from after supper until two in the morning. If I wasn't in the NBA, I'd still be playing twice a day, trying to think up more moves, do something I've never done before."

Wilkens said, "Ron isn't a great player yet, but he has the makings of one. He just has to play, to develop. Remember, in the MAC [Mid-American Athletic Conference] he could do anything he wanted. No one could stop him. It's safe to say that he probably was not only the most talented player to come out of his school [Miami of Ohio], but maybe the whole league. That has made him fearless and willing to challenge anyone. Now, he has to learn there are times when he has to pull back."

But this game in Boston Garden wasn't one.

8:47 *Bagley steals Parish pass.*

The Celtics wanted to isolate Bird in "The Hawk" on the right side of the court. The Cavaliers wouldn't allow the isolation. They insisted that Bird give it up. Larry threw it to Parish. The Cavaliers rotated well defensively, Harper sliding up to guard Parish because Daugherty went to help Hubbard with Bird. When Parish tried to hit a cutting Johnson with a bounce pass, Bagley alertly picked it off. This entire defensive sequence was exactly what the Celtics like to do unto others. They had now been done unto themselves, and the consequences would shortly be evident as the Cavaliers headed the other way with the turnover.

8:40 *Harper double-pump runner.*

BOSTON 68, CLEVELAND 68

Bagley dribbled up the court, setting up a three-on-two fast break. Bagley was in the middle of the floor when he spotted Harper on the right wing. Ainge and Bird were guarding the key for Boston. Bagley passed to Harper at the foul line. Harper took one dribble and simply soared over Bird and Ainge to bank in a five-footer. Harper's overwhelming leaping ability has brought the Cavs back into the game.

Gary Briggs yelled, "Deal on 'em, Ron."

Wilkens said later, "When Ron makes a move like that, it rubs off on the rest of the team. His confidence is contagious. His two quick baskets got us right back in the game and changed the momentum. Until these last two possessions, we were in real trouble."

Forty-six seconds earlier the Celtics led by four. Now it's tied. So much for momentum. The crowd could barely be heard in the men's room.

8:30 *McHale fouled by Williams (P2, T2). First foul shot, hits front of the rim and falls in. Second foul shot, swish.*

BOSTON 70, CLEVELAND 68.

The Celtics ran a two-man game on the left side. Bird handled the ball and McHale posted Hot Rod under the basket. Bird passed to McHale, who caught the ball and faked a jump shot. It's been a long time since McHale got the ball in his living room. The Celtics shifted the attack, first to Bird and then to Parish. Now they wanted to find out what the Cavaliers planned to do with McHale. Hubbard came over to help Williams, but he was too late. And the Celtics got their answer. Williams went for the fake and came down on McHale for the foul.

Talk about a deadly combination: Bird outside, McHale inside. Considering Bird's accuracy from three-point range and McHale's tendency to score inside, get fouled, and then make the foul shot, maybe the Cavs were lucky to get out of this situation only giving up two points.

McHale now has scored twenty-four points.

8:12 *Harper lay-up off offensive rebound of his own miss.*

BOSTON 70, CLEVELAND 70.

Harper cut across the lane and caught a pass from Hot Rod. He drove around Johnson and took a right-handed lay-up that went off the right side of the rim, but Harper stayed with it, tapping his rebound once and then bringing it down before laying it in. Two more points for Harper's legs. That gives

Harper nineteen points and he has all eight of the Cavs' points in the third quarter, including six in the last fifty-three seconds.

The Celtics do not have, never have had, and are unlikely ever to have a player like Harper. And other than Chicago, no one else does, either.

8:00   *Parish wheels in lane for thunder slam.*

Boston 72, Cleveland 70.

Ainge and Parish ran a two-man game on the left side. Bagley guarded Ainge, Daugherty was on Parish. Ainge passed to Parish, who took one dribble with his right hand and threw his left hand in Daugherty's side, effectively pushing Daugherty out of the way. Parish wheeled left and scored on a right-handed tomahawk dunk. All Daugherty could do is watch.

"Daugherty made a basic defensive mistake when you're guarding Parish," said Wilkens. "Parish is very quick once he gets the ball. You lean on him and fight him for position as he is trying to get set to receive a pass. But once he gets the ball, you have to step back away from him. Otherwise, he'll just blow by you as he did on Brad. When Parish has the ball and feels you on his back, he knows he can just wheel around you, in effect, leave you just standing there. But if you step away from him after he makes the catch, it gives you time to react to his move."

But when Parish beat Daugherty, the play didn't have to be over for the Cavaliers, and you'd like to think it wouldn't have been in, say, the last minute of play. Either Hubbard or Williams were in position to help their beaten comrade by contesting Parish. Neither moved.

7:44 *Parish blocks Daugherty.*

The Cavaliers tried their own two-man game with Bagley and Daugherty. The team may be young, but they're not too young to appreciate the law of payback. Bagley passed to Daugherty, who took a turnaround that was blocked by Parish.

"Parish played exactly the kind of defense that you want from a center," said Wilkens. "As Brad was trying to get position, Parish was on his back. When Brad caught the ball, Parish took a step backward. Then Brad went up for the shot and Parish had time to react and get the block."

There was another element to this play. "Taking this shot was a poor decision on Brad's part," said Wilkens. "I think he was a little frustrated because Parish had just driven around him and scored. He wanted to get the two points back quickly, and he forced a bad shot." In the first half the Cavaliers had continually disrupted the Celtics by beating them along the baseline. Daugherty may have been thinking he could take that route once again, but this time the mountain pass was closed. Parish had done what the coaches ordered, forcing Daugherty back to the middle. Daugherty, whose original idea was ruined, did not go up with authority, and Parish easily blocked the shot.

7:31 *Williams flip hook in middle.*

BOSTON 72, CLEVELAND 72.

Unfortunately for the Celtics, Parish's play did them little good because the Celtics couldn't retrieve the ball. Hubbard did. He threw it back out to Bagley.

"Bags was twenty-five feet from the basket," said Wilkens.

"He could have come in another step or two, but instead, he tried the three-pointer." And he missed.

Williams grabbed this rebound and passed it out to Hubbard, who threw it back into Williams, who scored on a jump hook, giving him ten points. Few things in basketball are as aggravating to a team as having a man make a superb blocked shot and then have the other team wind up scoring.

This was also the first basket by any Cavalier but Harper in the third quarter.

"We really went to the boards and Hot Rod got the basket because we got our heads back in the game and kept working," said Wilkens. "Harper's baskets meant so much because they bought us time to regain our composure."

Meanwhile, the Celtics and the crowd were both starting to get the message: The Cavaliers have no intention of playing the nightly Mickey the Dunce role for the Celtics. It's quite possible Cleveland has already taken Boston's best shot. It was 37–20, Boston after the Cavaliers had gone up by thirteen at 44--31, but the Celtics peaked about two minutes ago and now they're trading baskets, and damned difficult ones, too.

7:14 *Bird bricks twenty-footer.*

7:07 *Harper misses underhand lay-up.*

6:58 *Johnson misses underhand lay-up.*

6:47   *Daugherty six-foot baseline hook. Assist–Harper.*

CLEVELAND 74, BOSTON 72.

This basket ended a minute of up-and-down, YMCA-style basketball during which Cavs trainer Gary Briggs yelled, "Three seconds," not once, but twice.

Finally, the Cavs ended up with the ball. Harper had it on the wing; once, twice, three times Harper dribbled through his legs, just aching to make a move to the basket. Finally, McHale and Parish came out on Harper, who spotted Daugherty open under the basket. Harper threw an underhand pass to Daugherty, who sank the short hook to give him nineteen points.

"This play showed that Brad learns," said Wilkens. "This was the move he should have made on Parish the last time he had the ball when Parish blocked his shot. The little, short hook is a great shot for a guy like Brad who is seven foot and 255 pounds. When Brad puts his big body between himself and the opponent, who can block his hook shot?"

Wilkens believes in the hook, and he teaches it. That's because it was one of his main shots as a player.

"I was only 6-1 and I could drive and get off a hook shot in the lane," he said. "If I could do it, a seven-footer should be able to. But the kids coming out of college don't use it. That's because of the zone defenses. When you catch the ball and three guys swarm around you in a zone, the best move is just to go up with the jumper. You need a little more time to get off a hook. But in the pro game against man-to-man defenses, the hook is a great shot, almost unstoppable. But we've had to teach Daugherty and Hot Rod the hook because they never really used it in college."

Even so, you wonder why the hook fell into disfavor, zone

or no zone. After all, shouldn't Kareem Abdul-Jabbar have
been the role model for all young black big men for the past
twenty years? And isn't his staple shot—what Bill Fitch would
call his basic—the sweeping move long ago nicknamed by
broadcaster Eddie Doucette the "Sky Hook"?

But Lenny is right. The hook is a fossil. The most you can
get out of today's typical young inside stud is the jump hook,
which is certainly a most devastating weapon. This shot
differs from the hook in that the shooter jumps straight up with
both legs perpendicular to the ground when he releases the
shot, whereas with a hook shot he pushes off one leg or the
other (his left if he's shooting right-handed, his right if
shooting left-handed) and tucks the lower half of his other leg
in. A man shooting a hook shot has far more thrust and can
make the shot from a greater distance. A jump hook is a nice
weapon from two to eight feet, but very few players have ever
had consistent success with it beyond that range. The great
hook shooters of yore could make them from fifteen feet and
beyond. Kareem routinely makes hooks, especially on the
right baseline, from that distance, the most famous being the
game-winner in the second overtime of game 6 of the 1974
championship series against the Celtics.

In the last fifteen years, very few centers have featured
hooks as a primary weapon. Bob Lanier, perhaps the most
individually versatile offensive center of his time, had a nice
hook. Willis Reed had one. Dave Cowens, who also had a very
reliable jump hook, had one. Bill Walton has one. Swen Nater
had a beautiful hook, although he was so mechanical in his
release he always conveyed the impression he was listening to
an inner tape recording taking him through the shot by the
numbers. Jeff Ruland has one. But the average modern center
relies on a turnaround jumper and assorted little inside moves.
It takes time to acquire the timing and feel of a hook shot, and
few players are interested in putting in that time once they
have reached the professional ranks.

Young players aren't taught the hook, and over the years

the feeling has grown that the shot just isn't, well, you know, cool. But take the hooks away from Kareem and it's doubtful he would have scored ten thousand points in his career, let alone thirty thousand.

6:27   *McHale leans in for scoop.*

CLEVELAND 74, BOSTON 74.

This play and the last one slow the game down. The helter-skelter "YMCA" sequence that has just ended came about because both teams suddenly started seeking the easy way rather than the prudent way. The physical pace of the game has been furious, and by now each team has expended a tremendous amount of mental energy. The minds have grown collectively soft. Neither team is paying great attention to detail.

The Celtics need a basket, so they go to the most likely source, Kevin McHale.

The Celtics called a "21 Flash" for Kevin McHale. When all the picking and shuffling was done, McHale had John Williams in the Torture Chamber. McHale maneuvered Williams practically into the organist's lap. From the sidelines, Wilkens was yelling for Bagley to leave Ainge and double down on McHale. "Ainge is a good three-point shooter from the corner, but not at the top of the key," said Wilkens. "Ainge was twenty-five feet from the basket. We said if we could double McHale and force him to throw it back out to Ainge for the twenty-five-footer, we'd live with Ainge." But Bagley couldn't hear Wilkens above the crowd, and he continued to guard Ainge, who was so far from the basket that he has taken Bagley out of the play and opened things up for McHale. Daugherty made a half-hearted attempt to double-team as Williams offered his impression of a matador avoiding a frisky bull. McHale flipped up the scoop shot and tied the game.

6:17 *Harper misses twenty-one-footer.*

The Cavaliers reached their offensive nadir here in what may very well be their most useless possession thus far in the game. Harper had the ball on the right wing, guarded by D.J. Harper obviously was feeling very good about his "invent'em on the way up" shots and may have started to think that Boston's green and white jerseys were starting to look like Ohio U.'s again. For whatever reason, Harper almost set an NBA record by dribbling through his legs five times without making any move toward the basket. Then he just heaved a boulder at the rim with four seconds left on the shot clock. This twenty-one-footer was not what Wilkens wants from Harper, and it is exactly the kind of shot Boston was inviting him to take. "This play is a rest stop for Cleveland," said Rodgers. "There's no movement. But it's a rest stop for our defense, too. There's a whole lot of inactivity going on out there."

6:07 *Ainge misses three-pointer.*

Bird rebounded Harper's shot and passed to Ainge, who dribbled it up the floor and let loose a concrete block of his own from three-point range on the right wing.

Both Ainge and Harper have taken the shots the defense has given them, and both missed badly, just as the defense expected.

"Anything you can do, Ron," Ainge seemed to be saying, "I can do worse."

5:46 *Parish blocks Hubbard.*

After Ainge's miss, the Cavs brought the ball up the court, and Harper passed to Hubbard under the basket. Hubbard went up for the lay-up in a crowd, and it was swatted away by Parish.

5:38 *Williams blocks Johnson.*

Johnson picked up the loose ball and drove the length of the floor. He tried to go over Hot Rod—not a good idea as Williams blocked the lay-up attempt.

"That was a great play by Hot Rod," said Wilkens. "He is so smart under the basket and you can tell because he blocks a lot of shots but almost never gets called for goaltending. He came from behind Parish to make that block on D.J. He just sensed that D.J. was going up for the shot and he timed his jump perfectly to make the block. Hot Rod read the whole thing right from the moment D.J. brought the ball over the half court line."

5:26 *Harper reverse offensive rebound slam.*

CLEVELAND 76, BOSTON 74.

After Williams's block, the Cavs started a three-on-two fast break. Harper got the ball on the right wing and drove on McHale. His shot banged against the glass and off the rim. The Celtics look dead, defensively and on the boards. Daugherty and Williams tried to tip in Harper's shot but missed. The ball ended up on the floor. Bird had a chance to get the ball, but he couldn't react quickly enough, and Harper grabbed it. Harper not only came up with the ball, he kept going up until he slammed the ball in, making it a reverse dunk.

Finishing off with a reverse dunk is a great dramatic flourish which seems to be saying, "Hey, Old-Timers, this game is *mine.*"

Daugherty waved to Wilkens, indicating that he was tired and needed a rest.

5:00   *Bird twenty-footer right side.*

Cleveland 76, Boston 76.

The play started out as a "Bull," in which Parish comes up high, the entry pass is made, the passer cuts ("rubs," in the Celtics' lexicon) off him, and there are various down-picks along the lane designed to free up a man popping out behind a screen.

The play broke down. Bird and Parish set up a two-man game, with Bird hoping for an inside-out three-point attempt. When nothing materialized, Bird dumped the ball off to Ainge on the baseline. He looped it back to Bird, who hit from a little beyond twenty.

4:58   *Cleveland calls timeout.*

Wilkens made what may be a daring move by taking not only Daugherty out of the game but Harper, too. Ehlo and Lee came into the lineup.

"Brad let us know he needed a rest," said Wilkens. "Harper had been working so hard that it was taking a toll. I noticed that he seemed to drag a bit the last couple times he went up and down the floor."

But Harper has scored 10 of the Cavs' 14 points in the third quarter. Daugherty is a strong presence on the boards. For the game, Harper and Daugherty have combined for 40 of the Cavs' 76 points.

"We stayed in the game when Boston jumped on us (68–64) early in the quarter so I felt I could go to the bench now," said Wilkens. "Look, you can't play everybody the entire forty-eight minutes. All week I had been saying this would be a close game and nothing I had seen so far changed my mind. I wanted to get Ron and Brad a little rest and I thought Ehlo and Lee would play well enough to help us stay close."

At this point in the third quarter, Boston was 7 for 11 from the field, Cleveland 7 for 18. The Cavs have outrebounded Boston 10 to 4.

"Young fresh legs were why we had that edge on the boards and why we were tied," said Wilkens. "I wanted to keep those legs young and fresh. Boston had experience on its side, we had youth and enthusiasm."

In the first half, Wilkens went with Johnny Newman for Harper and Ehlo for John Bagley.

"But Johnny's inexperience really hurt him," said Wilkens, remembering that Newman was called for traveling and had trouble staying with Dennis Johnson. "At the half, I decided to use Ehlo to back up at both guard spots. Craig doesn't have much experience compared to the Celtic players, but he had more than most of the guys on my team and it showed."

Remember, Ehlo had played in a championship game, even if he was best remembered for dunking over a Boston fan.

With Harper and Daugherty out of the game, Wilkens really stressed the need for ball movement. The Cavs didn't have the option of putting the ball in Harper's hands and getting out of the way so he would have room to invent two points.

In the huddle, Wilkens said, "Run the plays hard, set good picks. Don't hold the ball, move in. Pass it from one side to the other."

As the buzzer sounded, Wilkens added, "On defense, see the ball. Remember, guys, see the ball."

NEW MATCHUPS

POINT GUARDS	Ainge vs. Bagley
SHOOTING GUARDS	Johnson vs. Ehlo
CENTERS	Parish vs. Lee
POWER FORWARDS	McHale vs. Williams
SMALL FORWARDS	Bird vs. Hubbard

4:36   *Bagley twenty-footer from top of key.*
        Assist—Hubbard.

CLEVELAND 78, BOSTON 76.

The Cavs indeed did move the ball, five passes swinging the ball to both sides of the court. Bagley ended up with the ball at the top of the key, wide open. The Celtics were again in "Rover," with Ainge as the chaser. They were still quite prepared to live with John Bagley shooting twenty-footers, if it came to that. As Bagley went up for the shot, Ainge ran at him.

As Bagley released it, Ainge ran past Bagley and down the court toward the Boston basket in the hope of being in position for a fast break. But Bagley hit the shot. He is seven for ten from two-point range and zero for five on three-pointers.

"People don't realize how a step or two changes a guy's shooting percentage," said Wilkens. "Some players don't realize it. Bags is reliable from eighteen to twenty feet, but three-pointers are a tough shot for him, and we're only talking about one more step back."

4:15 *Bird nineteen-footer right foul line. Assist—Ainge.*

CLEVELAND 78, BOSTON 78.

Guess what? Boston also knows how to move the ball and how to throw five passes that produce a wide-open jumper. Only it was Larry Bird taking the shot, not John Bagley, and Bird buried it for his twenty-third and twenty-fourth points.

Seven years of Bird-watching have left everyone taking his astonishing shooting ability for granted, because this was one helluva shot and no one seemed to think much of it. Bird started off on the low right box, guarded by West. He moved to the middle, banged off John Williams, drifted back to his right, and with 6-foot-11-inch John Williams running at him, dropped in a fadeaway shot. You very often hear people in the NBA moan, "How am I supposed to defend *that?*" Harper's contortionist effort back at 68–66 is one such example. This shot is another. Remember, we are not far removed from an era in which a man 6-feet-9 taking a shot like this would either be removed from the game, fined, or brought in for a psychiatric examination.

·

Larry Bird is not as good a shooter now as he was in college. The general public is unaware that Larry Bird goes around sinking shots like the one he has just made with 40 percent of his fingers on his shooting hand a mess.

Bird has to play professional basketball with a badly mangled right index finger and a permanently bent and dislocated right pinky. Since becoming a Celtic, he has had to reconstruct his shot in order to overcome his—there really is no other word—*deformities.*

In the spring of his senior year at Indiana State, Bird, a big baseball fan, was playing a pick-up softball game. He was in left field when his brother Mike hit a line drive in his direction. Bird, being as orthodox in baseball as he is in basketball, eschewed the fancy one-hand catch. He did it by the book, bringing his open right hand in to close the glove as he caught the ball. But he got his hand in too soon and the ball smashed into the index finger.

Two operations later, he was left with the finger he has now. It is swollen and bent. He cannot make a fist with his right hand. Celtics team physician Dr. Thomas Silva once described the break in Bird's right index finger in terms of the difference between snapping a pencil in half and having someone smash it with a hammer. Bird's right index finger was smashed with the hammer.

How traumatic was this for Larry Bird? Only he knows. He never brings up the finger in public, never curses his misfortune and never allows any prolonged discussion of the finger. To him, it is something that happened, and something he has learned to deal with.

He was very concerned about the finger when he first signed with the Celtics. Throughout both the weeklong rookie camp in August 1979 and the entire training camp that year, he played with the injured finger heavily taped to his middle finger. He was very fearful of having the finger bumped or hyperextended.

On opening night he took the floor against the Houston Rockets with the same taping arrangement. He scored fourteen points on six-for-twelve shooting. He tried an experiment the following evening in the Richfield Coliseum against Cleveland. Rather than taping the index finger and middle finger together from top to bottom, he simply taped the fingers loosely above the joint, thus allowing himself more flexibility. He shot twelve for seventeen and scored twenty-eight points.

He maintained this arrangement for the next nine games. On the night of November 9, 1979, a home game against the Kansas City Kings, he again started the ballgame with the fingers loosely taped. But when he emerged from the locker room after intermission, the tape was gone. He finished the game with seventeen points on six-for-eleven shooting. He did make the game's key basket, but it was a left-handed jump hook.

Afterward he explained what prompted him to tear off the tape—forever. "I decided I had to stop babying myself," he declared. "If it gets bumped, it gets bumped."

But he does wear tape every night on the pinky. That finger has been so continually mauled that it now is permanently crooked. Bird has devised a taping method to protect the finger, while allowing it sufficient mobility for shooting and passing purposes. Compared to the gravity of the damaged right index finger, his injured right pinky can be classified as a mere annoyance.

The fact remains that Larry Bird has adjusted to an injury that could easily have ruined the career of a less tough-minded person. The two most important fingers for a shooter are the index finger and the middle finger. The ball rolls off these two digits, and Bird has had to compensate for a whole new feel. Bird has put in the time to remake his shot because he is a man of uncommon resolve. The adjustment has clearly been ongoing: From a shooting percentage of .474 as a rookie Bird gradually improved to a career-high of .522 in the 1984–85 season. His three-point accuracy has likewise gone upward.

Bird has occasionally made reference to his shooting prowess as a collegian, as opposed to the way he is now. As great a shooter as he is, there is absolutely no doubt he would have been substantially better as a professional had he never damaged that right index finger. This is not a sufficiently comforting thought for the rest of the NBA.

3:56 *Williams ducks in for scoop. Foul by McHale (P2, T1). Foul shot missed.*

CLEVELAND 80, BOSTON 78.

The Cavs set up a two-man game on the right side of the basket with Bagley handling the ball and Williams posting up McHale. Hot Rod caught the pass from Bagley and gave McHale a pump fake. McHale jumped and Hot Rod jumped into McHale. It's not too often that anyone lays a first-class McHale move on Kevin McHale. As McHale made contact, Hot Rod sort of pushed the ball at the basket, the ball settling into the net as McHale whacked Williams's shoulder. Mel Whitworth blew the whistle, indicating the basket is good and the foul is on McHale.

"He jumped into me," McHale told Whitworth.

Whitworth turned his back and walked away.

"It's a charge," said McHale.

Meanwhile, Ainge yelled that Williams traveled; Whitworth didn't like that claim much better and made a point of also staying away from Ainge.

One thing McHale could glean from this play is exactly how strong John Williams is. The Cleveland rookie may or may not have initiated the contact, but once it was there, the shot could very well have been lost. Instead, he had enough muscle on it to score the basket. Score one for the Kid.

In the broadcast booth, Joe Tait was not impressed by the Celtics' complaints, "That is only the first foul on the Celtics this quarter and they don't like it, if you can believe that."

On the Cavs' bench, Gary Briggs can believe it. "Those guys think no one has the right to call a foul on them."

Meanwhile, Williams's move has excited Wilkens. "That was something a small forward would do. Like everyone else in the league, Hot Rod has trouble covering McHale. But on offense, Hot Rod is quicker than McHale and he gives McHale problems, too. We wanted Hot Rod to take the ball at McHale. Make him work on defense, get him tired."

3:42   *Ainge eighteen-footer right baseline. Assist—Johnson.*

CLEVELAND 80, BOSTON 80.

Sometime between Williams's missed free throw and the next Cleveland possession, John Bagley's mind took a leave of absence. How else can anyone explain his behavior on this particular play?

As Johnson brought the ball up to the right side of the court in a leisurely manner, Bagley trotted alongside Ainge. No problem. But once he hit midcourt, Bagley freaked out. He ran over to assist Craig Ehlo on Johnson. Ehlo didn't need any help. Johnson was thirty-five feet from the basket, out toward the right sideline, and D.J. wasn't going anywhere.

But Ainge was. Realizing that Bagley had gone off on a mission of some sort, he raced to the right baseline. Johnson saw him and threw him the ball. Danny had enough time to set his feet, clear his throat, and recite the Koran before hitting a jump shot.

3:30 *Johnson blocks Lee.*

When Keith Lee was a freshman at Memphis State, people covering the team needed a thesaurus handy. They were ready to alert the authorities at the Hall of Fame in Springfield, Massachusetts, to clear a spot for Keith Lee's plaque.

The young Lee was skinny, mobile, and creative. But as he got older, he bulked up and became stiff and very uncreative. In his senior year he developed a frightening propensity for fouling. On June 18, 1985, the Cavaliers made one of those dumb decisions that characterized them in the pre-Embry era. They worked a draft-day deal in which Charles Oakley, whom they had just chosen, and Ennis Whatley were shipped to Chicago for Lee, just taken by the Bulls, and rookie Calvin Duncan. Oakley immediately blossomed into one of the league's great rebounders. He is a star of the future.

This play may have been the ugliest of the night. Bagley brought the ball up the court and passed to Lee, who was on the wing. Lee uncorked a ten-footer that went about thirteen feet and came down on the other side of the basket. The rebound went through Ehlo's hands, then bounced off Johnson's head and out of bounds.

The Cavs took the ball out under the basket. Bagley inbounded the ball. On one side of the lane was Ehlo, guarded by Johnson; on the other was Lee, guarded by Parish. Lee ran toward Ehlo and set a pick on Johnson. Getting Johnson on his back, Lee turned and received the pass from Bagley. He had an open lay-up, but he brought the ball behind his head before he shot and Johnson blocked it. Lee had no idea where Johnson was or how he blocked the shot.

"These things can be frustrating," said Wilkens. "We run our out-of-bounds play exactly as we want, we get the good

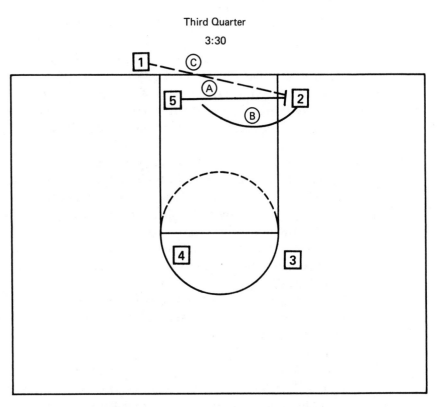

1 — Bagley	(A) Lee cuts across the lane to pick for Ehlo.
2 — Ehlo	(B) Ehlo goes around the pick.
3 — Hubbard	(C) After setting the pick, Lee turns and faces the basket, catches the pass from Bagley, and goes up for the shot.
4 — Williams	
5 — Lee	

ILLUS. 5

pick, the good pass, and the good shot, but we don't score. Keith never should have hesitated. He just should have powered the ball up." (See Illus. 5.)

3:27 *Lee offensive foul (P3).*

Lee got his own rebound after Johnson's block. He went up for the shot, this time making a lay-up. But Earl Strom blew off the play, indicating that Lee had thrown an elbow.

Wilkens bolted off the bench.

"Earl where was the elbow?"

Strom again threw out his elbow.

"Earl, he didn't do anything," yelled Wilkens.

Strom nodded, as if to say, "Yes, he did."

Lee jogged back on defense, his head down, seemingly embarrassed or perhaps frustrated. In three seconds he had had a shot blocked by a guard and then picked up an offensive foul for throwing what the Cavs thought was a phantom elbow.

Wilkens said, "Sometimes, guys just blow the whistle and then think up something to call later."

Sounds like what Ron Harper would do if he were calling the game. Call it the "invent 'em as you blow" style of officiating.

3:12 *McHale left lane flip. Lee goaltends.*

BOSTON 82, CLEVELAND 80.

Sure, Lee is frustrated. Sure, he thinks he got a bad deal from Strom on the offensive foul. But this goaltend was so

Mickey Mouse, so classically unthinking, that it could only be excused if Lee were a rookie. He isn't. He is just a player of moderate NBA talent with no latent aptitude for the game.

The Celtics ran a two-man game with Ainge and McHale. Ainge passed to McHale, who took a five-foot hook over Hot Rod. Lee cut across the lane and, about a foot from the rim, whacked the shot away. The play was purely a manifestation of Lee's frustration. Things have gone from bad to worse for him—Johnson's block, the offensive foul, and now the goaltending—all in eighteen brutal seconds.

The Celtics, meanwhile, have scored on eleven of their fifteen possessions in the third quarter, and they only lead by two points. The crowd is squirming.

2:53 *Williams misses hook in lane.*

2:45 *McHale called for three seconds.*

McHale posted Hot Rod in the lane. "Three seconds," yelled Gary Briggs. Mel Whitworth agreed. "About time they called it. It was more like six seconds. Why don't they just let McHale lease an apartment in the lane?" asked Briggs.

•

NBA referees are much like the Motion Picture Academy of Arts and Sciences in that they sometimes make cumulative calls rather than actual calls. To wit, the 1987 Oscar for Best

Actor went to Paul Newman for his performance in *The Color of Money*. He was a heavy favorite for the honor, not because he had threatened the best of Olivier when he reprised the role of Fast Eddie Felson (although he was certainly very good), but because the Academy was known to feel it was Newman's "time" to win the award. Though one of the most respected and well-liked men in Hollywood, Newman was a perennial also-ran when it came to Oscar nominations. He was good enough in *The Color of Money* that a guilt-ridden Academy saw fit to give him what amounted to a meritous service Oscar. Nobody complained.

We turn now to Kevin McHale and his overstay in the three-second zone. All night long Gary Briggs has been badgering Earl Strom and Mel Whitworth to call three seconds on Kevin McHale. This is one of the things trainers do best. It seems to be what they were put on this earth to do, at least once the game starts. Former Knicks trainer Danny Whelan started shrieking "Three! Three!" from the opening tap-off in a voice that could have alerted the beleaguered citizens of London to take the shelters in 1940, had the sirens suddenly ceased to function.

This scenario is repeated every night in the NBA. At the exact moment Briggs was hollering at Strom and Whitworth to call three seconds on McHale, for example, Detroit trainer Mike Abdenour was probably screaming at Ed Middleton and Mike Laverman to call three seconds on Houston's Akeem Olajuwon in the Pontiac Silverdome. Once the game starts, trainers do three things. They keep track of fouls, both personal and team; they keep track of timeouts; and they yell at the officials to call three-second violations on the other team's inside people.

Referees are not deaf. They can absorb information during the course of a game, and they certainly want to get things straight. Kevin McHale does continually set up shop on the edge of the foul lane. He does stray into the forbidden three-second area on occasion, and logic dictates that if this game has progressed through thirty-three minutes and fifteen seconds of playing time it's entirely possible McHale has been guilty of a three-second violation, at least once.

It is, furthermore, entirely possible that Mel Whitworth had decided to monitor the three-second situation a little more closely. Gary Briggs's incessant carping on the subject was impossible to ignore. There certainly *could* be some validity to the charge.

The Celtics had come into possession of the basketball when Williams attempted a hook and Parish rebounded. The Celtics came upcourt at a moderate pace, and McHale went to work on the left hand side of the lane. Time, perhaps, to take John Williams back into the Torture Chamber.

He moved into the lane. Mel Whitworth was on that side of the court, standing a few feet out of bounds. Gary Briggs was there to remind him about McHale's affinity for the real estate inside the foul lane. McHale was in there and Whitworth started his count. *One thousand one*—McHale is still in there—*one thousand two*—McHale is still in there—*one thousand thr*—McHale is now exiting the lane—*eee*. McHale is now out. This may have been a two and seven-eighths second violation. It may have been a two and nine-tenths second violation. It may have been a two and ninety-nine one hundredths second violation. But it was *not* a three-second violation.

But Whitworth has decided that it is time to cite McHale. Now we know who Mel Whitworth would have voted for in 1987 had he been a member of the Academy.

2:22 *Ehlo three-pointer from top of key.*

CLEVELAND 83, BOSTON 82.

The Cavs tried to work the ball inside, and finally hit Williams in the lane with six seconds left on the shot clock.

But Williams was closely guarded by McHale. He threw the ball out to Ehlo at the top of the key. The ball went off Ehlo's hands and he chased it down at the three-point arch. From the bench, Wilkens yelled, "Shoot it!"

Ehlo grabbed the ball and went up for the twenty-five footer from the top of the arch. The ball banged in front of the rim, bounced straight up about five feet and fell right in. You could see Ehlo yelling at the ball after it hit the rim.

"Ehlo talked that bitch in," said Gary Briggs.

Later, Ehlo said, "That may have been the worst-looking three-pointer in basketball history."

The shot restored the lead to the Cavaliers and started people in attendance who believe in NBA omens thinking that perhaps the Celtics weren't meant to win this game.

2:02   *Bird bad pass. Daugherty in for Lee.*

Bird tried to hit Ainge, who was cutting across the lane, with a bounce pass, but it was too far ahead of him and went out of bounds.

Mercifully, Wilkens replaced Lee with Daugherty.

"Keith had been playing well for us, but he was just having a tough time this quarter," said Wilkens. "Still, with Keith on the floor, we didn't lose any ground."

In fact, the Cavs outscored Boston 7–6 in the 2:56 that Lee played. Boston had yet to make a substitution in the third quarter.

1:39   *Williams right baseline jam.*

CLEVELAND 85, BOSTON 82.

The Ehlo shot has perhaps jolted the Celtics into realizing how hard they might have to work if they intended to win this game. The passive play of a few minutes back is history now, because right here the Celtics dig in.

Johnson started off chasing Ehlo through a weak-side pick set by Hubbard. Bird, who has been guarding Hubbard, now elected to ignore him and start playing a little "Rover" defense of his own. McHale picked up Ehlo, leaving John Williams unattended. Johnson should have rotated toward Williams, but he didn't, and now there were two Celtics— Bird and Johnson—playing free safety.

They might get away with this if Bagley didn't react to the open man, who was Williams. But he flipped him a pass while Williams was on the move, and Hot Rod stuffed it. The Celtics have established a different defensive mindset, but the Cavaliers still won this little confrontation. (See Illus. 6.)

The man who botched things up for Boston was McHale. There was no need for him to switch onto Ehlo. "He switched without need," confirmed Rodgers. It's a nice gesture to help out his buddy, but after he does Johnson never reacted accordingly by rotating back to Williams. Still, there is a lot of basketball to play, and, in the long run, McHale's thought is what counts. If he does something this weird in the final minute of the game, he can change his name to Keith Lee.

Earl Strom accidentally blew his whistle at the conclusion of the play, then quickly waved it off, yelling, "No foul! No foul!"

1:33   *Ainge fouled by Bagley (P3, T3). Roberts and Sichting in for McHale and Johnson.*

Ainge brought the ball up the floor and was setting up a two-man game with Bird when he got whacked by Bagley. Since Ainge wasn't shooting and the Cavs weren't in the penalty, Boston got the ball out of bounds. During the stoppage of play, K. C. Jones made his first substitutions of the

Third Quarter

1:39

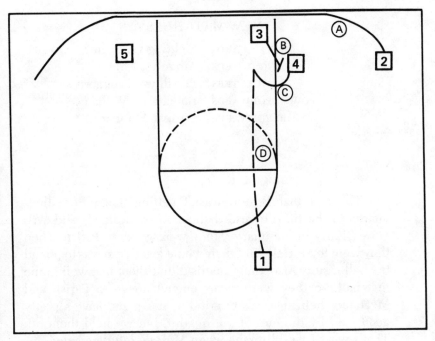

1 — Bagley
2 — Harper
3 — Hubbard
4 — Williams
5 — Daugherty

(A) Harper runs across the baseline.

(B) Hubbard picks for Williams.

(C) Williams cuts around Hubbard's pick into the middle of the key.

(D) Bagley passes to Williams, who is open for the short shot.

ILLUS. 6

half. Going this long without a second-half substitution is the norm for Boston. As Johnson went to the bench, the Celtics had only two points from their guards in the third quarter.

NEW MATCHUPS

POINT GUARDS	Sichting vs. Bagley
SHOOTING GUARDS	Ainge vs. Ehlo
CENTERS	Parish vs. Daugherty
POWER FORWARDS	Roberts vs. Williams
SMALL FORWARDS	Bird vs. Hubbard

"The fact that Boston wasn't getting much from their guards in the third quarter happened by design," said Wilkens. "Early in the quarter, they were going to Parish. Then they went to McHale. But their whole game plan was to pound the ball inside. Also, their guards didn't shoot that well in the first half, so they were smart enough to go to Parish and McHale. Their idea was to grind us down and have a pretty good lead by the end of the quarter, but we held them off. That's what I was thinking when McHale left the game."

With Roberts in for McHale, Wilkens said, "We knew that Parish would become the focal point of their inside game. Roberts just isn't big enough or strong enough to hurt us in the post. With Fred, the main thing to do is block him out because he likes to sneak in there and get offensive rebounds."

As for Sichting, Wilkens said, "I have respect for Jerry as an outside shooter. When he had the ball twenty feet from the basket, we had to play up on him. Basically, I was just thrilled to see McHale go take a rest. He had worn us out."

McHale sat down with twenty-eight points.

1:23   *Parish fouled by Ehlo (P1, T4). Swish, swish.*

CLEVELAND 85, BOSTON 84.

Ah, Larry Bird. His unique shot-pass capability separates him from all other forwards playing the game, as this play demonstrates.

Ainge again set up a two-man game with Bird on the right side. Hubbard was guarding Bird. Ainge dumped the ball in and Bird turned to shoot. Or did he? Nothing is ever certain with Larry Bird. While his first thought as he turned was to take a turnaround jumper from a safe, medium distance, he was aware of what has been going on behind him. Because the odds are that Bird will shoot, Parish is moving in from the foul line for a possible rebound.

Meanwhile, because the odds were that Bird will shoot, Brad Daugherty decided he would help out Hubbard by making a rush at Bird. This would be a very intelligent course of action were the ball in the hands of all but two forwards who have ever played. The first is Rick Barry, and he's been retired since 1980. The second is Larry Bird, and he was now about to do what he may do best: make rival players look foolish.

There is no other active forward who makes the pass Bird will now make. The instant Daugherty abandoned Parish, Bird whipped a two-hand bullet to the rolling Chief. Ehlo, the nearest bystander, made the citizen's arrest, hoping to save two points. But Parish made both free throws.

1:04   *Daugherty left lane lay-up.*

CLEVELAND 87, BOSTON 84.

Bagley and Daugherty played a simple pick-and-roll game with Bagley passing to Daugherty, who drove around a confused Parish for a lay-up. D.J. and Parish couldn't have worked this little scam any better. Bagley and Daugherty are a shade quicker and a shade more alert than Sichting and Parish. Daugherty wound up making Parish look like the rookie, and don't think the Chief didn't file this away for future reference.

Daugherty has scored 21 points, and seemed very happy to get back at Parish. On Boston's last possession, Daugherty knew he should never have left Parish open.

:49   *Ainge nineteen-footer left corner. Assist—Sichting.*

CLEVELAND 87, BOSTON 86.

The panic has set in, although Wilkens would no doubt prefer to think of it as intelligent team defense.

Teams playing the Celtics must make a decision when Bird receives the ball in an isolation situation. Will we risk him beating us with a shot? Or will we risk Bird beating us with a pass? The last time Bird received the ball he was double-teamed and he created two points with a brilliant pass. He's been known to have as many as six or seven assists in a period of play when teams double-team him, but some clubs still prefer the ball out of his hands.

This time, Bird posted on the right side. When he received the entry pass, Daugherty again came over to help out Hubbard. This time Bird wasn't concerned with Parish. Anticipating the sequence of events perfectly, he whipped a quick pass out to Sichting, who was standing at the top of the key, and who was open because Bagley dropped down to protect the middle.

Sichting was now playing the role of a second baseman.

Over at first base, awaiting another delectable open jumper, was Ainge, whose man left him as part of the Cavaliers' defensive rotation. So if you're keeping score at home, it's Bird-to-Sichting-to-Ainge. Swish.

:37   *Williams dunk. Assist—Daugherty.*

CLEVELAND 89, BOSTON 86.

Among Brad Daugherty's many attributes is his ability to put the ball on the floor. He made a play on this sequence beyond both the physical and mental capabilities of any rookie big man in the league. The idea that some knowledgeable pro people might have preferred a raw talent such as Chris Washburn to a well-rounded *basketball player* like Brad Daugherty is scary.

The Celtics have gotten very, very serious. For at least eight minutes now they have realized it won't be easy to win this game, and on the last several possessions they have been playing some big-time defense.

Daugherty received the ball, and Bird immediately moved in for a double-team. Daugherty extricated himself from trouble by taking off along the baseline. "A tightrope walk along the baseline in a size sixteen or seventeen shoes," laughed Jimmy Rodgers later. When Bird left Hubbard to pick up Daugherty, Fred Roberts, assigned to Williams, moved up to pick up Hubbard. This left Williams free but, given the situation, this was the least of Roberts's worries. Daugherty, still dribbling, was surveying matters and he not only saw Williams making his way to the basket, but had the dexterity to deliver the ball. Williams caught the pass, faked a late-arriving Roberts, and dunked the ball while just about everyone on the Boston bench screamed for a traveling violation. They didn't get it, and the Cavaliers still led by three.

"There are very few centers who could have made that kind of pass to Hot Rod," said Wilkens. "I just wish some of those people who knocked Daugherty in college would take the time to see what he does on the court. They talk about all that Mr. Softee garbage. I mean, this kid is tough, he's aggressive, and he likes contact. Boy, they nail you with a label and that's it. Some people never give you a chance.

"And what about Brad's offense? He has good moves under the basket, and he knows the game. He gets the ball and he knows where it should go. In another year or two, it will be impossible to double-team Brad because he'll just hit the open man for a lay-up. I love to watch him pass and our guys love to play with him."

:32 *Ainge three-pointer from left wing.*

CLEVELAND 89, BOSTON 89.

Strategy time. With 37 seconds left the Celtics must make a decision. If they advanced the ball at a routine pace, and presuming there was no turnover committed, they would have one shot and the Cavaliers would have one before the period ends. But if they moved the ball upcourt quickly enough, they could get a shot off and still get the ball back for a second shot before the period closed. The big question is what kind of a shot they can get off. Will it be worth it? Would they be better off taking one good shot rather than two poor ones?

All things considered, the Celtics are a confident enough team, especially at the Boston Garden, to go for the big payoff. "We like the two-for-one exchange," Rodgers said.

And that was why Danny Ainge, who had awakened as an offensive threat just as Lenny Wilkens feared, pushed the ball up with four quick dribbles against a furiously backpedaling Ehlo and launched a long jumper a step behind the three-point line. Ainge has blossomed into a major three-point threat this season, and the ball dropped cleanly through for his third consecutive field goal.

Before the game, Tom Heinsohn had told his TV audience, "Danny Ainge makes the key shot in the key situation."

Plays like this are what make people first-round draft choices. The next ninety-nine guys trying this shot air-ball the sucker.

•

As any baseball fan knows, Danny Ainge *wasn't* a first-round pick. He was a second-round pick, because he wasn't supposed to be playing professional basketball to begin with.

He had signed a baseball contract with the Toronto Blue Jays while still an undergraduate at Brigham Young University. While the rest of his teammates were spending their collegiate summers at basketball camps, beaches, or flipping hamburgers at McDonald's, he was spending his playing professional baseball. The Blue Jays started him at Syracuse in 1978, and he advanced to the big leagues for eighty-seven games the following year, hitting .237 while swatting his only two home runs (both in Seattle, which means he never hit one outdoors) in 665 major-league at-bats.

NCAA rules no longer prohibit an athlete from playing professionally in one sport and on an amateur level in another, so his baseball playing didn't jeopardize his college basketball career. He had been a great player for the Cougars in his first three years, but in his final season he elevated his game to new heights, scoring twenty-four points a game. He was named the College Player of the Year by the National Association of Basketball Coaches. When he went into the NCAA tournament and scored thirty-seven points against UCLA, the pro basketball people really started to drool about him, even though he was under contract to the Blue Jays and had never given anyone reason to think his future wasn't in baseball.

Were he not involved in baseball, he would have gone in the top five in the 1981 draft. But he was, so everyone shied away from him. Figuring he had nothing to lose, Red Auerbach chose him in the second round, the thirty-first player picked. This is the same Red Auerbach who took Charlie Scott, already under contract to the ABA, in the seventh round in 1970 and who traded the rights to him to Phoenix for Paul Silas, a man who would win him two championships. This was the same Red Auerbach who selected Larry Bird as a so-called "junior eligible" in 1978, thereby giving him negotiating rights to the greatest all-around player the game has yet produced.

Four months later Danny Ainge was a Celtic.

In order to get him, the Celtics went to court with the Blue Jays. Ainge had claimed that he had been given a verbal release from his contract. The Blue Jays had denied it. Toronto won the case but, knowing that they had lost his heart to basketball, accepted a settlement. Ainge signed a contract with the Celtics and was activated in December of 1982.

He did not blossom immediately. He never did figure out what it would take to please Bill Fitch, and even when Fitch left, K. C. Jones took over, and Gerald Henderson was traded away (in part to open up a spot for him), Ainge had periods where he didn't seem to fit. He had shooting and driving ability, he could play defense, and he had a championship heart, but unless your name is Dennis Johnson, the Celtics are a very difficult team on which to be a guard. D.J. will play his game, no matter what. Normal guards—that is, people with consciences—worry about whether or not a shot should be taken. D.J. takes what he feels like taking.

If there was a turning point in Ainge's basketball career it was in game 2 of the 1986 opening-round series with the Chicago Bulls. Ainge was kind of hanging around, minding his own business midway through the third quarter of that game. The Bulls were leading the Celtics by ten, and Ainge hadn't scored a point.

About three minutes later, after Danny had finally gotten into the scoring column, K. C. Jones decided to make a substitution. He wanted to put Sichting in for Johnson.

"I told him, 'Go in for Dennis,'" K.C. recalled.

Sichting thought he heard, "Go in for Danny."

But when Sichting walked on the floor, Johnson said he wanted to come out because he was tired. That was fine with Ainge, who later said, "I figured I'm going to go get a couple of buckets before they *can* take me out."

Which he did, starting with a left-handed drive down the lane to cut the Chicago lead to four. Before the third quarter was over he had scored eleven of Boston's final thirteen points, all in less than three minutes. He would go on to score twenty-four points in the Celtics' epic 135–131 double overtime triumph, a game in which Boston had to overcome a record-breaking sixty-three-point performance by Michael Jordan.

A star was born. Ainge went on to score fifteen points a game in the playoffs, a startling increase of five points a game over his regular season average. He would provide continual heroics, such as in the fourth Milwaukee game, when he held the team together during the first half and finished with twenty-five points.

Ainge's confidence grew and grew, but he has no illusions. "I play with four All-Stars," he would later say. "If this was a four-man game, I wouldn't be playing."

Maybe, maybe not. The Danny Ainge raining down deadly jump shots on the Cavaliers is the same Danny Ainge who on defense seems to be covering each and every one of the 264 squares that comprise the Boston Garden parquet floor. He now has supreme confidence. He knows there will be nights when he'll score thirty, and there will be nights when he'll score six. But he is smart enough not to define his value solely in terms of offense. He knows the team relies on his extraordinary defensive range (it's easy to imagine him becoming the next Mark Belanger, had he remained in baseball), and he doesn't have to worry about being unappreciated any longer.

By the players and coaching staff, that is. Ainge's acceptance as a superior player has been much slower among fans, both inside and outside of Boston. In a sports fandom where most people who care at all about the Celtics either love them dearly or despise them totally, Ainge is the most hated of them all. His image is that of a spoiled brat. He does have the aura of the high school hero in the faces he makes at officials when things don't go his way, and there is just something about the mercurial nature of his game that strikes rival fans as loathsome.

He plays hard and he seems to have a way of winding up in compromising positions defensively, so much so that Milwaukee's respected coach Don Nelson once called him "the dirtiest player in the league," a charge he has since retracted. Much of Ainge's infamy stems from a 1983 playoff fight with Atlanta center Wayne (Tree) Rollins, an altercation in which the 7-foot-2-inch Rollins wound up biting the finger of the 6-foot-4-inch Ainge. Ainge must live with the fact that people still think the biting roles were reversed.

His own fans aren't always fully appreciative of his defensive contributions. There is still a significant percentage of the Boston Garden populace that simply can't accept the fact that Ainge is now a highly regarded player around the league, that there really aren't that many guards who can hurt opponents in as many ways as Danny Ainge can. Even though he has been a very successful three-point shooter all season, he has failed to get much credit for his achievement. It's as if his threes don't count, but Bird's do.

Ainge gives the Celtics a fifth take-charge player. He was bred to be a star. At North High School in Eugene, Oregon, Ainge starred in baseball, basketball, and football. In fact, Oregon reporters claim his best high school sport was football (wide receiver). He once performed in high school all-star games in baseball and basketball on the same day. He is also a low-handicap golfer. At every step on the athletic ladder, coaches have recognized his special qualities. "He has unusual defensive quickness, instincts, and actions," Bobby Mattick, then manager of Toronto, said of Ainge back in '81. "And we know he's something you can't teach—he's a winner."

Ainge simply has "star" quality. He has always taken the big shot and made the big play in both high school and college. It has always been the normal course of action for him. Coming to the Celtics was a tough adjustment. For three years it wasn't so much that he was low on the pecking order; he wasn't even *in* the pecking order.

Now he is, and when Danny takes it upon himself to attempt this vital three-pointer, he does so with the knowledge that nobody will chastise him if the shot won't fall. He has earned the right to fail here; that's what being a Celtic is all about.

:15   *Bagley three-pointer left wing.*

CLEVELAND 92, BOSTON 89.

How typical of this game that when the Celtics make a gutsy and brilliant play that the Cavaliers respond with a slap in the face of their own.

The Celtics went to the "Rover" defense for the final Cleveland possession. Ehlo and Daugherty set up a two-man game on the right side. Ehlo puts the ball in Daugherty's hands, and he is double-teamed by Ainge, acting as the rover. Ehlo made a move into the middle, and Roberts, for some reason, reacted, leaving Williams. Sichting, worried about an unguarded Williams lurking in scoring territory, went toward him, leaving Bagley alone.

Daugherty spotted Bagley by himself on the other side of the court and heaved a thirty-foot cross-court pass. Bagley might have been covered had Roberts not strayed toward Ehlo, but Bagley still had to put the ball in the basket. He did, and the Cavaliers again led by three, this time with a matching three-pointer.

In their last three possessions, the Cavs ran two-man

games with Daugherty and those three possessions produced seven points.

"We knew Brad was rested and we decided to ride him for a while," said Wilkens.

The three-pointer gave Bagley eighteen points, but it was the first time he'd scored in six attempts from three-point range.

Speaking of Roberts, Rodgers said, "You can never fault a reaction to a teammate in trouble on defense. They ended up with a cross-court pass and a very low percentage shot. What can you do?"

:01   *Parish eight-foot turnaround jumper. Assist—Bird.*

CLEVELAND 92, BOSTON 91.

Who else but Larry? The Celtics rushed upcourt and posted Bird up on the right side. Daugherty again double-teamed, and Bird fired the ball to Parish, who had come rolling down to the right baseline from the foul line after the departure of Daugherty. Bagley picked up Parish, and the seven-footer hit an eight-footer over the six-footer, just as you might expect.

The "two for one" has worked. The only problem is that the two Boston baskets aren't supposed to be sandwiched around a John Bagley three-pointer.

•

In the third quarter, Boston shot 13 for 17 (74 percent) from the field. Considering that, it's remarkable that the Cavs were only outscored 32–30.

The Cavs were 14 for 29 (48 percent) from the field. But the difference was that Cleveland took 12 more shots than Boston.

The Cavs outrebounded Boston 11–6, including 7–0 on the offensive boards. Those seven offensive rebounds became six points, and that was why Wilkens wanted to keep those young, fresh legs in the game.

"What I was really happy about was that we were able to get Harper some rest and it didn't hurt us," said Wilkens.

Harper had 10 points and 4 rebounds in the third quarter, even though he sat out the last 4:58. In fact, the Cavs outscored Boston 16–15 with Ehlo subbing for Harper.

"That's because Ehlo didn't do anything stupid," said Wilkens. "He didn't turn the ball over, he got it inside to our big men and he helped on defense. I'm telling you, his experience showed. Even if you're on the bench in this league for three years, you have to learn something."

For the game, Boston was shooting 60 percent, the Cavs 50 percent. Boston had only 9 turnovers, but the Cavs were even better with seven. From the foul line, Boston was 18 for 19 and Cleveland was 8 for 11.

In the third period the Celtics scored 3 points in transition (the Ainge three-pointer) and the Cavaliers 2; the Celtics were called for just one team foul; and they have posted 5 times and scored 5 times.

"One thing that bothered me was that we took only one foul shot in the third quarter," said Wilkens. "You mean to tell me that we got fouled only once and we were all over the boards? When things like that happen in Boston Garden, it makes you wonder."

7

Fourth Quarter

Boston Garden fans, having been exposed to basketball at its best for so many years, can be blasé. It takes a lot to get them excited. They've seen too much. Many times they don't cheer what other fans would cheer, because they know not only good from bad but, more important, good from great.

There are crowds around the league who cheer indiscriminately, mindlessly, and who boo every obvious call against the home team. Portland comes to mind; the mentality is such that the Trail Blazers should take the floor wearing uniforms with the lettering "PHS," for Portland High School. It's different in Boston. If the home team isn't hustling, or is performing in a manner that besmirches the honor of those championship flags hovering above, they won't hesitate to boo. But if the team is playing the basketball the way it should be played, there is no more appreciative audience. None. They have been educated; they've got *standards*.

They have combined with the team to make Boston Garden an imposing place to play. A team entering the Garden is truly playing more than just the five men in white. It is playing five pretty good basketball players, plus a crowd plugged into history, a crowd that views itself as a viable force. The crowd has a way of letting an opponent know its place.

These fans don't waste their vocal cords unnecessarily. They know what the team needs, and when it needs it. They know a real crisis from a mere dead spot in the game. They know when the Celtics are screwing off, and are undeserving of their support or sympathy. And they know when the Celtics have come up against a team playing at the top of its game. Since the middle of the third period, the Celtics have recognized that not even the Los Angeles Lakers have played the Celtics any tougher in this building during the past fifty-four games than the Cleveland Cavaliers are doing right now.

The score at the end of three quarters is Cleveland 93, Boston 92. There is only one reason for this state of affairs: The Celtics are playing well, and they are still being outplayed. The crowd knows its role in the scenario. The Cavaliers aren't walking out of here without hearing from the ghosts.

The 287th consecutive Boston Garden capacity crowd is ready to start working.

MATCHUPS

POINT GUARDS	Sichting vs. Bagley
SHOOTING GUARDS	Ainge vs. Ehlo
CENTERS	Parish vs. Daugherty
POWER FORWARDS	Roberts vs. Williams
SMALL FORWARDS	Bird vs. Hubbard

11:45 *Parish eleven-foot jumper in lane. Assist—Ainge.*

BOSTON 93, CLEVELAND 92.

Boston had possession because they got the opening tap. They went to the "Thumbs-Up" play in which a forward comes up high, the pass is made by the guard, and the first option is the give-and-go handoff. Johnson and McHale ran it successfully in the second quarter, with D.J. going in for a left-handed lay-up.

This time the first option wasn't there. Ainge took the ball from Fred Roberts and hit Parish, who took the ball in his rhythm and hit a turnaround in the lane. Daugherty just stood there looking surprised that Parish would just catch and shoot the ball. Parish now had twenty-two points.

11:36   *Boston illegal defense.*

As the Cavs brought the ball up the court, Wilkens yelled, "Who's Roberts playing?"

The answer was nobody, and Roberts was called for an illegal defense for standing in the middle of the key, nowhere near his man, Williams.

"Some coaches get really hung up on the illegal defense," said Wilkens. "I know guys who run plays just so the other team gets called for an illegal. In my mind, that is sort of egotistical. The point of a play is to score, not to get an illegal defense. A coach shouldn't run a play just to show how smart he is or to trick the other guy. There are times when you know the other team is playing a damn zone and they've got all five guys packed in the key. Then I might run an isolation for Harper or maybe a two-man game with Harper and Daugherty, so they either have to play us straight up, man-to-man, or get called for an illegal defense. But the main reason for running those plays is to score, it's not to stand there staring at the officials and waiting for them to make a call."

This was the first illegal defense call of the game for either team. Each team gets a warning. The second illegal defense call is a technical.

Ever since outlawing the zone defense when the league was formed, the NBA has struggled to write proper guidelines to enforce the prohibition.

The current rule dates from the start of the 1982–83 season. It is very involved and essentially unpopular. About the only thing everyone understands about it is that it is illegal to double-team a man who *does not have the ball.*

For purposes of the illegal defense rule, the court is divided, both horizontally and vertically, into zones. The horizontal zones are the "inside area" (from the baseline to an imaginary horizontal line whose upper boundary is the second hash mark along the foul lane), the "middle area" (from the hash-mark line up to the foul line), and the "upper defensive area," (from the foul line to the top of the circle). (See Illus. 7.)

There are ten paragraphs and five subparagraphs outlining the restrictions. Strictly speaking, a defender cannot remain more than one "zone" away from the man he is supposed to be guarding for longer than 2.9 seconds without being cited for an illegal defense violation. The rule, in its dazzling complexity, is repeated in its entirety in the glossary at the back of this book. After reading it, your sympathy for the officials will increase.

11:21 *Ehlo fouled by Parish (P4, T1).*

The Cavs took the ball out of bounds after the illegal defense warning. Ehlo ended up with the ball at the top of the key, just beyond the three-point arch. He dribbled toward the corner around a Daugherty pick. Parish switched off onto Ehlo, while Sichting cut off the inside pass to Daugherty. Ehlo got stuck in the corner with Parish all over him, but Parish then made a play that was not the brightest of his career, trying to whack the ball out of Ehlo's hands. He got Ehlo across the wrist. The worst thing about Parish's play was that it was his fourth personal. He runs enough risks as it is without picking up nonshooting fouls on rival guards a long distance from the basket.

As Parish's foul stopped the action, Wilkens replaced Bagley with Harper.

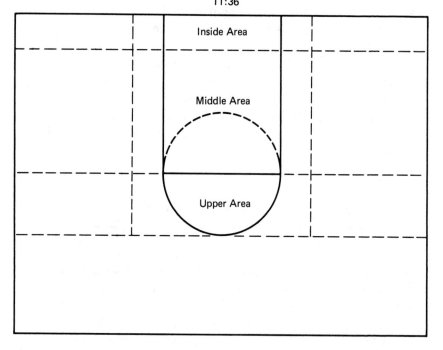

Fourth Quarter

11:36

Inside Area

Middle Area

Upper Area

Illus. 7

"I was glad to get Ron a good, long rest while we stayed in the game," said Wilkens of Harper, who sat out the last 4:58 of the third quarter. "Ron also sat through the fourth-quarter break. So that gave him at least fifteen minutes on the bench. I thought about waiting until the ten-minute mark to bring him back, but Bagley had been on the floor for the entire third quarter and he started to look pretty tired to me, so I brought back Ron at this point and moved Ehlo to the point."

11:16   *Williams slam in middle.*

CLEVELAND 94, BOSTON 93.

The Cavs got two points on an out-of-bounds play. Hubbard inbounded the ball from the sidelines. Harper and Williams stood together at the top left corner of the box. As Hubbard got the ball, Harper broke to the corner while Williams took a step or two up toward the top of the key. Hubbard passed to Harper in the corner, and Williams reversed direction, breaking toward the basket. The move was too quick for Roberts, the Celtic on Hot Rod, and as he broke wide open Harper hit him with a pass and he slammed it home. (See Illus. 8.)

"Most inbound plays are relatively simple," said Wilkens. "What makes them work is effort. Both Harper and Hot Rod were thinking about what they were doing. Some coaches are just content to get the ball inbounds, but I like to try and score on inbounds plays. We had one game this season against Indiana where we got eight points alone on plays where we took the ball out under the basket. That can be the difference in a close game."

Fourth Quarter

11:16

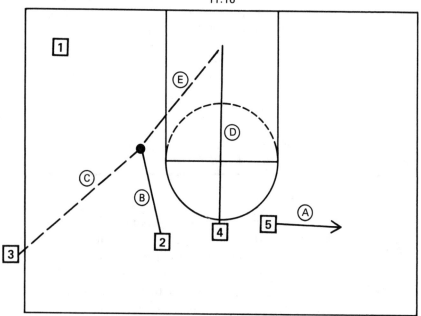

1 — Bagley   (A) Daugherty runs away from the play.
2 — Harper   (B) Harper runs down the side of the lane.
3 — Hubbard   (C) Hubbard passes to Harper.
4 — Williams   (D) Williams cuts down the middle of the key.
5 — Daugherty   (E) Harper passes to Williams, who scores.

Illus. 8

11:04   *Roberts fouled by Hubbard (P2, T1).*

Roberts set a pick on Hubbard, and Hubbard tried to get through it by giving Roberts a forearm to the head. Stevie Wonder could have made this foul call.

Both coaches went to their bench. Jones substituted McHale and Johnson for Roberts and Sichting, thus reuniting Boston's starting five for what is presumed to be for the remainder of the game. Wilkens sent in West for Williams.

Did Lee's tough third quarter—a shot blocked by Johnson, an offensive foul, and a goaltending—cause Wilkens to come back with West instead of Lee?

"Let's put it this way," said Wilkens. "Mark had looked a little better in this game than Keith, so I went to him."

NEW MATCHUPS

POINT GUARDS	Ainge vs. Ehlo
SHOOTING GUARDS	Johnson vs. Harper
CENTERS	Parish vs. Daugherty
POWER FORWARDS	McHale vs. West
SMALL FORWARDS	Bird vs. Hubbard

10:51   *McHale nine-footer on the baseline.*

BOSTON 95, CLEVELAND 94.

The Celtics value the inbounds play as much as any team in basketball, which is why K. C. Jones and Red Auerbach are so chagrined when the other team makes it work, as Cleveland did in their last possession. Auerbach prided himself on the efficiency of his inbounds plays when he coached.

But the Celtics have never been more devastating on inbounds plays than they are now, and the reason is Larry

Bird. He racks up a disproportionate number of assists on inbounds plays from underneath, and he is particularly deadly on sideline out-of-bounds plays. Chicago coach Doug Collins goes so far as to label Bird as "the best inbounds passer in the history of the game."

Bird's favorite trick is to throw the ball in to a big man posting up high, race in behind the three-point line, take a return inside-out pass, and then deposit a home-run ball. Teams say they're catching on, but he keeps doing it.

This time, McHale posted up low, and Bird inbounded to him. McHale leaped to receive the pass, and put it back in Bird's hands before hitting the ground. Bird cranked up a twenty-footer that banged off the rim. In the midst of the trees, Ainge came up with the ball and gave it right back to Bird. Larry thought about a shot but crisply dumped the ball in to McHale, and the Scoring Machine hit a turnaround jumper to give Boston the lead as the crowd roared its approval of the entire sequence.

10:37 *McHale steals Harper's pass to West.*

Harper brought the ball up the floor and passed to West. But McHale cut in front of West and intercepted the pass.

"Everyone wants to blame Harper for this turnover," said Wilkens. "But West was standing out there, twenty-five feet from the basket, real nonchalant. He just never thought McHale would come that far out to guard him. But McHale is a smart player. Kevin saw that Mark had no idea where he was. And Kevin saw that West was just going to wait for the ball to get there. A guy catching a pass has to come to meet the ball. West just stood there. McHale stepped in front and made the steal. I know West just came in the game and he was a little cold and not into the flow, but you still have to be aware of what is going on."

McHale is a man of many skills and accomplishments as a basketball player, but the second coming of Alvin Robertson he's not. Allowing Kevin McHale to steal a pass this far out on the floor could very well be a capital offense.

The truth is that Kevin is too inherently lazy as a defensive player to get very involved in working for steals. He would much rather have his man catch the ball and try to shoot over him down low. When forced to play a man as far away from the basket as West was, he's usually quite content to allow an uncontested entry pass.

But Kevin realized the entire situation here. The game is tight, much tighter than the Celtics want it to be, or think it should be. A couple of scores here and the crowd might take over. The Cavaliers might realize the futility of this effort. Cleveland might fold and Kevin might get a few more easy baskets. He might even wind up with a forty-point night.

So McHale made the effort. He came up with his fifteenth steal in this, the thirty-sixth game of the season.

10:34 *Johnson fast-break lay-up.*
        Assist—McHale.

BOSTON 97, CLEVELAND 94.

After stealing the ball, McHale raised it over his head with both hands and fired a two-hand overhead pass ahead to a streaking Johnson for the easy lay-up. In three seconds he has made two totally uncharacteristic Kevin McHale plays. One, Kevin McHale averages one steal every other game and *never* makes one in the open floor. Two, Kevin McHale does not ordinarily throw a two-hand overhead pass to spring people for sneakaway lay-ups. He really wants this game.

Incidentally, this was the first Boston fast-break basket

since Sichting hit his jumper to make it 44-37, Cleveland, back in the second quarter.

10:34   *Cavs call timeout.*

In the huddle, Wilkens was livid, "Dammit, step up and catch the ball. Come to the ball, show some intensity. If we're gonna run a play, dammit, come to the ball. Everybody has got to be aggressive. I don't want us just standing there, arms at our sides. Now, let's get the ball down low to Brad."

Later, Wilkens explained the timeout. "Once again, this was a critical part of the game. I didn't want Boston to run off a couple of quick baskets and blow it open. We've all seen them do that so many times, and the way we were standing around to start the quarter, it could happen. The crowd was starting to get into the game. That's why I wanted to stop things and get our heads back in the game."

Boston has hit sixteen of its last twenty-one field-goal attempts.

•

As the Celtics broke the huddle, Ford, who was known as a superb cheerleader even during his playing days, yelled "One stop! One stop! C'mon!"

Catch phrases come and go in the NBA, and right now a key one is "stop." If a team on defense prevents the rival from scoring, this is a "stop." Frequently a coach will say something like this in his postgame analysis: "Well, we played pretty good offense in the fourth quarter, but we just couldn't get a stop when we needed one."

Ford was articulating the feelings of everyone in the Celtics' entourage, as well as those of all veteran fans up there in the seats. The Celtics have had just about all the Cavalier effrontery they can take. Ainge has grabbed a big rebound. McHale has hit a tough shot and has then stolen the ball and produced another basket for Johnson. The crowd has responded accordingly, disturbing a man taking an after-dinner nap in Lawton, Oklahoma. The Cavaliers have failed to get a rebound they should have had and have gotten careless on offense. They appear ready to fold.

If the Celtics can come up with a "stop," Bird might then throw in a devastating three-pointer and the crowd can start thinking about where it would like to go for a bite to eat on the way home.

10:09   *Ainge steals from Daugherty.*

The Celtics are clearly prepared to play as much tough defense as it will take to put the Cavaliers away. First the Cavaliers tried to post up Harper, but D.J. knocked the ball out of bounds. Cleveland inbounded the ball. Hubbard tried to drive, but found himself surrounded underneath by Parish, Bird, and D.J. He dished back to Harper, who, as Wilkens had asked, was looking inside to Daugherty. But so was Boston. When Daugherty got the ball in the lane, he had Parish, McHale, and Ainge all over him, and Ainge knocked the ball out of his hands.

9:57   *Ainge misses eighteen-footer.*

After gaining control, Ainge pushed the ball upcourt and passed to D.J. on the left wing. D.J. got the ball into McHale down low, but Cleveland had cut off the fast-break opportunity. No problem. It was still a fine secondary break, since the

Cleveland defense packed in the lane left Larry Bird all alone behind the three-point line at the top of the key. McHale whipped the ball back to Bird, who spotted Ainge on the right wing. As Harper ran out at Bird, Larry hit Ainge for the open eighteen-footer. A perfect secondary break, thanks to the Celtics' deadly ball movement, but the shot was off the front rim, and Daugherty controlled the rebound.

9:49   *Harper lay-up spins out.*

Daugherty threw out to Harper, who sped downcourt on the right side. He drove to the basket, but his lay-up spun in and out, and the rebound was knocked out of bounds by West. Harper was closely contested by Bird—too closely, according to Wilkens.

"Earl, he was all the way down his back," yelled Wilkens. "He was all over him."

Earl Strom just waved off Wilkens's complaint as he turned and ran down to the other end of the court.

9:33   *Ainge foul-line jumper.*

Boston 99, Cleveland 94.

Back to the "Bull," a Celtics staple tonight. The entry pass to Parish was made by Bird, who picked off Ehlo. Ainge had the equivalent of a free throw, and he's a 90-percent foul shooter. For a brief moment, Wilkens closed his eyes and looked up to the heavens.

Chris Ford jumped up and screamed "One stop!"

9:17   *Daugherty fouled by Parish (P5, T2). First foul shot hits back of rim and misses. Second foul shot, swish.*

BOSTON 99, CLEVELAND 95.

Once again, the Cavs ran a play to Daugherty, this time isolating him down low on Parish. (See Illus. 9 and Illus. 10.) Daugherty tried a reverse lay-up and Parish grabbed his arm for his fifth foul. The foul shot halted a 6-point Boston run. Ford's "stop" was not forthcoming.

"That should have been his sixth," said Wilkens later, referring to the first half when Parish appeared to have been whistled for a foul but the call was changed to Sichting. "I watched the tape of this game several times. Sichting wasn't even around the play when he got that foul. That was a turning point. We could have had Parish out of the game for most of the second half if he had gotten the foul he deserved. It's little things like these that drive coaches crazy."

Yeah, Lenny, but if Parish had had five fouls when Daugherty made this move, he surely wouldn't have contested the shot, not with so much time left. In the past two seasons, Parish has played 199 games, playoffs included, and has fouled out six times. The Chief knows what he's doing.

On the dead ball, Wilkens sent Williams in for Hubbard.

9:04   *Briggs yells, "Three seconds on McHale."*

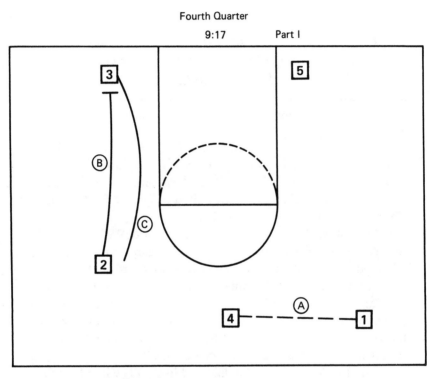

Fourth Quarter

9:17   Part I

1 — Ehlo	Ⓐ Ehlo passes to West.
2 — Harper	Ⓑ Harper picks for Hubbard.
3 — Hubbard	Ⓒ Hubbard breaks up to Harper's old spot.
4 — West	
5 — Daugherty	

ILLUS. 9

Fourth Quarter

9:17   Part II

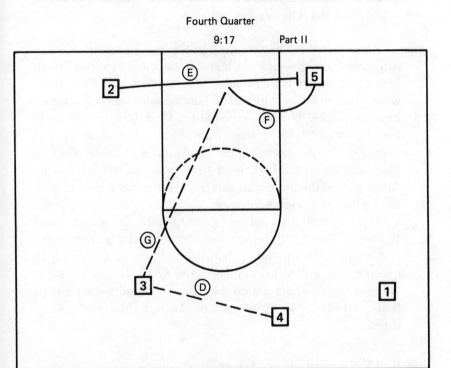

1 — Ehlo		
2 — Harper	Ⓓ	West passes to Hubbard.
3 — Hubbard	Ⓔ	Harper cuts across the lane and picks for Daugherty.
4 — West	Ⓕ	Daugherty cuts around Harper's pick into the key.
5 — Daugherty	Ⓖ	Hubbard passes to Daugherty, who is open for the shot.

ILLUS. 10

9:00   *Ainge eighteen-footer from the right foul line.*

BOSTON 101, CLEVELAND 95.

Ainge got the ball at the top of the key, guarded by Ehlo. Ainge dribbled through his legs and took a couple of steps to his right, running Ehlo smack into a McHale pick. Ehlo made what should be considered a shrewd play as he wrapped himself around McHale, preventing McHale from rolling to the basket to catch a pass from Ainge. But none of that mattered. Ainge was confident, looking for the shot. He saw that McHale's pick had freed him to shoot. Not hesitating, Ainge put up the jumper; it was true. Ainge has scored nine of the Celtics' last eighteen points.

"I keep trying to get our guys to think the game," said Wilkens. "To pay attention to who is hot and who went cold, and we have to remember that it can change from quarter to quarter. Ainge didn't do much in the first half, but he had it going now. Veterans notice that. Rookies tend to just go out there and play. You really have to play and think at the same time."

8:41   *Ainge steals from West.*

Daugherty tried to pass in to West from the top of the key, but the pass was behind West. It went off his hands and Ainge grabbed the loose ball.

8:30   *Bird misses three-pointer.*

The Cavaliers are blessed by the schedule. Bird is coming off a debilitating back injury and is not in a three-point groove.

If they had caught him before he hurt his back, as Chicago did (3–4 on three-pointers), as Seattle did (3–3), as Sacramento did (1–2), or as Phoenix did (3–5), this game could be over right here. If Bird nails this, the Celtics lead by nine and Wilkens will almost undoubtedly call timeout. The crowd will bury the needle on the yellometer.

Bird loves this type of situation. Up by six . . . a little over eight minutes left . . . the momentum clearly shifting to the Celtics . . . a Garden crowd ready to make its contribution . . . this is when he loves to drop the bomb. "He wanted to drive a stake in them," Rodgers declared. He prides himself on being the king of the three-pointer, and there is no question that in the eight years the three-point rule has been in effect, no other NBA player has made such good strategic use of the home-run ball.

Bird has never actually won the NBA three-point percentage championship, but this is of no importance. He proved himself when they actually threw the money on the table the year before in Dallas. The league's best three-point shooters were vying for a $10,000 first prize at the 1986 All-Star Game in Dallas, and Bird blew them away, wiping out Milwaukee's Craig Hodges by sinking eleven in a row from downtown in the finals. Bird had been struggling with a variety of physical ailments prior to that competition, but that triumph seemed to lift his spirits. He came charging out of Dallas to win the NBA Player of the Month Awards in both February and March of 1986, and he went on to become the MVP for the third time in succession.

He utilized the three-pointer with great success in the playoffs, most notably in the fourth Milwaukee game, when he hit four in a row to close out the game, and in the vital fourth Houston game in the final series, when he clinched the game with a three-pointer in the final minute of play to give Boston the one road victory it needed during the three-game set in the Summit.

He came into this game having made more three-point

shots than any man in NBA history; indeed, he had made more three-point shots during his career (which spans the existence of the rule) than many *teams*. Since returning to the lineup two games earlier after missing three games with a bad back, Bird had gone zero for four on three-pointers. He didn't appear to be 100 percent recovered. But if Larry Bird were *not* to pull up and take this three-pointer, in this instance, he just wouldn't be Larry Bird.

Anyway, the shot was short, and Mark West rebounded.

8:22 *Johnson steals from Harper.*

Johnson may be thirty-two years old, and Harper may be four days shy of his twenty-second birthday and in possession of much greater reflexes and physical talent, but right here D.J. taught the kid not to get careless with the rock. Back in the first quarter, a little over four minutes into the game, D.J. had tried to reach in and "poke check" the ball away from Harper, and he had been left staring at the championship flags while Harper had gone in for a lay-up. This time D.J. deftly stuck his right arm in and separated Harper from the basketball at a far more significant moment than the 7:56 mark of the first quarter. With the Celtics up by six, a basket here would do a great deal to insure a Celtic win.

8:15 *Johnson misses jumper.*

Having stolen the basketball, Dennis Johnson was now thinking about turning his theft into a transition basket and an eight-point lead. The Cavaliers retreated well, however, and his path to the basket was blocked. At this point he has a choice between setting up for a jump shot or pulling the ball back out and going into something from the set offense menu. All his basketball life, D.J. has been an erratic outside shooter; his jumper comes and goes without warning, making him one of the great trick-or-treat jump shooters of our time.

In the first game of the Boston-Chicago 1986 playoff series, Johnson went zero for seven from the floor in the first half. He then came out in the third period and hit seven consecutive shots, some turnarounds and others standard face-up jumpers. That's life with D.J.

The rational decision here is for D.J. to pull up. He's not Larry Bird. He's not Danny Ainge. He's not Jerry Sichting. He's now in the right corner, and this is not *his* shot, or anything like it. But there are two important factors at work here: (1) A basket here could be demoralizing to the Cavaliers, and (2) Dennis Johnson has unwavering confidence. So when he passed the ball to Bird and Bird put it back in his hands, he fired it up, but the shot wouldn't go. Brad Daugherty rebounded, and Lenny Wilkens wanted a timeout.

8:11   *Timeout, Cleveland.*

Did Lenny Wilkens know what a break he gave the Boston Celtics here? True, he has to discuss some things with his team, but has he not noticed in the last few minutes that the Celtics look like an old, tired ball club? Johnson has just made a nice individual move, but did Lenny see anyone sprinting downcourt to help D.J. turn his steal into a fast break? The Celtics are in desperate need of a rest, and Lenny has given them one—at his own expense.

The truth is that the Celtics have just lost their opportunity to assume real control of the game. Bird had a chance, but his three-pointer wouldn't fall. Johnson had a chance, but he took a jumper that wasn't in the team's best interest. The Celtics had Cleveland's shoulders on the mat for a count of two, but two isn't good enough.

The last two possessions have showcased the veteran Celtics' macho instincts, but these judgments by Bird and Johnson have indicated that the Celtics have lost some mental tenacity. They've been looking for the easy, dramatic path to victory. But they've got to think the Cavaliers can be had. The teams have played almost four minutes in the fourth period, and Cleveland has four turnovers, and only two official field-goal attempts.

•

In the Cavs' huddle, Wilkens said, "First, I want us to spread the floor when we run our offense. We can't keep drifting towards the key. That lets them just stand in the middle of the lane. Now look, the ball is a valuable possession. We just can't afford to go down the court and not get a shot. Damn it, step to the pass, get the ball. Settle down, take your time and move the ball around. And hit the boards. We gotta get back on the boards."

As the Cavs broke the huddle, Wilkens put Bagley into the game for Ehlo. "I wanted more of our starters out there for the stretch run," said Wilkens. "Craig had given us solid minutes, but we needed Bags to get out there and settle down the offense."

NEW MATCHUPS

POINT GUARDS	Ainge vs. Bagley
SHOOTING GUARDS	Johnson vs. Harper
CENTERS	McHale vs. Daugherty
POWER FORWARDS	Roberts vs. Williams
SMALL FORWARDS	Bird vs. West

Meanwhile, K. C. Jones, concerned about Parish's serious foul trouble, has brought in Fred Roberts. Do not look for this to be a long-term proposition.

7:48   *West rebound and follow-up in middle.*

Boston 101, Cleveland 97.

Cleveland brought the ball upcourt, and it became immediately apparent that the brief rest during the time out has refreshed the Celtics, who have on a playoff-style collective game face as they dig in on defense. Ainge, that relentless "rover," tipped away a pass intended for the low post, giving Cleveland the ball out of bounds. Harper, going nowhere, was forced to crank up a three-pointer on the right wing with three seconds left on the shot clock. The rebound was long, and Daugherty managed to get a hand on it in the middle of the lane, inadvertently tipping it in the direction of West, who sank the little flip shot to give Cleveland its first basket in three minutes and twenty-nine seconds.

"This was why West was in the game," said Wilkens. "He isn't very talented, but he is relentless on the boards. That is important at this juncture of the game because both teams are tired. Effort in rebounding could make the difference."

"We played very good defense," said Rodgers. "But defense isn't over until you get the rebound."

7:32   *McHale fouled by Daugherty (P3, T2).*

Johnson and McHale ran a two-man game on the left side of the basket. Daugherty was guarding McHale. As Johnson passed to McHale, Daugherty made a pass of his own by throwing McHale across the floor. All of this inspired Gary Briggs to yell, "Take that guy's head off, Brad."

7:30   *West ties up McHale.*

The Celtics took the ball out on the side. Bird inbounded to McHale on the left box, and as Kevin turned on Daugherty for a shot, West made an excellent double-team, enabling the two tall Cavaliers to have McHale trapped in a perfect sandwich. "Kevin was kind of pinballing around in there," laughed Rodgers. A jump ball was called between McHale and West.

"That makes up for those turnovers," said Wilkens.

7:22   *Bagley fouled by Ainge (P3, T3). Swish, swish.*

Boston 101, Cleveland 99.

West got the tap over to Bagley, who sprinted toward the Cleveland basket, drawing a foul from Ainge. The Cavaliers have been held to four points on transition since their explosive eleven-for-eleven first period.

7:14   *Johnson give-and-go lay-up. Assist—McHale.*

Boston 103, Cleveland 99.

The Cavaliers were again done in by the first option on "Thumbs-Up." Johnson brought the ball up the court and set up the same give-and-go play with McHale that worked in the first half. Johnson was in the middle of the floor, about thirty feet from the basket. He threw a bounce pass to McHale at the foul line, broke for the basket, and took a handoff from McHale. Either Harper has to take the inside route on defense, back toward the middle, or he's got to get some help from a big man. But Harper trailed D.J. around McHale to the left, Daugherty didn't react, and Williams was immobile on the weak side. The 1925 playground play is now two for two.

6:55   *West turns and slams in Bird's kisser.*

BOSTON 103, CLEVELAND 101.

Larry Bird is a great defensive player—sometimes.

Larry Bird is a good defensive player—most of the time.

Larry Bird is a physically vulnerable defensive player who can be badly exploited—on occasion.

When Bird was a collegian at Indiana State, the debate raged on about his capabilities as a professional, given the fact that he was (a) white, (b) slow, and (c) no threat to make the Olympic team as a high-jumper. There were many who thought defense would be his downfall as a pro.

He has proved himself to be a major defensive asset, good enough to be named to the league's official All-Defensive squad as a second-team member on three occasions. His forte is team, not individual, defense. When trapped in isolation situations, his physical shortcomings are highlighted. But when allowed to roam the floor as a defensive helper, Bird has no peer among contemporary forwards as a source of disruption. He is the smartest defensive forward alive in double-team situations.

So notorious has Bird been as a rover over the years that he gets credit for sparking the current illegal-defense rule. There were so many complaints about Bird's camping in the lane under the old rule that the committee drafted a new proposal, nicknamed by those in the NBA inner sanctum as the "Bird

Rule," at the 1981 league meetings in Danvers, Massachusetts.

Teams with only one scoring threat at forward have always dreaded playing Boston, because it seemed as if there were six men playing against their five. Bird will automatically ignore a rival forward he doesn't deem to be a scoring threat, spending the evening poaching on everyone else's defensive territory. One club he delighted in tormenting was Philadelphia, when Marc Iavaroni was a starter. Then the 76ers drafted Charles Barkley and paired him up with Julius Erving. "Now," said Jack McMahon, then the Sixers' player personnel director, "Bird will have to *guard* somebody."

During his career, he has played both small and big forward, and he has had his successes and his problems at both positions. Strangely enough, small, quick forwards have not really been that big a bother to him. Most of them have no hope of guarding him at the other end, and Bird has lost few individual battles to small forwards. His biggest defensive problems as an individual defender have come with the tough inside players.

Bill Fitch lived in fear of Bird being posted up. He refused to play Bird and Scott Wedman as a combination because he thought they'd both be abused inside. Bird's vulnerability lies in his jumping problem. As a rule, he cannot bother the shot when a big forward either takes a turnaround jumper or uses an inside power move.

In order to compensate, Bird must contest the post-up man's position and his entry pass. Having little chance to rectify a bad situation with sheer physical ability, Bird must outwork his opponent if he is to have a chance to stop the man from scoring. History has shown that Bird does not summon the energy to do this until it is absolutely necessary. He yields position easily for forty-four, forty-five, or forty-six minutes a game, or perhaps even all forty-eight if the Celtics are comfortably ahead.

But in a close game, opponents get a surprise when they

attempt to post up Bird in the final two or three minutes. The same passive opponent who has yielded juicy scoring position in the first forty-five minutes turns into a snarling, clawing, maniacal defender in the last three. He bangs, he bumps, he fronts, he three-quarters, and he does absolutely anything imaginable to deny the pass. Three-Finger Brown would find it quite easy to tally on his pitching hand the number of games in Bird's entire career when opponents have taken advantage of him in the low hole with a game on the line.

Bird has not reached that mental state yet in this game. The Celtics are leading by four and there are over seven minutes remaining as Cleveland comes up the floor. Throwing the ball in to Bird's man in the low post, even if the recipient is a journeyman such as Mark West, is a good idea.

In this case, it turned out to be a great idea. Bird was as helpful to West as John Williams was to McHale in the first quarter. West received the ball in a very dangerous area, from the Boston perspective. "There was too much green showing, where West caught the ball," said Rodgers, meaning that there was a vast expanse of the green-painted foul lane showing between the passer and receiver. Bird was supposed to be in a "Fist" defense. He should have been fronting West more. Instead, he played directly behind him, and West was allowed to get much too close to the basket.

By the time West caught the ball, Bird was already beaten. More than that, he *deserved* to be beaten. West wheeled and only had to take one step before he jammed the ball with his left hand right in the kisser of the $1.8 million man. Let the record show that Fred Roberts tried to help at the last instant. Given the weight and body mass difference between the monstrous West and the wispy Roberts, Fred is fortunate he was late, or else the game might have been delayed for a wake.

Wilkens said, "When West first came in, I was on the verge of pulling him after he had trouble handling the passes. But I decided to let him try to get settled down, and this was his third good play in a row. It started with the basket on the offensive rebound, then he tied up McHale and won the jump ball and now this. Mark played a big role in getting us back into the game. That is why coaching can be so tricky. How long is too long to go with a guy? That's what you ask yourself."

6:46 *Johnson fouled by West (P1, T3). First foul shot, swish. Second foul shot, in and out and in.*

Boston 105, Cleveland 101.

Johnson brought the ball up the floor. The play started out as an "Iso-Kevin," a two-man game with D.J. and McHale, but Daugherty was all over McHale, so D.J. just kept going, right by Harper and to the basket, up for a lay-up that spun in and out but drawing the foul from West. Mel Whitworth made the call, and it was a late one.

"Hey, Mel, why wait so long?" yelled Wilkens. "Don't wait to see if the ball goes in before making the call."

Whitworth turned his back on Wilkens.

Wilkens's point was that officials sometimes act as if this were a pickup game. On the playground, a player will drive to the basket, take the shot, and wait to see if the ball drops in. If the shot is good, he says nothing. But if not, he calls a foul.

D.J. made the first free throw easily, but the second one rattled around before falling in. The Celtics have now made nineteen consecutive free throws. They are the league leaders in this department, and were they any less proficient they would be in a great deal of trouble in this game.

During the dead ball, K.C. sent Parish back in for Roberts. The Chief's breather lasted a total of 1:26. He also had five personal fouls, a development the Cavaliers would love to exploit.

Here is an example of how the Celtics are vastly different than they were a year before. With Bill Walton available, K. C. Jones would not have to risk inserting Parish with a four-point lead and 6:46 to play. But now his alternatives are to employ a front line of McHale, Bird, and Roberts, which effectively leaves the Celtics without a "true" center, or to bring in backup center Greg Kite, a player who in ordinary times would be the twelfth man and nothing more. Kite is a notably clumsy player who for the past six weeks has been playing far below even his limited potential. K.C. has chosen more and more to go without a center rather than to risk using the foul-prone Kite, who is singularly lacking in individual offensive skills.

This substitution spoke volumes. It indicated K. C. Jones's respect for the Cavaliers, for one thing. He felt that even with this lead he needs all his weapons to pull out this game. It indicated that Roberts has been ineffective. It indicated that Kite has become the thirteenth man on a twelve-man team. To an extent, it indicated confidence that Parish is a clever enough veteran to avoid the disqualifying sixth personal foul.

Trainer Ray Melchiorre has never claimed a Ph.D. in Hoopology, but he's been around professional basketball for sixteen years, and he's aware that bringing Parish back in this circumstance is a bit, shall we say, unorthodox. He felt compelled to make an observation.

Melchiorre said to Jones, "Do you guys know he has five fouls?"

6:30

A member of the Boston stat crew walked to the Cavs bench and asked, "Is Scooter McCray here?"

Gary Briggs said, "Yeah, down there."

Briggs pointed to McCray at the end of the bench, where

he was, in his own words, "layin' down some real D. on the water cooler." The stat man nodded and walked away.

"Wonder what that was all about?" asked Briggs. No one answered.

It has been a long night for McCray. The man who wanted to dunk on someone, anyone, only got a chance to slam a paper cup into a trash can.

6:25   *Bagley loses ball out of bounds.*

The Celtics demonstrated to Cleveland what top-of-the-line team defense is all about.

They were again in "Rover," and that perpetually frisky pup Ainge was darting around. Cleveland wanted to isolate Daugherty on Parish here. Lenny Wilkens isn't fooling around; Parish has five fouls, and Wilkens has a center who can score. He's trying to get Parish out of the game in a hurry.

Daugherty got the ball on the left side of the lane, and as soon as he did Danny the rover dropped down from the foul line, abandoning John Bagley for what seems like the thirty-fourth time this evening. Bird immediately rotated up to the foul line from his defensive position with West. Daugherty got the ball up to Bagley, but thanks to Bird's rotation Bagley had nothing better to do than to send the ball back down to Daugherty.

Daugherty was now in trouble. He couldn't shoot it, and he chose to salvage this by-now broken play by relying on his mobility. He started dribbling toward the endline. Bird took notice and now injected himself into the play by leaving Bagley and heading toward Daugherty. The young center was really flustered now. He momentarily lost control of his dribble, barely recovering it. Bagley knew he was accomplishing nothing at the foul line, so he moved toward Daugherty, stationing himself on the left wing, near the three-point arc. Daugherty, who had yet to regain either full control of the basketball or his composure, threw a hard bounce pass out to Bagley. Bags couldn't handle it, and the ball went out of bounds off his hands, and over to Boston.

6:25   *Celtics call timeout.*

Boston has three full timeouts and a twenty-second left. Cleveland has one full timeout and a twenty-second left.

"Are we in the penalty?" asked Wilkens.

"We've had only three team fouls," said Dick Helm.

Wilkens nodded. When the players got to the huddle, he said, "Look, we've got a couple of fouls to give before they're in the penalty. I want aggressive defense. Let's get all over them, force them into a mistake. Guys, let's run the ball and when we bring it down court, let's make them pay. Let's get good shots."

Daugherty said, "We gotta keep moving the ball."

Wilkens said, "That's right. Let's push the ball at them, let's see if we can get a break going. If not, let's set up in our half-court offense."

As the buzzer sounded, Wilkens says, "Guys, see the ball."

In the broadcast booth, Joe Tait said, "When you stop to realize that the Celtics have hit nineteen of their last twenty-six shots and are six for nine this quarter, it is amazing that the Cavs are still in the game. That also gives you some idea just how well the Cavs have played tonight."

That is especially true when you consider that in the fourth quarter Harper hasn't scored, Daugherty has one point, and Williams has two.

6:07 *McHale dip-in lay-up. Assist—Bird.*

BOSTON 107, CLEVELAND 101.

The Celtics emerged from the huddle and ran a "Special." Said Rodgers, "The first look was a lob to Robert. But Bagley did a good job of bumping Parish and holding him up." No problem. The Celtics quickly went to the second option. Bird set up on the right and gave it to McHale. He gave West a pump fake, all but assuring West he will be going for the jump shot. West rose to block the shot that wasn't there, and McHale leaned forward and softly laid it in.

5:39 *Cleveland twenty-four-second violation.*

One of the major differences between the Boston Celtics and other teams is that its players tend to remember things they are told.

Almost ten hours earlier, during the shootaround at Hellenic College, Jimmy Rodgers had told the Celtics that Cleveland codes their play numbers by position. *If they call a "2," look for the two guard, Harper.* Dennis Johnson was paying attention.

The Celtics had created a turnover on the last Cleveland possession, and now the lead was up to six points again. The crowd, itself the most experienced set of third-party observers in the league, sensed the import of this possession. There was an ever-growing rumble leading to a roar as Ron Harper ambled upcourt, dribbling the basketball with his left hand and holding his right index and middle fingers over his head.

Dennis Johnson, seeing the two fingers, turned his head and alerted Kevin McHale, guarding Mark West, what the play would be. *If they call a '2,' look for the two guard, Harper.*

"It was going to be a '21,' or a 'UCLA Rub,'" said Rodgers. "In any event, the first option was going to be Harper."

With nineteen seconds left on the twenty-four-second clock Harper, under no great pressure from Johnson, crossed midcourt. He was on the right of center. West came up from the right side of the lane to take the entry pass. McHale, responding to D.J.'s warning message, got up close to West, refusing to allow an unmolested pass. West caught the ball with fourteen seconds left on the twenty-four.

McHale had pushed West out a little farther than he wanted to go. After Harper made the entry to West, Daugherty stepped up and Harper cut off him and made his way toward the basket. He was hoping to get free for a lob pass and a dunk, but Parish, guarding Daugherty, put a little body on him, slowing him down just enough for Johnson, taking the inside route through the lane, to catch up to his man.

"In essence," Rodgers explained, "we had the entire first option covered," in that:

—there was no alley-oop to Harper;

—there was no quick post-up for Harper;

—there was no cutting route whatsoever on the play.

With twelve seconds left on the twenty-four, Daugherty, stationed high on the right side of the lane, almost to the foul line, turned and received the ball from West.

Any comparable young team would have been in big, big trouble right here, but the Cavaliers were playing intelligent basketball all night long. They weren't about to give up on this play.

As Daugherty was receiving the ball, Bagley was setting a good back-pick on Bird, who was guarding Williams. Given Daugherty's great vision and execution as a high-post passer, this could have been a damaging development for Boston. But the 6-foot-4-inch Ainge unhesitatingly switched to the 6-foot-11-inch Williams and banged him, holding up his progress as he cut across the lane long enough for Bird to return to Williams. Bagley has now drifted to the left of the lane while Williams headed for the low left box to post up Bird.

With ten seconds left, Daugherty gave the ball off to Bagley. Ainge stepped up in what the Celtics call an excellent "close-out" defensive position, his right foot forward, his right hand up in Bagley's face, his left hand out. If Bagley was going anywhere, he was going to the middle, where Danny had help.

"At this point," said Rodgers, "Danny is actually playing two men. He's got Bagley, and he's paying attention to Williams, too. Not only is Danny closing out well, but he's also discouraging a pass to Williams. Meanwhile, Larry is doing a good job of fighting Williams, not letting him back him too deeply into the paint."

Harper now materialized to the left of Bagley. The chief object of Cleveland's attention was now Williams. After all, isn't posting up Larry Bird supposed to be so damned easy? But Bagley has been prevented from making an entry pass. If he gave the ball to Harper, the Cavaliers could try the entry from a different passing angle.

Harper received the ball with nine seconds left on the twenty-four.

He dribbled once, then succeeded in getting the ball in to Williams. There were now five seconds remaining on the twenty-four-second clock.

As Williams got the ball he was confronted by Bird and, of course, by Mr. Rover himself, Danny Ainge. Bagley, by now used to the way Ainge keeps leaving him right in the middle of the conversation, alertly moved to his right, setting up residence at the foul line. Williams, who may not be much with the readin' and writin', but who sure has an inner sense of right and wrong when it comes to basketball, spotted Bagley and looped a pass. He has had the ball for a second and a fraction. Bagley received the ball, but by the time he did he was no longer open. Dennis Johnson started heading for

Bagley the instant Ainge left him to go help out on Williams. In NBA terms, this is known as "rotation," and the Celtics have made it an art form in this game.

Bagley caught the ball with four seconds left on the twenty-four. "This had now evolved into a one-on-one," said Rodgers. "All their options were exhausted." Bagley was now wearing an iron overcoat named Dennis Johnson. Bagley started left, spun back right, kept dribbling, and finally got off an off-balance jumper. The shot was immaterial. The buzzer went off before he could shoot, and Earl Strom signified that the Cavaliers had committed a twenty-four-second violation.

During this possession every Cavalier has touched the ball. Every Celtic defender has performed his defensive chore as if he had a radio receiver from the bench implanted in his brain. "It was just the way you would have charted it during the Shootaround," said Rodgers. "'Off-the-drawing-board' defense."

This was Cleveland's sixth turnover of the quarter. The Cavs had only seven turnovers in the first three quarters. Wilkens sends Hubbard in for West.

"It was time to get all the starters back," said Wilkens.

NEW MATCHUPS

POINT GUARDS	Ainge vs. Bagley
SHOOTING GUARDS	Johnson vs. Harper
CENTERS	Parish vs. Daugherty
POWER FORWARDS	McHale vs. Williams
SMALL FORWARDS	Bird vs. Hubbard

5:22   *McHale misses turnaround.*

The Cavaliers are supposed to be demoralized. It's in the script. Been that way for thirty years.

The Celtics set up, hoping that the third try for an eight-point lead will be, you know, the charm. "We went to what we call '21-Dribble Out,' " Rodgers said. "We had a nice triangle on the left side. Got the ball in to Kevin. He's triple-teamed. Gets it back out. Then back in. He goes for the corner turnaround. Can't get it. They did a nice job of keeping him from the paint."

Perhaps the demoralization would come on the next possession.

5:13 *Williams misses a dunk.*

The Cavs blew a big, big opportunity. Harper rebounded the McHale miss and turned upcourt. Williams sneaked away from the pack along the right sideline. "Everybody else," said Rodgers, "was running. He was *sprinting*." Harper threw him an alley-oop pass, but Williams's slam went back rim, front rim, back rim, and out, Parish grabbing the rebound.

"That was an excellent opportunity for them to get a big hoop," said Rodgers. "That's psychologically devastating if they score a basket like that."

4:55 *Parish throws the ball away.*

Tempo, tempo, tempo. Suddenly the game has picked up. The Cavaliers have tried to make a statement play, and so the Celtics automatically started thinking about making one of their own. They wanted desperately to get beyond this six-point barrier.

The ball was in Johnson's hands. He was moving quickly along the left sideline, scanning the floor and evaluating his options. "He had a chance of two things there," said Rodgers. "He can retaliate with a break, or he can slow it down and go to our half-court game." He made a quick decision: A break is too risky; he will get the ball to one of the big men. "D.J. did what a great guard should do in that situation," Rodgers declared. "He slowed it down."

He saw Bird and Parish on the right. He gave it to Bird high as Parish took his posting-up position on the low right box. Bird dumped it in, but Parish, feeling defensive pressure from behind and seeing Ainge spotting up on the right wing, slapped the pass back out toward Ainge. Danny, unprepared for this Birdlike gesture, had already vacated the spot, heading for the right corner. The ball sailed out of bounds. Since making the great defensive stop a while back, the Celtics have been unable to capitalize. But the lead is six; and the clock is starting to become a major factor.

"If we had scored on either of the last two possessions," said Rodgers, "we might have been able to bust open the game."

4:51   *Bagley seventeen-footer from right wing.
Assist—Harper.*

BOSTON 107, CLEVELAND 103.

Harper was allowed to make a left-to-right penetration in the lane. An overeager Parish stepped out on him when he didn't have to. Ainge, too, got involved without reason, and again Bagley was left alone. "We had a breakdown," said Rodgers. "It was nice they were thinking team defense, but this wasn't the way to do it." This time, Bagley took Wilkens's advice. He disdained the three-pointer, took a step in, and hit the shorter shot.

Bagley now had twenty-two points.

4:38 *Bird throws ball away.*

The Cavs were aggressive on defense as Wilkens again reminded them that they have a couple of fouls to give before the penalty. The Celtics wanted an unadulterated "Hawk," a right side post-up isolation for Bird. Daugherty wouldn't allow it, however, double-teaming aggressively. Bird tried a difficult backward bounce pass in the lane to a cutting Parish, but the ball went off the knee of John Williams, bouncing back directly into Daugherty's hands.

4:33 *Harper fouled by Ainge (P4, T4).*
Breakaway foul. First foul shot, swish.
Second foul shot hits the front of the rim
and goes in.

Boston 107, Cleveland 105.

After coming up with the loose ball, Daugherty spotted Harper breaking down court and hit Harper with a long pass. Harper was headed for a dunk when Ainge grabbed him. That much is agreed upon.

"Ainge tackles Harper," Joe Tait said matter-of-factly in the broadcast booth.

Wilkens yelled, "Breakaway."

Mel Whitworth agreed.

The Celtic bench protested, and the crowd booed.

Joe Tait said, "These folks here don't like reality. You're not supposed to give Boston a breakaway foul in the Garden. It's sacrilegious."

"Ainge," said Rodgers later, "made a great hustle play to save a lay-up. The intention of the breakaway foul is to penalize people who come from behind and run the risk of hurting someone. Danny made a great effort and got his body *to the side.* He actually fouls Harper from the *front.* It's just a great play. Danny knows the rule, or he wouldn't attempt to do this. This was a very big play."

The breakaway-foul rule was instituted because players were trying to put each other in the emergency ward. A guy would be running down the court for an open lay-up and a defender would rush down and throw a body block into him. The thing was to foul him, put him on the line, and make him earn the two points.

But this was leading to bashed skulls, broken limbs, and other injuries. So the league passed a rule saying that if you grab a guy from behind who is going for an open lay-up, it's a breakaway foul. The player who is fouled goes to the line for two shots. After his shots, his team also gets the ball out of bounds.

This means that Harper was at the line, alone. Would he heave one of his spirals?

Not on the first shot, which swished. But the second shot would have made Dan Marino proud, a spiral all the way. But it banged against the front of the rim and then crawled in. An excited Harper made a fist and then clapped for himself.

"Man, I didn't want to stand out there and miss them shots with all those people watching me," he said. "Ain't nothin' worse than bein' out there all by yourself and throwin' bricks."

The lead is now down to two, and it's Cleveland ball.

4:21   *Harper travels.*

Bird wants this game. He *really* wants this game. He is now playing defense as if he must do everything himself. He will leave absolutely nothing to chance.

Harper wanted Williams down deep because he's got Johnson there on a switch. Bird came over to double-team, making Williams give the ball back out to Harper. Harper was now guarded by McHale, Williams's man, because of that same switch. He faked a jumper, sending McHale flying past, and drove into the lane. Bird alertly switched over to him, and as Harper went up for the shot, Parish, too, went over to help out. Harper had done some phenomenal things in this game, but the defensive attention of the entire Celtic front line was too much even for him. He lost control of the ball in midair, landed, caught it, and was called for the up-and-down violation.

4:07　*Bird leaner in lane. Fouled by Williams (P4, T4). Foul shot, swish.*

Boston 110, Cleveland 105.

The Celtics ran an option off "21-Dribble-Out," the play they ran three possessions ago. As Johnson looked over the chances of getting the ball low to McHale on the left box, Parish and Bird lined up in a stack on the right foul lane. Parish came down and picked off Hubbard. Bird circled out and took a bounce pass from Johnson as he entered the lane.

Among Bird's many offensive attributes is a very well-developed left hand. He drives just about as well right-to-left as he does left-to-right. He took it hard to the basket. Both Williams and Daugherty converged, shutting off Bird's access, but he forced up a difficult left-handed shot that crawled up and in, while drawing a foul on Williams. The foul shot gave Bird twenty-seven for the night.

"We could have folded right here," said Wilkens. "We had a chance to tie the game after the breakaway foul, and Ron lost the ball. Then Bird comes back and hits us with a three-point play. The crowd was going crazy. I knew we had to get the ball inside and get some points."

3:53 *Hubbard fouled by Parish (P6, T5). Swish, swish.*

BOSTON 110, CLEVELAND 107.

Bagley got the ball in to Hubbard, who was posting Bird on the left box. Parish came over to help. Bird and Hubbard were going at it pretty hard, with no call. At one point Hubbard simply lowered his left shoulder and banged it into Bird's chest. No call. But when Parish arrived, Hubbard made a nice pump fake to get Parish into the air, went up, got bumped slightly, and the disqualifying sixth foul on Parish was called. What contact there was between Hubbard and Parish was minimal, and yet the obvious banging for position earlier was sanctioned. Refereeing is certainly a very strange profession.

The Cavs could not have asked for more. They defused Bird's three-point play by getting two points from Hubbard and knocking Parish out of the game. Parish left with twenty-two points, and Roberts came in with none.

NEW MATCHUPS

POINT GUARDS	Ainge vs. Bagley
SHOOTING GUARDS	Johnson vs. Harper
CENTERS	McHale vs. Daugherty
POWER FORWARDS	Roberts vs. Williams
SMALL FORWARDS	Bird vs. Hubbard

3:39 *Johnson lay-up no good. Roberts follow-up no good. Bagley steals from Roberts.*

D.J. cut off McHale and got free underneath when Bird picked off Harper. McHale got him the ball, but Williams came from the weak side to contest the shot and Johnson missed the lay-up. Fred Roberts couldn't knock in a flying follow-up, and after he grabbed the rebound, he was stripped of the ball by Bagley.

"It was a well-executed play," shrugged Rodgers. "We just came up empty on it."

3:33 *McHale fouled by Hubbard (P3, T5). Swish, swish.*

Boston 112, Cleveland 107.

Bagley pushed the ball upcourt, and the Cavs had a four-on-three break. Daugherty got the ball for a drive in the lane, but his running hook wouldn't fall. McHale got the rebound, and Hubbard jumped on McHale's back. And now the Cavs didn't have any more fouls to spare as this one put them over the limit.

3:17 *Williams six-footer.*

Boston 112, Cleveland 109.

The Cavs ran a two-man game with Bagley and Hot Rod. Since Parish fouled out, McHale had to guard Daugherty. That left Roberts on Williams. Wilkens leaped on the chance to call a play to get Hot Rod the ball under the basket. Williams caught the pass and went up for the turnaround, which rattled around the rim three times before dropping in. Williams now had twenty points.

3:05 *Bird fouled by Hubbard (P4, T6). Swish, swish.*

Boston 114, Cleveland 109.

Johnson threw a pass to Bird at the top of the key. Hubbard went for the steal and got a hand on the ball. He also got a finger in Bird's eye, and Bird grabbed his face as if he has been gouged. The whistle blew, and Hubbard put his hands on his hips and glared disgustedly at Whitworth.

"Mel, that's a cheap foul," yelled Wilkens.

Whitworth had no reply.

Wilkens turned to the bench and said, "At this time of the game, that's a cheap foul. With all the banging they're doing out there, they call Hubs for that. You tell me that call wasn't cheap."

No one on the Cavs' bench tells Wilkens.

Wilkens turned back to the court and yelled, "Ah, come on, Mel."

Whitworth has probably made the right call, but for the wrong reason. A few counts before Bird received the ball, he was banged hard by Hubbard from behind. That's the foul Whitworth is actually calling. At least, that's Rodgers's view. "Whitworth saw Hubbard make the contact initially," said Rodgers later. "Officials do this all the time. They see something, and they're sort of digesting it, when something lesser happens. Then they blow the whistle." After making that first contact, especially against Larry Bird, Hubbard was going to draw a foul for breathing.

Rodgers is fascinated by the thought process of officials. He espouses what he calls the "1-2-3 Theory," which means that if a defensive player goes up to contest a shot and blocks it twice, that's usually the limit. If he can't get control by the third block, the whistle will blow ninety-nine times out of one hundred, and he'll be called for a foul. You could probably call the phenomenon at work here the "After-the-Fact Theory."

•

As the teams headed upcourt, Chris Ford jumped and yelled, "One stop, Danny! One stop! Get the loose ball!"

2:48   *Bagley twenty-footer top of key.*
Assist—Daugherty.

BOSTON 114, CLEVELAND 111.

The Cavaliers won a sweet little two-man battle against Ainge. Danny wound up trying to protect against the drop-down pass to Daugherty while not giving Bagley a very good shot. But when Daugherty began backing into the lane, Ainge rightly chose to double-team, leaving Bagley open for the twenty-foot jumper. "Bagley made a tough shot," said Rodgers. "But we did what we wanted to do. Up by five, you want to make them do it from the outside. You've got to take away any inside game, and we did."

Just to stay with Boston, the Cavs needed a great game from Bagley. To beat the Celtics, they needed an outrageous game, almost a career game from the 5–11 point guard. With a season-high twenty-four points and deadly shooting from two-point (but not three-point) range, Bagley had given the Cavs an almost shocking boost, especially since he could barely walk eight hours earlier at practice because of the mysterious knee injury.

At Boston College, Bagley was known as a penetrator. The Eagles pressed and drove to the basket. Chaos was their game plan, which was terrific for Boston College but awful training for a pro point guard. Only in this, his fifth season, is Bagley beginning to understand all that it takes to run an NBA team on the floor, and the reason is Wilkens.

"I told Bags that if he's open and he's set, shoot the ball," said Wilkens. "He doesn't have to drive through three guys and then get in trouble under the basket. He is a good, sensitive kid who has worked hard to improve his outside shot. He'll never be a great outside shooter, but if he picks his spots, he can hurt a team."

Just as the Cavs elected to let Ainge shoot, Boston took the same tack with Bagley, and he has made the Celtics pay.

2:32 *Both Gary Briggs and Lenny Wilkens yell, "Three seconds on McHale."*

2:28 *McHale eight-footer in middle. Assist—Bird.*

BOSTON 116, CLEVELAND 111.

Bird initiated things by setting a back-pick on Daugherty, guarding McHale. When that happened, Hubbard should support his teammate by slowing McHale down, but he was too worried about the prospect of Bird standing alone at the free-throw line. The pick freed McHale to set up in the middle of the lane; Daugherty was by now out of the play, and Hubbard had to make a decision. He came running at Bird, who dumped the ball down to McHale for an eight-footer. McHale has scored thirty-six points.

"Get McHale out of the lane," yelled Wilkens. "He's living in there."

Both officials ignored Wilkens.

2:17 *McHale fouls Daugherty (P3, T5). Swish, swish.*

BOSTON 116, CLEVELAND 113.

"After The Fact Theory," Part II.

As Harper brought the ball up the court, Wilkens yelled,

"2–5," calling for Harper and Daugherty to run a two-man game. They set up the play on the right side of the basket; Harper passed in to Daugherty, and Bird, the designated rover for this sequence, left Hubbard to help McHale double-team Daugherty. Daugherty went up for a shot, and Earl Strom whistled McHale for a foul. McHale made what appeared to be a perfect block. But seconds before Bird's arrival, McHale and Daugherty had staged a reenactment of Wrestlemania III, off the ball. They were emulating Hulk Hogan and Andre the Giant, but there was no whistle. So, naturally, the next *appearance* of possible contact drew a call.

Many reasonable NBA people say that if you don't believe in your heart that all these things even themselves out over the course of a season, you'll never survive in this league.

Daugherty stood at the line, holding the ball. Wilkens yelled, "Fingers."

Daugherty made the first shot, then the second. Wilkens nodded. Daugherty was now six for eight from the line.

1:57 *Johnson twenty-footer left corner. Assist—Bird.*

BOSTON 118, CLEVELAND 113.

For the third time in the game the Celtics tried "Thumbs Up." For the first time, option one didn't result in a Dennis Johnson lay-up. The Cavaliers have finally reacted properly to the ol' give-and-go.

McHale came up high and took the entry pass from Johnson. But as D.J. cut diagonally from right to left, Daugherty stepped to his right and protected the lane, diverting D.J. to the left corner. Bird, wasting not a second, popped up to the line, took a pass, and started into the lane, attracting an impromptu convention of Cavalier folk, one of whom is

Harper. Bird ducked in and got off a bounce pass to the unguarded Johnson in the left corner, and D.J. hit the jumper.

"That might have looked like a broken-down play," said Rodgers, "but it wasn't, because everybody did what they were supposed to do. Larry created some one-on-one action and then hit the open man. They played us tough defensively, but we maintained our poise. This play showed the versatility of Bird. After that last left-handed drive, they all reacted. Now he breaks their hearts with his great vision and passing ability."

"That was Johnson's first real outside shot of the game," said Wilkens. "We did the right thing in leaving him open and going for the double-team on Bird. As I said, I usually don't like to double Bird, but at this part of the game and with Bird driving to the basket, you have to stop him and let someone else shoot, especially when that someone else is almost twenty feet from the basket."

The Cavaliers weren't about to be beaten from the inside any more than Boston was.

1:45   *Daugherty misses ten-footer.*

1:35   *Hubbard blocks McHale.*

After Johnson's basket, the Cavs brought the ball up the court and got it to Daugherty in on the baseline, but his shot was long. McHale rebounded and passed to D.J., who drove the length of the court and missed the left-handed lay-up. McHale grabbed the rebound and started to go up for the shot, but Hubbard came from behind and blocked it.

The Celtics could have won the game on this possession. McHale with an offensive rebound is usually two points, and two more points would have made it a seven-point Boston lead with ninety-five seconds left.

But in the last minute, some things were happening for the Cavs that weren't supposed to happen.

For example, John Bagley continued to hit from the outside. For example, Brad Daugherty continued to hit from the foul line. For example, Phil Hubbard blocked McHale's shot. Not only was this the first time all season Hubbard blocked McHale, it was the first time Hubbard blocked anyone.

1:30   *Harper fouled by Ainge (P5, T7). Brick, swish.*

BOSTON 118, CLEVELAND 114.

After blocking McHale, Hubbard dribbled to midcourt and passed to Harper, who was thinking one thing—*get to the basket as fast as possible.* Ainge, meanwhile, was also thinking one thing—*don't let Harper get to the basket.* The result was high-level confrontation between the two best athletes on the floor and two of the best in the league. Harper moved to the hoop, and Ainge threw his body between the rim and Harper. This was a classic race to the crossing, with a decision awaiting Judge Whitworth. They collided, Whitworth blew the whistle and pointed the finger at Ainge, who was flat on his back, yelling it was a charge.

The first foul shot went off the front of the front rim, but the second swished.

1:09   *Bird fouled by Hubbard (P5, T7). Swish, swish.*

BOSTON 120, CLEVELAND 114.

The Celtics elected to try "Bull," the high-post split that had gotten Bird an open twenty-footer on the first possession of the game. Daugherty spoiled the plan by deflecting Mc-Hale's pass to Bird, however, and now it was Improv City.

D.J. picked up the loose ball in the right corner and hit Bird, who was now posting up Hubbard on the right baseline, about fifteen feet from the basket. He got it in to Larry as the clock started running down. Harper injected himself into the situation, by leaving Johnson to come at Bird from the right, but Bird froze him with a great fake and spun back to the right for a scoop shot. A foul was called, and it's a very good thing for Bird, since there were only three seconds remaining on the twenty-four second clock.

"Come on, where's the foul?" yelled Wilkens. "He never touched Bird."

No response from either official.

Wilkens turned to the bench and said, "Tell me where Bird got fouled."

No one tells Wilkens.

Bird hit the first foul shot and Wilkens said, "Are these guys ever going to miss one?"

No one says anything to Wilkens. Bird's second shot means the Celtics have hit twenty-seven free throws in a row.

This was Hubbard's fifth foul, and his fourth in the last four minutes. Bird's foul shots gave Boston its biggest lead of the fourth quarter. Bird has scored thirty-one points.

:53   *McHale blocks Daugherty.*

In the first half the Celtics' coaching staff was unhappy about the way their big men had defended individually. Daugherty had extricated himself from a number of sticky situations, twice moving along the baseline to create baskets for teammates. There would be no giveaways now—and no double-teams, either.

"Stay at home!" the Boston coaches yelled, primarily because they didn't want to surrender a three-point shot, which was more likely to develop if the Celtics were scrambling around trying to rotate from open man to open man. Secondarily, the Celtics wanted to make Cleveland work hard and long for whatever they got on this possession. They didn't want to give up any "quickies," as they call them. Finally, they didn't want to foul. Fouling lets the Cavs score with the clock not running, and they have the opportunity to set up their defense. To accomplish these objectives, the Celtics were in their "Strict" defense, a tough man-to-man.

Wilkens yelled, "1–5," a two-man game for Bagley and Daugherty on the left side of the lane. Bagley passed to Daugherty, who passed back to Bagley. Bagley took a dribble toward the top of the key and passed back to Daugherty, who received the ball in good low-post scoring position. McHale played him expertly, taking away any move the rookie might make toward the middle and sending him to the baseline and into McHale's own right hand. Daugherty put up a scoop shot. McHale blocked it but couldn't keep it in play. The ball went out of bounds with eight seconds left on the twenty-four and fifty-three in the game.

:51   *Harper fouled by Johnson (P2, T8). Swish, swish.*

BOSTON 120, CLEVELAND 116.

Bagley took the ball inbounds, passing to Harper, who drove the baseline, put up a prayer for a shot, and was fouled by Johnson.

At the line, it was now no sweat for Harper, just another game against a team in a green and white uniform like Ohio U. He sank both shots, cleanly.

:34   *Harper steals from Johnson.*

There were dazzling plays, electrifying plays, awesome plays, stupid plays, weird plays, and creative plays made from the beginning of this extraordinarily well-played game, but there was only one truly *shocking* play—and this was it.

OK, so Harper had hit the two free throws. The Celtics still led by four. What they were most concerned with was the clock. Chris Ford was up off the bench. "Use it up!" he yelled at Dennis Johnson, a superfluous bit of advice, since D.J. was well aware of the situation.

Johnson moved slowly and carefully past the midcourt line and then stopped his advance without losing his dribble. Bird was standing unguarded at the foul line, but Johnson ignored him. He was half-turned, watching the clock on the auxiliary scoreboard until he was ready to initiate the play.

"Even if we took the whole time and never got off a shot it would have been all right," said Rodgers. "They'd have twenty-seven seconds left, and there aren't any four- or five-point shots you can pull off. Our objective was to use as much time as we could."

With ten seconds left on the twenty-four, and forty-one in the game, Johnson was still crouched, dribbling, at midcourt. Harper quickly stuck his arm in there and jarred the ball loose. He had flat-out D.J.'d D.J. himself with a poke check, and the ball went rolling loose into the Cleveland half of the court. A horrified Johnson caught up to it but couldn't control it and the ball belonged to the Cavaliers with thirty-three seconds left, down by four.

"They just reversed roles here," Rodgers said. "He did what D.J. does so well."

:33 *Cavs call twenty-second timeout.*

"We have the ball out under their basket," Wilkens told his players. "Let's run our regular out-of-bounds play, and let's run it right. Concentrate. Hubs, you take the ball out."

"A three [point shot] would do them no good if it didn't come quick enough," Rodgers said later. "We were up by four, and if we could hold them for nine seconds, we could get the ball back and not have to shoot again. Whatever they wanted to do, we had to make sure it took them a little time to do it."

:30 *McHale blocks Bagley.*

On the in-bounds Williams picked off Ainge, and Hubbard threw the pass to the open Bagley, as Roberts was slow to switch over. Bagley thought someone was behind him, and he took a dribble before going up for the shot. Well, Bagley was right; by the time he took that dribble, someone *was* behind him. That someone was McHale, who stuffed Bagley from behind as he went up for the shot, but remember what

Rodgers said earlier about defense not being over until you come up with the damn basketball.

:29   *Williams fouled by Bird (P2, T9). Swish, swish.*

Boston 120, Cleveland 118.

Hot Rod picked up Bagley's blocked shot, went up for the shot, and was whacked by Bird. Williams easily made the two shots. Only four seconds had elapsed. For the Celtics, this was, as Chester A. Riley would say, a revolting' development.

The Cavs, who are the worst foul-shooting team in the league, a team that had been losing games at the foul line, was staying in this one because they were twelve for fourteen from the line in the fourth quarter, including seven for eight in the last 2:17, and all of those shots were taken by Cleveland's three rookies—Harper, Williams and Daugherty.

Chris Ford was up again. "Use it up!" he implored.

:13   *Johnson fouled by Harper (P3, T8). Swish, swish.*

Boston 122, Cleveland 118.

The Celtics will be required to shoot the ball now. Again the ball went to Johnson. McHale came up high to set a pick on Harper, but the rookie eluded it and this became another one-on-one duel between the Jedi master and the apt pupil. Wilkens started screaming, "Ron, no foul." Harper was trying to reach in, dreaming of another steal.

Both Wilkens and his assistant, Dick Helm, were standing, stomping their feet, screaming, "No foul."

But the Boston crowd was louder.

Harper kept reaching.

"Just don't foul," yelled Wilkens.

With eight seconds left on the twenty-four, and D.J. going nowhere in particular, Harper commited a rookie foul.

Wilkens looked up to the heavens as Johnson went to the line and made the shots.

"I never heard anybody," said Harper. "I just wanted to get the ball back."

"The crowd noise was tough," said Wilkens. "But there were only eight seconds on the shot clock and Dennis was a long way from the basket. We might have gotten a twenty-four second call. I don't fault Ron. I know he couldn't hear us, but . . ."

:13   *Cleveland calls its last timeout.*

Wilkens lives for these moments.

"I love close games," he said. "I feel I can do something directly to help us win a close game. I like it when we have a timeout and the guys come to the huddle and I have to come up with a play that will get us a good shot.

"It's funny, twenty-point games make me more nervous than close games. I just feel that I am as good as any coach in a close game and that my teams play well in these situations."

Entering this game, the Cavs were 6–2 in games decided by four or fewer points.

In the Cleveland huddle, Wilkens said, "All right, we gotta go to the hoop right away. When we score, we have to press them, go after the ball. If we foul, we foul."

Wilkens drew up a play with Hubbard taking the ball out of bounds at half-court. Williams and Harper will line up at the opposite sides of the top of the key. Williams will pick for Harper at the top of the key, Harper will cut around the pick toward Hubbard. As he gets around the pick, he'll receive a pass from Hubbard and drive to the basket.

"All right," said Wilkens. "Stay with it. We don't know what's going to happen. We can make this work."

:10 *Williams slams.*

BOSTON 122, CLEVELAND 120.

The play worked, exactly as Wilkens diagrammed. (See Illus. 11.) The whole building knew that Harper was going to get the ball, but Hot Rod's pick on Johnson freed Harper to receive the pass. Harper went to the basket hard, but his lay-up rolled off the rim. But here came Hot Rod down the lane with a vengeance. Among the people who had futilely tried to stop Harper was Fred Roberts, the man guarding Williams. When Harper missed, Williams had an open path to the basket. The ball came off the rim and he was there to jam it home.

"We just didn't do a good job of taking away Harper's curl and drive," Rodgers said. "No one stepped in with the body. Larry reached. Danny reached. Fred reached. It was all arms and hands; no movement of feet and lower bodies. The last line of defense was Kevin, but that was too late. And when he missed, the offensive rebound was there."

:09 *Johnson called for traveling.*

The Celtics have no interest in a timeout. They want to get the ball inbounds and move it around to avoid a foul, if possible. But in almost every comparable situation, you can

Fourth Quarter

:10

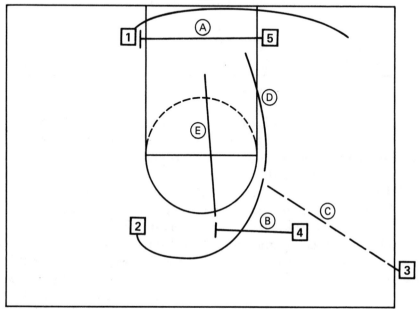

1 — Bagley   Ⓐ Daugherty screens for Bagley.

2 — Harper   Ⓑ Williams screens for Harper.

3 — Hubbard

4 — Williams   Ⓒ Harper comes around Williams's screen and catches pass
                   from Hubbard.

5 — Daugherty

                Ⓓ Harper drives to basket, misses shot.

                Ⓔ Williams crashes boards, gets Harper's rebound and scores.

Illus. 11

expect to get fouled. In order to wrap up this game they'll most likely need to make two more free throws.

Ainge took it out as the pumped-up Cavaliers tried to press. He ran from right-to-left behind the end line, which is perfectly permissible after a score, but would not be after a violation. Cleveland was in a total scramble, and Johnson broke free along the left sideline. Ainge spotted him and threw a long lead pass, the ball reaching Johnson near the midcourt line.

Johnson picked the ball up on a short hop (this is a crucial detail, in light of what is to come). Either he has already seen a wide-open Fred Roberts before he received the ball, or he saw him as soon as he got it, because he immediately wanted to unload the ball. He released it before his foot hit the floor—or, at least, that's what he and the Celtics think.

But Mel Whitworth believed otherwise. Whitworth called Johnson for traveling. The ball went over to Cleveland with plenty of time to tie or win this ballgame.

"That was a great call, a gutsy call in Boston Garden," said Wilkens. "There was no doubt. D.J. ran with the ball before he threw the pass. You expect Earl Strom to make a call like that, but Mel really showed me something there. You gotta give him credit."

In the broadcast booth, Joe Tait said, "What a call by Whitworth. You have to admire him for that. Don't look now, but as incredible as this sounds, the Cavs still have a shot at this game."

Here is what Rodgers saw, and has seen time and again via the magic of videotape since then: "D.J. picks the ball off the floor, takes a step, and then gets rid of it before step two," Rodgers said. "The only thing I can figure is that Whitworth was not in position to see that D.J. had caught the ball on that short hop. If he *had* caught the ball on the fly and taken those steps, it *would* have been traveling."

Had traveling not been called, Roberts would have had the ball on the right side of the court. Williams was coming in from the left, and had Roberts chosen to take it all the way rather than to pull up, there would have been an interesting confrontation at the hoop.

As long as the principals in this play are alive, there will be no agreement as to what actually happened. The only certain thing was that the Cavaliers, who had been down six with sixty-nine seconds to go, now had a chance to tie or win.

The Cavs are out of timeouts, so all Wilkens can do is watch them throw in the ball.

"What I would have given for just one more timeout," Wilkens said. "Just one more."

:00   *Harper left corner jumper beats the buzzer.*

BOSTON 122, CLEVELAND 122.

The Celtics were disoriented. In one instant they figured the game was over, and in the next they were supposed to be setting up a defense to save the ballgame. Worse yet, we're not talking one or two seconds. There were *nine seconds* left. In nine seconds all sorts of unspeakable horrors could be perpetrated.

Hubbard passed the ball to Bagley, who broke down the right sideline, step-for-step with Ainge. Bagley drove toward the top of the key and passed behind him to Daugherty, who was at the three-point arch near the top of the key. Bird and McHale converged on Daugherty, leaving Hubbard open on the right wing. At this point the Celtics' brass knows the team is in trouble. "We're in what we call 'Chase,'" said Rodgers. "We were worried about the three-pointer. At one point two guys were guarding John Williams in three-point land. There were Larry and Kevin all over John Williams at the three-point line. He's not a three-point shooter, but you know from experience that anybody can just *throw* it in."

Daugherty passed to Hubbard, just outside the three-point arch. Harper was in the right corner, arm up asking for the ball. Johnson left Harper and ran to Hubbard. Hubbard heard Harper, saw him open, and threw a pass to Harper, who caught it just inside the three-point arch.

Ron Harper, of all people, has been left alone in this furious station-to-station scramble, and he is now standing in the right corner directly in front of the Celtics' bench.

"I knew when I saw Harper standing in the corner," said K. C. Jones, "that we had left the wrong man open." Fred Roberts was under the basket when Harper got the ball with no more than a second left. He came flying at the rookie as he let the shot go. The buzzer went off before the ball swished cleanly through the cords. Earl Strom, standing under the basket, signaled emphatically with his left hand that the basket was good. The Celtics were fortunate that Harper hadn't spotted up *behind* the three-point line, or that he hadn't had either the time or the presence of mind to step behind it. At this moment, the Celtics were fortunate to be heading into overtime.

Harper jumped up and down, waving his fist in the air.

"I just knew if I could get that shot, I'd make it," said Harper.

Wilkens clapped his hands and, smiled.

"He was under duress, with a man 6-foot-10 running at him, and he maintained his poise," said Rodgers later. "They all did. They made two critical passes to beat the defense around the horn. But most of all you credit Harper. That's when you look at a person like that and you put the tag on of 'Future All-Star.' The big ones deliver shots like that at the buzzer. How many times have we seen Larry Bird make a shot like that to tie or win the game?"

Hot Rod was jumping up and down. Later he confessed, "I thought we were only down a point and that Ron's shot won it for us."

"It's overtime, baby," said Harper.

Hot Rod wasn't the only one who thought the game was over. One individual, after watching Harper hit the big shot, walked over to the scorer's table, picked up his jacket, and started walking down the runway. We'll give you a hint: His initials are Mel Whitworth.

8

Overtime

Overtime? At Boston Garden? Against the Cleveland Cavaliers?

This was the first overtime the Celtics had been forced to play all season. In the last two years overtime had only been an issue once in Boston. The Celtics needed the five extra minutes to defeat Utah by a 115–106 score on November 20, 1985. Since then the Celtics' home-court opponents had seldom come closer than ten points. About all the Celtics could think of during the huddle was that if Whitworth had not called traveling on Dennis Johnson they could all be enjoying a hot shower right now.

Yet the Celtics also realized how easily this game could already have been lost. Only one previous Garden opponent (Philadelphia, on December 5) has played the Celtics anywhere near as well as the Cavaliers have. The Celtics have been forced to play some of their best basketball of the season in order to survive. True, they were unable to hold a six-point lead with a little over a minute to go, but this is where Whitworth and his traveling call came in. In their minds, they already *have* won the game, even if the scoreboard says Boston 122, Cleveland 122.

"We did the things we had to do," Rodgers said. "We got good shots, even if we didn't make them all. We played very good defense. They just didn't crack."

The pressing reality for Boston entering the five-minute overtime is that Robert Parish is gone. He has taken his twenty-two points and nine rebounds to the bench with six personal fouls. A year ago, this would mean playing time for Bill Walton, and the Celtics might conceivably be better off. But this season there is, as yet, no Bill Walton. K. C. Jones's alternatives are to insert Greg Kite or to stick with Fred Roberts and let Kevin McHale play center. McHale prefers to play the big forward spot, but in the past few weeks he has been forced into the backup center role because Kite has been dreadful, even by his own modest standards.

•

In the Cavaliers huddle, Wilkens said, "OK, guys, what we need to do now is show a lot of poise. Take our time. It's a five-minute game. Let's run the plays all the way through."

Harper burst in, "Come on, baby, we can do it."

Harper slapped Daugherty's palm.

"Let's get the ball up the court quickly," said assistant Dick Helm.

"They're getting tired," said Wilkens. "Let's keep pushing the ball at them."

Harper said to Williams, "Come on, Hot Rod."

Harper slapped Williams's palm.

"We gotta stay on the boards," said Helm.

"Poise," said Wilkens. "Lots of poise."

As Harper walked on the court, he approached Hubbard and slapped his palm.

Later, Wilkens said, "At this point, I was a little worried because we were so pumped up. It's great to get the adrenaline flowing, but sometimes the emotions can be too high. I mean, it was a dramatic play that tied the game. The kids had every reason to be excited. But you can be too excited. I mean, I knew the Celtics were going to play smart and we had to do the same."

MATCHUPS

POINT GUARDS	Ainge vs. Bagley
SHOOTING GUARDS	Johnson vs. Harper
CENTERS	McHale vs. Daugherty
POWER FORWARDS	Roberts vs. Williams
SMALL FORWARDS	Bird vs. Hubbard

The overtime begins with a jump ball, and its a five-minute period. Each team gets an extra timeout, but not an extra twenty-second timeout.

4:46   *McHale fouled by Daugherty (P4, T1). First foul shot, swish. Second foul shot hits front of rim and rolls in.*

BOSTON 124, CLEVELAND 122.

The two teams lined up for the jump ball, McHale against Daugherty. McHale timed the toss and tapped the ball back to D.J., who passed to Bird on the right wing. Bird and McHale set up a two-man game. Bird lobbed the ball to McHale at the low post. McHale made his move, and Daugherty committed the apparently unpardonable sin of putting his arms straight up in the air. McHale made contact, and Mel Whitworth blew the whistle and called a foul on Daugherty. A frustrated Daugherty demonstrated to the official his perfect defensive position. He was ignored. The rookie walked away, sadly shaking his head.

"Whitworth," chuckled Jimmy Rodgers, "had pangs of conscience."

"Mel, he never moved," yelled Wilkens.

Whitworth ignored Wilkens.

"Daugherty was just standing there," yelled Wilkens. "McHale jumped into him."

Whitworth wasn't interested in Wilkens's comments. After

McHale made both shots, the Celtics were 31 for 32 from the foul line and McHale had 38 points.

"Be patient," Wilkens yelled to his team as they brought the ball up the court.

4:21   *Cleveland twenty-four-second violation.*

On almost every Cavalier post-up in the second half, Danny Ainge had played the role of rover, serving as the primary double-team man. When Daugherty received the ball on this particular play, the analytical Cleveland rookie appropriately anticipated the arrival of the pesky Celtics' guard and immediately assumed John Bagley would be standing unguarded at the free-throw line. But when he looked for Bagley, he was horrified to discover that Ainge hadn't gone anywhere. The Celtics weren't in "Rover" this time. Ainge was staying at home, and now Daugherty was stuck with the basketball. He dribbled once and tried to back into McHale.

"Move," Wilkens yelled at his players.

No one moved.

Realizing that the shot clock was down to five and that he had better do something, Daugherty started to go up with an awkward hook. When the ball got to shoulder level, McHale knocked it out of Daugherty's hands. Daugherty recovered the loose ball. Finally, someone moved as Hubbard came over and set up at the low post. Daugherty passed to Hubbard, who fell down as the buzzer sounded, indicating a twenty-four-second violation. The Celtics had created one twenty-four-second violation because they double-teamed and rotated expertly, and they had created another because they fooled the Cavaliers by not double-teaming at all.

Still on the floor, Hubbard pointed to Bird.

"Man, he pushed me," said Hubbard.

Whitworth shrugged.

"It was a damn push," said Hubbard, getting up.

As Whitworth ran down the floor, Wilkens yelled, "What about the push? You think he just fell down by himself?"

Whitworth shrugged again.

4:10   *Roberts misses lay-up.*

The Celtics don't quite understand what makes Fred Roberts tick. He does some smart things on the floor and he does some dumb things. He says some intelligent things off the floor and he says some incomprehensible things. He's 6-feet-10, but he uses his body in such an unproductive way that most of the time he might as well be 6-feet-7. He's got a beard one day, and he doesn't have a beard the next. He's been wearing this 1955 short haircut all year. He dresses like a high school sophomore. He's just kind of, well, weird.

His nickname on the team is "Norman," as in Norman Bates. You know, *Psycho*. The Bates Motel.

Roberts signed with the Celtics in the summer of 1986 after spending the previous year and a half with the Utah Jazz in his home town of Salt Lake City. The Brigham Young University graduate had originally been drafted by Milwaukee in the second round of the 1982 draft, the twenty-seventh man selected. His immediate introduction to the NBA was to find himself traded to New Jersey before his first season. He wound up spending the 1982–83 season in the Italian League. Returning to the States the following season, he found he now belonged to San Antonio, and it was with the Spurs that he spent his rookie season, scoring 7.3 points a game as a substitute forward.

The Spurs found that he could certainly run better than the average 6-10 forward, and better than just about any 6-10 *white* player. But he also had some major holes in his game, one of them being a very inconsistent outside shot, and it was with no great remorse that they shipped him to Utah for a pair of second-round draft choices in December 1984.

The Jazz are always happy to stock the roster with local talent, and Roberts was a welcome addition. He had his moments as a Jazz, playing a hero's role during a 1985 playoff game when a desperate coach Frank Layden inserted him at guard, of all things, and earning national notoriety in a game against the Los Angeles Clippers when he scored five points in one second by getting a goaltending call that stopped the clock and then stealing the subsequent inbounds pass and canning a three-pointer.

Layden genuinely liked him but was unable to find much playing time for Roberts due to the presence of 6-11 Thurl Bailey, a slender forward who can really shoot, and of Karl Malone, a potentially great player who was a viable Rookie of the Year candidate. That situation wasn't going to change, and Roberts realized he'd have to get out of Salt Lake City if his career was to have any additional meaning.

The Celtics, meanwhile, thought their backup forward problem was solved in June 1986 when they drafted University of Maryland forward Len Bias with the second pick in the entire draft. They had secured that cozy draft position by virtue of a trade just prior to the 1984–85 season, sending guard Gerald Henderson to Seattle in exchange for the Sonics' 1987 first pick. The trade was debated at great length in Boston, for the hustling Henderson had many fans and was viewed as a great hero by some due to a timely steal and basket that prevented certain defeat in the second game of the 1984 finals with LA. The Celtics, then down 0--1 in the series, went on to win the game in overtime and eventually capture the series as well. Henderson played well throughout.

But the weeping and wailing about trading Henderson ceased during the 1986–87 season, for two reasons. The first was that, as many had predicted, Ainge emerged as a good enough player to make people stop yearning for Henderson. Secondly, the Sonics had again settled in as one of the worst teams in the league. They were heading for the lottery. Who knows? The Celtics are lucky enough by nature to wind up with the championship *and* the number-one pick.

They did, in fact, win the 1986 championship. They did not get the number-one pick, although they came close. They wound up picking second. Philadelphia, who owned the Clippers' first pick (from an eight-year-old deal, no less), had the first selection.

In the weeks preceding the draft the discussions surrounding the first pick were endless. The prime candidates were Brad Daugherty; William Bedford, a mobile seven-foot center from Memphis State; and Len Bias, a 6-foot-8 forward from Maryland who was a superb shooter and rebounder and who was widely viewed as the best athlete among all the big men in the draft (Ron Harper was regarded as the best athlete of any description). The Celtics paid the appropriate lip service to Daugherty and even to Bedford (although he was scratched from the list quickly after they met him and talked to him), but as the draft drew nearer it was becoming more and more apparent that the man Boston wanted was Bias. Red Auerbach had long been partial to players with Washington, D.C., connections, and Bias was a Greater Washingtonian through and through, having gone to high school in Landover and college in College Park, both Maryland suburbs of the nation's capital.

Moreover, Bias had spent time at Auerbach's summer camp and Auerbach actually knew him and liked him. But the principal reason was that Bias was the single best player in the country, the surest bet to become an NBA star among all the available players. He was strong, mobile, and mean. He would bring an element of athleticism to the Celtics' frontcourt that had been lacking for years.

Red got his man. The 76ers traded their number-one spot to Cleveland in exchange for forward Roy Hinson and a lot of cash. That left Bias for the Celtics, who gleefully chose him. The master plan had worked. The Celtics had traded an expendable guard for the man who would be the regenerative link between Celtics present and Celtics future. In NBA thinking, trading any guard for a big man of equal stature is a fabulous deal. Trading this particular guard for this particular big man was a felonious assault on the Seattle consciousness. Larry Bird was so excited about having Bias as a teammate that he said he would come to rookie camp just to work with him. Bird even started telling friends that having a young stud like Bias around might prolong his career. Previously, Bird spoke only in terms of fulfilling his existing contract and heading back to Indiana. Bias's joining the Celtics was enough to make Bird think of rearranging his career plans.

Two days later Len Bias was dead.

Cocaine killed him. "Cocaine intoxication," the coroner called it. Big, strong Len Bias wasn't big and strong enough to say no to a killer substance.

A lot of people will never really get over the Len Bias tragedy, but the reality of his death for the Celtics was that they still had a major weakness at backup forward. Scott Wedman had undergone an operation on his left heel, and no one knew what his status would be for the following season. With no Bias to show for their labors, they had to do something to address the forward situation, which is where Fred Roberts came in.

He was invited to the Celtics' rookie camp, and he had been predictably dominant. Satisfied that Roberts would fit in, the Celtics signed the free-agent forward to a contract.

Roberts paid his first major dividend on the night of November 12. Nine minutes into the first period of a game with Milwaukee, Bird got into an argument with referee Billy Oakes. After getting a technical, a defiant Bird taunted the referee by daring him to call another. Oakes did, and the man most of the 14,890 in attendance had paid to see was gone.

K. C. Jones sent Roberts in to replace Bird. Fred proceeded to have a rather active evening, submitting twenty-three points, twelve rebounds, six assists, and seven turnovers to the cause. Roberts just kept running the lane and moving constantly without the ball in the half-court offense, finishing up with an eight-for-eleven night from the floor. Bird wasn't missed at all. The Celtics won, 124–116, not that it was anywhere near that close a ballgame.

On December 3 Fred came off the bench and did it again. Bird was nursing a sore achilles tendon, and K.C. decided to give Wedman a start. Roberts came off the bench to score nineteen points in twenty-nine minutes of play, displaying the same restless style of play. In the next few weeks he played solid backup ball. He was doing exactly what the Celtics hoped he could do when they signed him to a contract. With Kite totally ineffective as a backup center, Roberts was frequently sent in to replace Parish, with McHale assuming the center position. That is precisely what K. C. Jones had done when Parish fouled out with 3:53 remaining in regulation play.

In addition to being the fastest member of the Boston frontcourt, Roberts is the best jumper on the team. He delights in dunking at the end of fast breaks. Roberts is so skillful as a finisher on the fast break that he has even been compared to former Sixer great Bobby Jones in that regard. And as for his basic game, Clippers coach Don Chaney has compared him favorably with Seattle's Tom Chambers, an ex-Clipper who would go on to become the Most Valuable Player in the 1987 All-Star Game.

So Fred Roberts is not a turkey. But he is off in a nether world in this game, a participant during this overtime only because K. C. Jones can't bring himself to rely on Greg Kite. Roberts just does not seem to be in synch tonight. Perhaps Norman Bates is off on a reconnaissance mission somewhere.

But no one was prepared for Roberts's reaction when Bird threw him one of his nice double-team passes. When Roberts caught the ball, all he had to do was dunk it. No one was contesting him. Yet for reasons no one can discern, he tried to put it in off the glass, actually releasing the ball on a plane *below* the basket. Here he is 6-feet-10, and he's making like Tyrone Bogues. Norman, Norman, Norman!

The ball clunked off the rim and the Celtics had just blown a chance to grab a quick four-point lead in the overtime. Fred Roberts has just reminded the Garden fans and the coaching staff why he's Fred Roberts. Granted, Larry Bird, Kevin McHale, or Robert Parish could also have missed that lay-up. But none of them would have missed it because he chose to release the ball below rim level.

3:54   *Ainge steals Harper's pass.*

Daugherty rebounded Roberts's shot and passed to Bagley at half-court. Bagley spotted Harper on the right sideline about thirty feet from the basket. Bagley passed to Harper. Dennis Johnson, back-pedaling, had no inclination to get tricky here. There will be no gambles, no attempts to poke-check the ball away and make the crowd-pleasing, flashy steal here. He was going to defense Ron Harper by the book.

He assumed a good defensive stance, and he intelligently directed Harper to the right, toward two excellent potential allies: Kevin McHale and the right baseline. Harper looked like a man tooling along the interstate who sees an exit sign he's been looking for at the last moment. He went down the off ramp, and into trouble, because now he was caught in a triple-team caused by Johnson, McHale, and the out-of-bounds line.

Harper now did the only reasonable thing. He tried to throw a half-blind bounce pass back to Daugherty. Danny Ainge, doing what any well-taught player would do, simply retreated into the passing lane and stole the ball. He may have gotten the steal, but credit Dennis Johnson with the mythical assist.

3:44   *McHale misses turnaround.*

Ainge's initial instinct was to think about a possible quick strike, but the Cavaliers have been making exemplary offense-to-defense transitions all night, and they didn't deviate from that policy here. Ainge reconsidered, did a 360-degree turn, and brought the ball up at a more leisurely pace.

Ainge saw that McHale was in the low post on the right side, and he dumped the ball in on another secondary break. McHale took a quick baseline turnaround on Daugherty but the ball wouldn't drop. Roberts suddenly materialized. Nobody had blocked him out, and he had a put-back available that a junior high school kid could make. But the Hoop God had no intention of approving anything Fred Roberts did in this game. Instead of putting the ball back up, Roberts tried to tap it out to the guards, and Daugherty picked off the tap.

Lenny Wilkens wanted a timeout. The Celtics have had three excellent scoring opportunities in three possessions, and it's been nothing but good fortune that the Cavaliers are only trailing by two. At this point Wilkens would like to see to it that his team gets a shot at the basket. Thus far, in two overtime possessions they've had a twenty-four-second violation and a pass stolen.

3:41   *Cleveland timeout.*

In the Cavs' huddle, Wilkens said, "Guys, when they double-team us, the pass has to be out along the sidelines. You can't just throw the ball into the middle of the key, hoping someone is there. They're cutting off the passing lanes, sagging to the middle. That means guys are open on the perimeter, right?

"All right, let's set up a two-man game with Ron and Brad. Take our time and let's think."

3:31   *Bagley misses three-pointer.*

The Cavs took the ball out at half-court. Once again, they couldn't find anyone open inside. Daugherty was the only player trying to post up as the other four Cavs just stood on the perimeter. Fatigue has become a factor, as the players don't cut to the basket; they barely move. Harper never moved to get a pass and set up the planned two-man game with Daugherty. Daugherty came out to the top of the key and caught a pass from Hubbard. With eight seconds on the shot clock, Daugherty knew he had to do something with the ball. Finally, he passed to Bagley, who was on the left wing, twenty-five feet from the basket. Bagley heaved a three-pointer that banged off the rim and was rebounded by Roberts.

"Why do that?" asked Wilkens.

No one has an answer.

"We're only down by two, why take a three-pointer?" said Wilkens, shaking his head.

3:06   *Bird fouled by Daugherty (P5, T1). Swish, swish.*

Boston 126, Cleveland 122.

The general belief among casual basketball fans is that talented black athletes such as Michael Jordan, Dominique Wilkins, and Ron Harper do nothing but perform wondrous physical contortions, while plodding white guys such as Larry Bird make nothing but mechanical jump shots behind picks.

The reality is that in addition to imitating the Flying Wallendas, Messrs. Jordan, Wilkins, and Harper can play a little backyard "H-O-R-S-E" and that Larry Bird has some extraordinary body control when he needs it. He definitely needed it here.

Bird began by isolating himself with Hubbard. Phil went for a fake, and Bird put it on the floor. "Once he got by Hubbard," Rodgers said, "Bird knew he was going to the line because he saw Daugherty coming. But he wanted more than just the free throws. Daugherty came in from Larry's left, and he really nailed him. Larry gets off a very makeable shot, anyway. The left side of his body absorbed heavy contact, but at the same time the right side of his body doesn't seem to acknowledge it. It was like nothing was happening over there on the left."

Bird made the foul shots, making the Celtics thirty-three for thirty-four from the line, including thirty-two in a row.

"Don't these guys ever miss one?" asked Wilkens.

Again, no answer. Celtics by four.

2:51   *Hubbard misses lay-up.*

Bagley brought the ball up the court and set up a two-man game with Hubbard on the left side. Ainge started out guarding John Bagley, but, as usual, expanded his horizons when the situation changed. Hubbard posted Bird five feet from the basket, Bird leaning on Hubbard's back. Suddenly, Hubbard took a step as if he were breaking to the foul line, then cut back to the baseline. Ainge assumed a one-on-two posture, paying good "close-out" attention to Bagley in front of him while darting back and forth in the direction of Hubbard. Hubbard caught a pass from Bagley and drove along the baseline. Ainge tried to cut Hubbard off, but was too late. Ainge tripped as Hubbard went up with a right-handed lay-up from the left side. A very tired Hubbard banged the ball off the board, and it was rebounded by Johnson.

Ainge's momentum carried him backward off the playing surface, and as he stumbled behind the baseline the sprained right ankle that had made him a questionable performer prior to the game simply caved in. Ainge went down in very obvious pain. Johnson brought the ball across midcourt and the Celtics called for a twenty-second timeout. Ainge was helped off the court by trainer Ray Melchiorre and a ball boy. K. C. Jones sent in Jerry Sichting to replace him.

2:44   *Boston twenty-second timeout.*

The Celtics, who have already lost their starting center on fouls, would now be forced to play the remaining 2:44 of the overtime, and conceivably beyond, without the irreplaceable defensive menace. Ainge represents the biggest dose of athleticism on the squad, and he has injured himself making a play that he and he alone among the twelve Celtics in uniform could have made. "He's like a fly at the beach," lauds Los Angeles swingman Michael Cooper, himself a nonpareil defender. "You know how a fly's bothering you and you swipe at it with a magazine, but by the time you do the fly is gone? On defense, Ainge is that fly."

Ainge exited with eleven points, eight assists, and three steals. And if anyone wonders how tough Danny Ainge is, he had just played forty relentless minutes on a certifiably bad ankle.

•

On his little scorecard, Cavs trainer Gary Briggs marked down the fact that the Celtics called a twenty-second timeout in the overtime. He figured the Cavaliers must also have picked up a twenty-second timeout.

2:32   *Harper blocks Roberts.*

The Celtics did it by the numbers here, but Ron Harper made a superstar play.

The play was "Iso-Kevin." Bird got it in. McHale couldn't make his preferred move and he hit D.J. at the point. D.J. immediately whipped the ball to Sichting, who was standing unguarded on the left wing. But a rotating 6-foot-11 Williams came flying at Sichting. Jerry knew that Fred Roberts must be open, and he was. Sichting slipped the ball to Roberts, but as Fred/Norman went up for his shot, Harper, who had been observing this exchange from the vicinity of the foul line, retreated to make a rather forceful rejection of the shot. Now Fred/Norman has an idea why the draft cognoscenti rated Harper as the best athlete in the draft.

2:10   *Williams misses ten-footer on baseline.*

After Harper's block, Williams picked up the loose ball and passed to Bagley, who dribbled up the court. Bagley passed to Hubbard at the top of the key. On the right side, Harper and Williams set up a two-man game. Hubbard passed to Harper, who passed to Williams. Hot Rod was on the baseline, about ten feet from the basket. He tried a quick turnaround over Roberts, and the shot bounced off the side of the rim. Bird grabbed the rebound.

The Cavs were now zero for three with two turnovers in the overtime, and they have yet to score.

1:48   *Williams blocks McHale.*

Celtics ran a two-man game with Johnson and Bird on the right side. As Johnson passed to Bird, Hubbard went for the steal and was too late. Bird caught the pass and drove past Hubbard to the basket. Daugherty left McHale to cut off Bird. Bird spotted McHale open under the basket and hit him with a pass. McHale went up for what he thought would be an open lay-up, but Hot Rod Williams came flying out of nowhere to block the shot.

Wilkens said, "We got in trouble early on this play because Hubbard was very tired and he went for the steal. When you're tired, you shouldn't try for a steal unless you *know*, not just *think*, you'll get it. I knew Hubbard was tired, but I was not about to take him out, not in an overtime game in Boston Garden. But Hot Rod bailed us out because after over forty minutes on the floor, his legs were still fresh and he was still jumping. I know McHale never expected Hot Rod to make that block."

1:39   *Harper drives for two.*

BOSTON 126, CLEVELAND 124.

Williams's brilliant block on McHale served two valuable purposes. The first, naturally, was that it prevented a high-percentage shot by the league's highest-percentage shooter. The second was that in addition to giving Cleveland possession it gave them an immediate advantage in terms of floor balance and matchups. Williams's block put Cleveland not merely in possession; with a man like Ron Harper on their side, it put them on the *attack*.

The Celtics were forced to match up by geography, not by

talent and attributes. Larry Bird cannot guard Ron Harper on the open floor in the half-court, let alone in transition. The only chance the Celtics had to stop Harper was by the use of smart group tactics.

Daugherty spotted Harper alone on the right wing, guarded by Bird; "Get him the ball!" yelled Wilkens.

Daugherty got Harper the ball.

"Take him!" yelled Wilkens.

Harper took him, all right. He dribbled on the right side and Williams came over to post up, but Harper waved at Hot Rod, sending Williams to the other side of the court with the rest of the Cavs. Harper wanted Bird, one-on-one. He relishes these moments.

"I just don't think anybody can stop me in the open court," said Harper, a guy who wasn't content to just drive past Julius Erving the first time the two players met; he drove on Erving, then did a 360-degree lay-up over the Doctor.

Fred Roberts, who had picked up Williams, was the key man. Bird knew he was in trouble, but he did the one thing he had to do—he angled Harper toward the middle, where help should have been forthcoming. Help here meant Roberts, but he was slow to react. "He was giving Williams too much respect from twenty feet," explained Rodgers. "The man he should have been worrying about was Harper." The kid put on his rat-a-tat between-the-legs dribble, bade Mr. Bird adieu, and sailed in for the Cavaliers' first two points of the overtime, almost three and a half minutes after play had begun. The Celtics' lead was down to two.

1:16 *McHale travels.*

Funny. People are always hollering about a travel that should be called on McHale, but not on this particular move. They're always moaning about the step count on some of his leaners and dip-ins. This one was a simple prelude to a jump hook, but Earl Strom's celebrated eagle eye caught Kevin doing a little carioca before releasing the ball. Good call.

The play started out as the ever-popular "Thumbs Up," but the Cavaliers have caught onto this in the fourth go-round. Johnson couldn't get free for option number one, the give-and-go, and Bird, popping out from the weak side, couldn't get a shot off, either. By the time McHale did travel, the Celtics were flirting with a twenty-four-second violation, anyway. The Cavaliers continue to astound the Celtics with the advanced level of their team play. No team starting three rookies is supposed to execute this well at this point in a ballgame.

:55   *Williams tip-in offensive rebound.*

BOSTON 126, CLEVELAND 126.

Oh, you crazy kids. Wilkens wanted the Cavs to run another clearout for Harper, and Cleveland did succeed in getting the ball to Harper at the top of the key. But Boston also knew the Cavs were looking for Harper. Harper drove down the left side of the key, where he was guarded by Bird and Johnson.

"Move the ball," yelled Wilkens.

Instead, Harper shot the ball, which was not a good idea, not with two guys on him. Here was Harper, out of control, taking a bad shot for any point in the game; in this context, it was a *ridiculous* shot. But he is, of course, good enough to make shots even more ridiculous than this.

So here he was, trying to salvage a broken play by inventing something. The shot wouldn't drop, but it was shot so hard and from such an angle that it did not come down in a predictable manner. For an instant it appeared that McHale would grab the long rebound as it caromed into the center of the lane. But the Celtics have not been getting either long rebounds or loose balls all night—*Defense doesn't end until you get the rebound*—and they didn't get this one, either.

Harper did. He put it back up without putting it on the floor, but missed again. The ball came off the rim, but it *still* didn't belong to the Celtics because Hot Rod, who apparently always does the right instinctive thing, came flying into the pack to tip the ball in underhanded, softly banking the ball into the basket. Tie score.

"Once Harper shot," said Rodgers, "this play was all reaction, a melee. Darn that Williams. He did the right thing." Williams, who has never heard of George Bernard Shaw, would dispute the playwright's most famous public observation. Youth (and fresh, strong legs) is not *always* wasted on the young.

:38 *Bird fouled by Hubbard (P6, T3). Swish, swish.*

Boston 128, Cleveland 126.

Larry Bird wants the basketball; it's that simple.

Bird has put up with this Cavalier impudence for fifty-two minutes and five seconds. He had on his "Popeye" look, and Phil Hubbard will serve as his Bluto. There was no need for fancy Xs and Os here. Just give Larry the ball. That's all I can stands! I can't stands no more! Larry doesn't even need the can of spinach.

Dennis Johnson knew where the ball should go. "D.J. has great sensitivity in these matters," said Rodgers.

Remember that Bird has already beaten Hubbard once in this overtime. He has no reason to think he can't do it again. He got the ball behind the three-point line and didn't indulge in any subtleties. He put his head down and drove to the basket.

The odds were with Bird. He is, after all, Larry Bird, the three-time Most Valuable Player. He knows very well that he is more likely to get the benefit of the doubt from the refs in any collision than is any Cavalier. That's the reality of NBA life. He may have a moderate worry with Earl Strom, but he shouldn't have much to worry about with Whitworth, especially since Mel has the memory of the controversial traveling call on Johnson fresh in his mind.

Going to the basket makes sense, also, simply because the Cavaliers have committed three personal fouls, and are thus in the bonus. Bird doesn't even need a shooting foul in order to get to the line.

Bird drove hard to the basket. Hubbard was right with him. When the inevitable collision occurred, Bird threw a wild shot off the glass whose sole intent was to draw a foul. Mel Whitworth blew his whistle. Were the roles reversed, and had Larry Bird done what Hubbard has just done defensively, this would be a very interesting call. Instead Whitworth took what Bob Cousy would refer to as "The path of least resistance." One gutsy call is enough for one night. The call was made on Phil Hubbard, whose primary crime appeared to be guarding a basketball demigod.

Brad Daugherty placed his right hand in back of his head, signalling his belief that it was a charging foul.

"Man, I was moving back," yelled Hubbard, holding his head.

The buzzer sounded, indicating Hubbard has six fouls and is through for the night.

"Mel, Bird jumped into him," yelled Wilkens. "My guy was moving backwards. Bird went right into him."

Later, Hubbard said, "Bird just went into me. He really isn't that quick; and I wasn't out of position. He should have been called for the charge, but this is one of those fouls that Bird gets because he is Larry Bird."

Wilkens sent Mark West in for Hubbard. Bird stepped to the line and swished both attempts. Cleveland immediately called timeout.

:38   *Cleveland timeout.*

Wilkens set up a play in the huddle. "OK, guys, now listen up," said Wilkens. "I want a 1–5." That means a two-man game with Bagley and Daugherty.

"Hot Rod, I want you on the other side, and crash the boards the minute you see Brad go up for the shot," said Wilkens. "Look, we got to get a shot off right away. We can't play with the ball."

•

During the timeout Boston trainer Ray Melchiorre informed K.C. that the Celtics have a foul to waste if need be. They had committed no team fouls in the overtime. NBA rules permit teams to commit one "free" nonshooting foul in the last two minutes of any period or overtime session. A second personal in the last two minutes puts the offending team over the limit and puts the rival on the line for two shots. This is a very beneficial situation for the Celtics.

As the Celtics broke the huddle, Chris Ford had a message to deliver. "One stop!" he screamed.

NEW MATCHUPS

POINT GUARDS	Sichting vs. Bagley
SHOOTING GUARDS	Johnson vs. Harper
CENTERS	McHale vs. Daugherty
POWER FORWARDS	Roberts vs. Williams
SMALL FORWARDS	Bird vs. West

:18   *McHale blocks Harper.*

As Wilkens planned, the Cavs set up a two-man game with Bagley and Daugherty on the right side. Bagley passed to Daugherty, who was about eight feet from the basket. The Celtics were not surprised by what they saw. They anticipated a two-man game of some kind, and they decided not to double-team anyone. "We were in 'Strict,'" explained Rodgers. "Everyone was supposed to stay at home. This threw Daugherty off again. He was looking for the open man, and there wasn't one." Instead of making a move to the basket, Daugherty dribbled out toward the foul line. Harper ran into the lane, setting up low-post position with Johnson on his back. Daugherty passed to Harper. Once Daugherty unloaded the ball to Harper, the Celtics changed the rules of the game. McHale was not going to allow Harper an unmolested shot. He came over to double-team with D.J. and blocked Harper's weak shot attempt out of bounds.

This was a painful sequence for Wilkens to watch, because "We set up a play for Brad to go to the basket and we get him the ball. Time is running out, and he's got to look for his shot. But his inexperience showed. He wasn't wide open, so he figured he'd try to get the ball to someone else. He ended up passing to Harper, who was in an even worse position than Brad to shoot. We were just lucky to get the ball back."

:14   *Johnson blocks Harper.*

The Cavs took the ball out under the basket with only five seconds left on the shot clock. Five seconds is a lot of time by NBA standards. The Celtics had to concentrate. Bagley got the ball in to Harper, who was straddling the three-point line on the left wing. His options were nil. He had to shoot.

He was not worried about getting off a shot, especially from that distance. But he should have been. Dennis Johnson loves this situation. He may be responsible for a man twenty-four feet from the basket, but it isn't in his nature to concede anything. Eighteen days earlier he had preserved a two-point Celtics' triumph in Seattle by making Dale Ellis eat a three-point attempt at the buzzer. Throughout his career he has been not merely a good defensive player, but a disruptive one.

Dennis Johnson went at Harper and got a piece of the shot. The ball dropped morosely from the air, into the waiting hands of Larry Bird.

:11 *Johnson lay-up. Assist—Bird.*

BOSTON 130, CLEVELAND 126.

Two consummate professionals were at work now. As soon as Johnson deflected Harper's shot he resisted the impulse to stand and admire his handiwork. Rather, he put his head down and started sprinting for the Boston basket. Bird, the contemporary master of the long outlet pass, grabbed the ball and immediately fired it to Johnson. There was no one within forty feet of D.J. as he laid the ball in the basket for a rare Celtics' transition basket, the first Boston hoop of the overtime. Celts by four. Timeout, Cleveland.

Tom Heinsohn told his TV audience, "Run when you need to run. That's what the Celtics have always done."

:11 *Cleveland calls its last timeout.*

"If you're Cleveland in this situation," Rodgers figured, "what do you do? Go for a quick two and then foul. Our objective was to play 'Strict' defense and slide our feet."

In the Cavs' huddle, Wilkens said, "Ehlo, go in for West. Now, guys, we need to score quick. I don't want a three-pointer. We're down by four, a three-pointer doesn't change things. We still need to get the ball twice and score twice. Okay, Ehlo will take the ball out at half-court. Hot Rod, you break up to catch the pass and let's isolate Brad alone under the basket. And after we score, we have to go for the steal. Man-to-man, full-court press. If we don't get the steal, we need to foul, right away."

Wilkens removed West in favor of Ehlo because Ehlo is a much better passer, and the inbounds pass from half-court is critical at this point of the game. This responsibility usually goes to Hubbard, but he has fouled out, so Wilkens needed someone else. At 6-6, Ehlo is tall enough to see the court.

NEW MATCHUPS

POINT GUARDS	Sichting vs. Bagley
SHOOTING GUARDS	Johnson vs. Harper
CENTERS	McHale vs. Daugherty
POWER FORWARDS	Roberts vs. Williams
SMALL FORWARDS	Bird vs. Ehlo

:07   *Ehlo seven-foot jump hook.*

BOSTON 130, CLEVELAND 128.

Four-point lead, eleven seconds. Even in the oft-bizarre world of the NBA, this game should have been over. But there had been something weird in the air all night. The Cavaliers had demonstrated a high Rasputin quotient. A six-point lead with 1:09 to go wasn't enough in regulation. Cleveland had performed some notable athletic feats, and they had also been the repeated beneficiaries of tipped passes, wildly angled rebounds, and improbable shots. When they desperately needed a phantom call, Whitworth provided it. The Celtics had been hanging on without Parish for the past eight minutes and two seconds and without Ainge for the past two minutes and thirty-three seconds. Every veteran Celtic and every longtime fan has a horrible tale of woe to relate, a story about a game that appeared to be sewn up and which instead oozed into the loss column. This game is not yet over.

The absolute worst Boston fears materialized. Ehlo inbounded crisply to Williams as Daugherty set an authoritative pick on Fred Roberts. Fred/Norman had been under siege all night, and now he was trapped guarding two men. What further misfortune could befall this poor man?

No time has yet elapsed. The count doesn't begin until Williams touches the ball. Hot Rod has an amazingly quick mind and surprisingly good floor vision. He attempted a slap-pass to Daugherty, who, having set the pick on Roberts, had not been picked up by either Roberts or McHale. But though the spirit was willing, for once the flesh was not strong enough. Fred Roberts got a piece of the ball.

Loose ball. If the Celtics had picked it up, the game really would have been over. They did not. The ball squirted into the grasp of Craig Ehlo, who threw up an off-balance jump hook rating a minus two on the artistic scale. It went in. Tear up those leads, boys. There's plenty of basketball to play.

:03   *Sichting fouled by Bagley (P4, T4). Swish, swish.*

BOSTON 132, CLEVELAND 128.

After Ehlo's basket, the ball was inbounded to Bird, who quickly passed to Sichting, and Bagley fouled Sichting. Sichting made his foul shots.

On the Cavs' bench, trainer Gary Briggs said, "Lenny, you have a twenty." Wilkens called a twenty-second timeout. The buzzer sounded, and Earl Strom went to the press table.

"Cleveland has no more timeouts," said the scorer. Strom signaled a technical foul on the Cavs. Briggs and Wilkens rushed to midcourt, confronting Strom in front of the scorer's table.

"Lenny, you're out of timeouts," said Strom.

"We got a twenty," said Briggs.

"You have no more timeouts," said Strom.

"But Boston called a twenty," said Briggs.

"You don't get an extra twenty with an overtime," said Strom. "That twenty was left over from regulation."

Resigned to the indignity of having called an illegal timeout, Wilkens walked back to the bench. A sportswriter offered to show Wilkens his play-by-play sheet, but Wilkens just shook his head and kept walking.

Briggs remained at half-court, arguing with the scorekeeper and anyone else who would listen. But no one was paying attention. Boston trainer Ray Melchiorre wandered along press row, smiling at Briggs's plight.

Briggs finally walked back to the bench and said, "Jesus, Lenny, I'm sorry." Wilkens dismissed the incident with a wave of his hand.

Later, Briggs said, "I've worked under six coaches in five years, and this never happened to me before. I couldn't find a big enough hole to crawl into. I mean, if that were a one-point game, my bags would have been packed and I'd have been headed home for Tampa. I wouldn't even have waited for them to fire me. I kept thinking we got an extra twenty-second timeout when the overtime started. Then I saw Boston call one, and I figured we had to have one. I was just being an idiot. I should have checked."

Wilkens said, "It was embarrassing for Gary. He's a good guy and works hard. What was I supposed to do, hang my trainer out to dry? I knew he felt worse about it than anyone."

:03 *Sichting shoots technical. Swish.*

BOSTON 133, CLEVELAND 128.

The contretemps concerning the illegal timeout left the Celtics as happy onlookers. "You say to yourself, 'How important is this technical?' " said Rodgers. "There aren't many four-point plays in anyone's repertoire. Then you think of a guy like World B. Free taking a three-pointer and sticking his leg out to draw a foul. It can happen. There were three seconds left. Five up was better than four."

Incidentally, notice that Sichting, not Bird, took the technical foul shot. Bird may be the league's best at the line, both in the books and in theory, but Sichting is a mid-eighties man himself, he's just made two, and he's in his rhythm. Sichting swished it. Since McHale missed the second of two free throws at the 9:23 mark of the first quarter, the Celtics have made 37 consecutive foul shots. And needed every one.

:01 *Bagley misses from half-court.*

FINAL: BOSTON 133, CLEVELAND 128.

For the third time in the game circumstance dictated that John Bagley take a desperation heave to end a period. There ought to be a category for these shots. The final sheet says he is ten for twenty-one. Take these impossible, but necessary, attempts away and he is a much nicer-looking ten for eighteen. This is a perfect example of the misleading nature of some statistics. Or perhaps Red Auerbach is correct; maybe they should just burn the damn stat sheets.

The only thing that really matters now is what's on the scoreboard. After fifty-three exhausting and exhilarating minutes of play, the Celtics as a team have scored 133 points and the Cavaliers as a team have scored 128.

Postgame

10:30 p.m.

The Celtics have earned their hot shower tonight.

"They showed me something," said Sichting. "I don't think we played poorly. Almost everything we didn't do well or failed to execute they had something to do with, and they had those springy legs to keep them in the game."

Harper has particularly gained Sichting's attention. "He's one of the best drivers I've seen," Sichting said. "He loves getting to the baseline. Everybody knows he wants to get there, but he blades through, somehow."

•

Wilkens had very little to say in the dressing room after the game.

"We played well and hard," he said. "But at the end, we made some bad decisions and it cost us. What we can learn from this game is that we are good enough to play with anyone in the league—but only when we play this hard. You have to play the Clippers, the Pacers, and everyone else as if they were the Celtics."

And that was it, less than a minute.

•

Dennis Johnson peeled off his uniform very, very slowly. "One thing we don't do is take anybody lightly," he insisted.

"We knew from the previous time they would be very tough. We would have liked to get it over with in regulation.

"Ron Harper? He can do quite a few things, with the ball or without the ball. He can score."

As to what won the game, D.J. had a definite opinion.

"Our team defense," he said. "That's what won us a title last year, and without that, we won't make it."

•

It's always hard to tell by looking at K. C. Jones whether the team has won or lost—or even played. Some coaches have that disheveled look of a soapbox orator, but K.C. invariably looks as if he's performing the role of the "After" subject in a deodorant ad. He's perpetually cool.

"Ah, you get drained," he claimed. "But it's not quite so much if you win. I really don't think we took them too seriously," he declared. "We wound up having to play great basketball in the third and fourth quarters and down the stretch."

•

An exhausted Phil Hubbard leaned back into his locker. Gary Briggs had taped an ice pack to Hubbard's right knee, and Hubbard looked like he wouldn't be able to stand up, much less play again, for a week.

"Man, I still didn't foul Bird," said Hubbard. "He jumped into me."

•

Jimmy Rodgers, who has prepared the hardest and who is by nature the most studious member of the Celtics' entourage, was dazzled by what he has seen. The Cavaliers have revealed themselves to be like no youth-dominated team he has ever encountered.

"They played a great first quarter and right away we knew we had a tiger by the tail," he said. "They established they could play with us right away. Looking back at that first game in Cleveland, you'd think we'd come out a little more psychologically prepared, but instead we came out and said, 'Show me,' again—and they did.

"It was a well-played game from start to finish. It was a very characteristic game for us. It was a game in which we did what we do best; that is, we *grew*. This ended up as a very strong defensive game by our team. Down the stretch we had some disappointing offense. We got too methodical. But the defense held up.

"The interesting thing is that with all their youth and so-called inexperience they played us as tough in the Boston Garden as anyone has all season, and that includes L.A. when they beat us. They would not crack. When we play this type of ballgame in the Boston Garden, in most cases we will expand that five- or six-point lead to fifteen or so. We have a way of snowballing games like this into blowouts."

The Celtics needed all their guile to defeat the Cavaliers. They posted up continually in the first half, and when the Cavaliers started to double-team McHale in the second half they went to more outside plays. They found their way to the line, both by design and reputation, and when they got there they cashed in, making thirty-eight of thirty-nine. On any number of occasions, they were certain they had applied, or were about to apply, the knockout blow. Yet after fifty-two minutes and fifty-seven seconds of play, the game was still undecided until Jerry Sichting went to the line. He needed to make his free throws, and he did. The Celtics would play thirty-eight games in the Boston Garden in the 1986–87 season, and the fans would not be as rewarded as on this particular occasion. Pro basketball was well served in Boston on the night of January 16, 1987.

"The Cavaliers were very poised," concluded Rodgers. "They might be a little disappointed with their offense, but their defense was excellent. We are not an easy team to defend because we read so well. We played the game in the second half the way we wanted to play. To play with an athletic team like this, we've got to play strong team defense and play fairly deliberately on offense. We could have done a lot better if we could have cut down on the loose ball element. But they did a nice job. Remember, they were playing the Celtics. There are nights when we get off to slow starts, but we evolve. We get to it eventually. We got to it tonight."

11:30 p.m.

The Cavs filed out of the Garden and onto the bus, where again they were greeted by the same middle-aged autograph seeker who was waiting for them when they got off the bus. The guy stuck a notebook in front of Brad Daugherty, who signed it and said, "I just did this a couple of hours ago."

Wilkens, who was next to sign, said, "I've been signing this guy's book for twenty years."

11:45 p.m.

Back at the Hyatt, the players found that the coffee shop was open, but they were no longer serving food, just cold snacks. Wilkens was at a table with five friends from Providence College. At another table were Gary Briggs and Ben Poquette.

"I'll buy you a beer," said Poquette.

"Make that a gun," said Briggs. "I feel like blowing my brains out."

Briggs settled for a beer.

Suddenly, the fire alarm sounded, and a tape came on

saying, "Everyone leave your room and report to the hallway. Wait there for further instructions."

Most of the players were either in the lobby or ignored the announcement, believing it was a false alarm. Keith Lee came out of his room, looked around, and went back inside. But Hot Rod Williams stood alone, in front of his room, in the hallway. He was told to wait for further instructions and he planned to do it.

Scooter McCray and Johnny Newman found a way to beat the coffee shop and make a statement at the same time. They walked down the street to the McDonald's, bought several cheeseburgers, french fries, and milk shakes. Then they brought the food back to the Hyatt, found a table in the coffee shop, sat down, and ate it.

Saturday, 12:15 a.m.

A half hour after the alarm, Wilkens went up to his room. He saw that Hot Rod was still in the hallway, only he was pacing.

"I think everything is okay," said Wilkens.

Hot Rod said, "I don't like no fires."

But he returned to his room. Williams had reason to be leary of fires. About two years before, his stepmother and sister were burned out of their home when their trailer went up in flames.

6:10 a.m.

The Cavaliers assembled in the lobby, checking out of the Hyatt and preparing to catch a 7:30 flight back to Cleveland, where they would face the New York Knicks.

Wilkens said, "You know, we got the calls until the very end. Whitworth made a great, gutsy call on the walk with D.J. He walked, but I didn't know if we'd get the call. But in the overtime . . . the call on Hubbard, that hurt. That killed us. We played so well and we came so close . . . . If we just could have executed a little better at the end . . ."

•

In the lobby, there was another autograph seeker. It was not the middle-aged guy with the notebook, but a guy about twenty wearing yellow and purple Magic Johnson tennis shoes.

"I guess these guys never sleep," said Wilkens while signing the guy's book.

•

As the players got on the bus, Scooter McCray asked the writers, "Anybody got a *Post?*"

"Yeah," said Joe Menzer. "But no Vecsey column."

"No rumors?" said Scooter.

"No rumors," said Menzer.

"Then what good is it?" asked McCray.

With that question hanging in the air, the Cavs' bus pulled away from the Hyatt and started the drive to Logan Airport. For the Cavs, the trip to Boston was over.

Glossary

box A small square painted along each side of the foul lane that directs the placement of players during a free throw. This is known as the box, and it is a reference point on offense, as in "He posted me up on the left box."

entry pass The pass in the half-court that initiates the play. Sometimes plays begin with what is known as a "dribble entry," but the majority of plays start with a pass. Contesting the "entry pass" is regarded as aggressive, winning defense.

fast break When a team converts immediately from defense to offense and gets an attempt at the basket via a missed shot, turnover, or even a successful basket or free throw, this is known as a "fast break." If you're fouled in such a circumstance and draw two free throws, this likewise counts as a "fast break."

illegal defense The following is the NBA rulebook definition of an illegal defense:

Section I—Illegal Defenses
a. Illegal defenses which violate the rules and accepted guidelines set forth are not permitted in the NBA.

b. When the offensive team is in its backcourt with the ball, no illegal defense violation may occur.

1. Penalties for Illegal Defenses.
On the first violation, the 24-second clock is reset to 24. On the second and succeeding violations, the clock is reset to 24 and one free throw (technical) is attempted. When a violation occurs during the last 24 seconds of any period (including overtime) regardless of the number of prior offenses, one free throw is awarded for the violation. On all violations, the

353

ball is awarded to offended team out of bounds at the free throw line extended on either side of the court.

EXCEPTION: If a field goal attempt is simultaneous with a whistle for an illegal defense violation, and that attempt is successful, the basket shall count and the violation is nullified.

2. Guidelines for Defensive Coverage

a. Weak side defenders may be in a defensive position within the "outside lane" with no time limit and inside the "inside lane" for 2.9 seconds. Defensive player must re-establish a position with both feet out of the "inside lane" to be considered having legally cleared the lane.

b. When a defensive player is guarding a player who is adjacent (posted up) to the 3-second lane, the defensive player may be within the "inside lane" area.

An offensive player shall be ruled as "posted up" when he is within 3' of the lane line. Hashmark on baseline denotes the 3' area.

c. An offensive player without the ball **may not** be double-teamed from the weak side. **Only** the player with the ball may be double-teamed, by a weak side defensive player.

Weak side and strong side restrictions shall not extend above the tip of the circle.

d. When an offensive player, with or without the ball, takes a position above the foul line, the defensive player may be no farther (toward the baseline) than the 'middle defensive area'. Defensive player may enter and re-enter the "inside lane" as many times as he desires, so long as he does not exceed 2.9 seconds.

e. When a weak side offensive player is above the free throw line extended, his defensive man may be no lower than the 'middle defensive area' extended for more than 2.9 seconds.

When a weak side offensive player is below the free throw line extended, his defensive man must vacate the "inside lane" unless his man is positioned adjacent (posted up) to the 3-second lane extended.

When a weak side offensive player is above the tip of the circle, his defensive man must be no lower than the 'upper defensive area' for more than 2.9 seconds.

When a strong side offensive player is above the tip of the circle extended, his defensive man may be no lower than the free throw line extended (upper defensive area) for more than 2.9 seconds.

When a strong side offensive player is above the free throw line extended (upper defensive area), his defensive man may be no lower than the 'middle defensive area' for more than 2.9 seconds.

When a strong side offensive player is below the free throw line extended (middle defensive area), his defensive man has no restrictions. He may double-team anyone with or without the ball. Should his man relocate to a 'spot' above the free throw line extended, he has 2.9 seconds to follow him into the proper defensive area.

In all of the situations above, the defensive player may always go and double-team the ball.

f. When an offensive player takes a position above the tip of the circle, with or without the ball, the defensive player may be no further (toward the baseline) from him than the 'upper' defensive area'.

g. A defensive player must follow **his weak offensive man**, switch to another man at the point where the two offensive players cross, or double-team the ball. There is no 2.9-second time limit on this play. Defensive player must do one of those three options or he is guilty of an illegal defense **immediately**.

h. A defensive player must follow his **strong side offensive man**, switch to another man at the point where the two offensive players cross, or double-team the ball. There is a 2.9 second time limit on this play which commences when the defensive player 'opens up' after reaching the weak side.

i. A double team is when two or more defenders aggressively pursue a player with the ball to a position close enough for a held ball to occur.

Failure to comply with paragraphs a through i will be adjudged an Illegal Defense.

isolation An offensive tactic whereby four players go to one side of the court and the fifth goes one-on-one with his defender. Also known as "clear-out."

paint The rectangle bounded by the end line, foul line, and foul lanes. Also known as the "lane," or "three-second area." Phrase coined by coach-commentator Al McGuire. Any offensive player caught standing in the paint for three seconds is guilty of a three-second violation, depending on the alertness of the official. In Boston Garden, the paint is Kelly Green.

penetrate To advance the ball as close to the basket as possible. Isiah Thomas is a superb "penetrator." John Bagley is a good one.

pick When an offensive player A stations himself so that a defensive player guarding offensive player B has his progress impeded. The rules state that a man must be stationary while setting a pick. Also known as a "screen."

pick-and-roll Two offensive players collaborate so that when Player A, without the ball, sets a pick for Player B, with the ball, Player A will cut, or "roll," to the basket, looking for a return pass. The defense is forced to make a decision, and a well-timed pick-and-roll is difficult to stop.

pivot Plays revolving around the center, assuming he is stationed reasonably close to the basket. A staple of basketball.

post   The "post" can be a simple synonym for the "pivot." A man is said to be "posting up" someone when he establishes position with his back to the basket. Anyone can "post up" a rival, not just centers, "but post play" generally refers to centers. Kevin McHale makes a living "posting up" people.

rotate   When defensive player A leaves to double-team an offensive player, and defensive player B leaves his man to take A's man, B is said to have "rotated." Teams try to stay a step ahead of the offensive by anticipating—in some cases even forcing—passes to be made in a certain direction.

rover   A defensive player who leaves his own man to chase the man with the basketball. Maurice Cheeks and Danny Ainge are superb "rovers."

rub   When you run a man off a screen, you are said to have "rubbed" him.

secondary break   When an offensive team attempts a shot before the defense is set, and without calling a play, this is known as the "secondary break."

shootaround   Universal NBA term for the day-of-game practice. This is a light workout, without taping, and normally involves going over some opposition plays and doing some shooting. Practice popularized by coach Bill Sharman with the 1971–72 Lakers. The team won thirty-three straight games and the championship, so it wasn't exactly a major shock when every team copied the idea.

stop   Any time the offense doesn't score when it has possession of the basketball, the defense is said to have come up with a "stop."

transition   All-encompassing phrase to describe offense in which an attempt is made to score without calling a play, and before the defense can be set up.

turnover   Any time a team on offense comes away from a possession without getting a shot at the basket, or a free throw, the team has committed a "turnover."

Xs and Os   When plays are diagrammed, "Xs" traditionally represent offensive players and "Os" defensive players. If a coach is regarded as a cagey tactician, he is said to be a good "X and O man."